BARRON'S

HOW TO PREPARE FOR THE COMPUTER-BASED TOEFL* ESSAY

TEST OF ENGLISH AS A FOREIGN LANGUAGE

By Lin Lougheed

*TOEFL is a registered trademark of Educational Testing Service. Barron's Educational Series, Inc. bears sole responsibility for this book's contents and is not connected with Educational Testing Service.

First edition published 2000 by Barron's Educational Series, Inc.

Text © copyright 2000 by Lin Lougheed
Text design and cover © copyright 2000
by Barron's Educational Series, Inc.

All inquiries should be addressed to:
Barron's Educational Series, Inc.
250 Wireless Boulevard
Hauppauge, New York 11788
http://www.barronseduc.com

International Standard Book No.: 0-7641-1479-4
Library of Congress Catalog Card No.: 99-55699

Library of Congress Cataloging-in-Publication Data

Lougheed, Lin, 1946–
    How to prepare for the computer-based TOEFL essay / by Lin Lougheed.—1st ed.
        p.   cm.
    ISBN 0-7641-1479-4
            1. Test of English as a Foreign Language—Data processing—Study guides.
    2. English language—Textbooks for foreign speakers.   3. English language—
    Examinations—Study guides.   I. Title.

    PE1128.L6434 2000
    428'.0076—dc21

                                                                                                    99-55699
                                                                                                    CIP

Printed in the United States of America

9 8 7 6 5 4 3 2

4. units
11 subunits
· model essays
· general test info

Contents

Introduction

1. Essay Writing in Twelve Steps

2. Planning the Essay

3. Writing the Essay

4. Revising the Essay

Appendix

Introduction

HOW TO USE THIS BOOK

There are three stages in creating an essay: planning, writing, and revising. When you write the Computer-Based TOEFL essay, you will have only thirty minutes to do all of this. In that short, thirty minutes, your writing must make an impression. Your writing must be clear, coherent, and correct. This book will help you do that.

How to Prepare for the Computer-Based TOEFL Essay provides a step-by-step guide for planning, writing, and revising your essay.

PLAN

This book will help you plan your essay. You will learn how to

understand the essay topic,

write a thesis statement, and

organize your thoughts with concept maps.

You also must have a plan for studying. Start with the first chapter of this book. Do every activity on every page until you reach the end. Follow the sequence of the book. When you write an essay, you start with the first word of the first sentence and end with the last word of the conclusion. Study this book the same way. Begin at the beginning and work your way through the book.

You will need to measure your success. The answer key in the back of the book will tell you how well you are doing. At the end of each chapter, there are Free Practice activities that ask you to write something on your own. There is, of course, no answer key for these activities. Share your writing with friends or teachers. They will tell you how well you are doing. You can find additional essays and topics, including any new topics from ETS, on Dr. Lougheed's Web site: *www.lougheed.com*.

WRITE

This book will help you write your essay. You will learn how to

state opinions,

write topic statements,

write supporting details,

write a conclusion, and

use syntactic and semantic variety in your essay.

The best way to learn to write is by writing. You will do a great deal of writing while you study this book. You will want to have a measure of how well you have progressed. Therefore, you will end each section with a self-test. You will be responsible for measuring your achievements.

The first self-test is at the end of the Introduction. You will be instructed to select an essay topic from the list in the Appendix and write on that topic. Pretend you are taking the TOEFL; write the essay in thirty minutes. When you are finished, don't show the essay to anyone. You will return to this first essay later.

At the end of the Planning section, you will take another self-test. Write a second essay on the same topic as your first essay. Write this essay in thirty minutes, too. Compare this second essay with the first one that you wrote on the same topic. Do you feel that you improved?

At the end of the Writing section and at the end of the Revision section, you will again write essays on the same topic. By the end of the book, you will have written four essays on the same topic. Compare all four essays. Compare your thesis statements, topic sentences, supporting details, and conclusions. Can you see your progress? Show your essay to someone else. What do they think?

REVISE

This book will help you revise your essay. You will learn how to

correct sentence fragments,

correct run-on sentences,

combine clauses and modifiers, and

use correct punctuation.

Writing is a solitary activity, but rewriting doesn't have to be. Get some help. Show your work to anyone who is willing to help you. Give them the Proofing Checklist on page 27 and have them rate the essays you write.

When you are learning how to write, you must, at the same time, learn to rewrite. You must make it a habit to rewrite the essays you write in this book. Try to incorporate your friends' suggestions into your revised essay. The more you write, the better writer you will be.

A good essay takes time: time to plan; time to write, and time to revise. On the Computer-Based TOEFL you only have thirty minutes. If you take time now to learn how to write, you'll easily be able to write your essay in thirty minutes.

WARNING Study the model essays carefully. Analyze them completely. **Do NOT memorize them.** Your essay will not be scored if it matches an essay in this book. Your essay on the TOEFL must be your OWN original essay.

TO THE TEACHER

This book is perfectly suited for use in the classroom. The activities are carefully structured and can easily be completed in class. The activities can also be done as homework and corrected in class.

This book contains two types of activities: structured and free. The structured activities present models and controlled writing activities for the students. The free activities encourage them to write on their own using the controlled, structured activities as models.

EXPANDING THE ACTIVITIES

This book is a gold mine. Each chapter has examples and structured activities showing how a particular part of an essay is developed. You can expand these activities by having the students find other examples in the model essays, which are located in the Appendix. For example, you are teaching your students how to support topic sentences with specific details. There are ten examples in that particular chapter, but more than 350 topic sentences with supporting details in the model essays.

Tell the students to turn to a model essay and find the topic sentence and the details. Similarly, they can use the same essays to find thousands of examples of transition words, cohesion, conclusions, or any other aspect of an essay that you want to illustrate.

THESE MODEL ESSAYS ARE FOUND IN THE SAMPLE ESSAYS IN THE APPENDIX AND THROUGHOUT THE BOOK.

You might advise your students that the model essays show a great diversity of writing. Everyone has a different writing style and the essays reflect this difference. This book is prescriptive in its approach to essay writing, but one can present one's ideas in many ways. By analyzing the style of a model essay (how the writer developed an idea and how the writer introduced and concluded the essay), your students will gain a broader understanding of essay writing.

GETTING STUDENTS TO DO MORE

Writing is a very personal activity, and students must be encouraged to write on their own. The Strategies and Tips section contains activities that the student can do to improve general writing ability (*General Writing Improvement Strategies*).

Students, of course, don't want to waste their time learning "general" writing, even though it will improve their essay writing. They want their preparation to be TOEFL-specific. To this end, there are more than 133 topics in the Appendix that have appeared or could appear on the actual TOEFL test. Assign essay topics from this list frequently. Have the students do one a night or one a week.

Even though writing is a personal activity, preparing to write an essay and revising it doesn't have to be. When the students bring their essays to class, let their classmates read them first. Let their peers use the Proofing Checklist on page 27 to rate the essays. Then have the students rewrite their essays incorporating the comments of their classmates.

Put your students in small groups. Small groups are also good for brainstorming on a topic. It is imperative that students begin to form opinions on these topics. They must get used to thinking about why a school needs more teachers, or why a landscaper is needed by our community. If time permits, you could even organize a mini-debate with students preparing opposite sides of the issue. The final activity is everyone writing an essay on his or her opinion on the topic.

You don't want to take home a lot of essays every night to correct. Let your students do the work. Photocopy a student essay and hand out copies to small groups. Have the groups critique the same essay. Emphasize that the group is to improve the essay. You can walk around from group to group focusing their attention on problems and comparing the comments. Once the groups have critiqued the essay, take some time to revise the essay as a class.

A variation of this activity is for each student in a group to read aloud his or her essay and have the group help improve it. Members of the group could also, on their own, rewrite the same essay and then compare their revisions with the group.

Whatever your students write, they will profit from doing it again. Even though they can't revise extensively on the Computer-Based TOEFL, learning to rethink and redo will help them develop sound writing habits.

A word of caution. Please remind the students not to memorize the essays in this book. An essay will not be rated if the reader suspects it was taken from the model essays.

QUESTIONS AND ANSWERS ABOUT THE COMPUTER-BASED TOEFL ESSAY

1. How long do I have to write the essay?
Thirty minutes.

2. Do I have to use the computer?
No, you can write your essay by hand. You can decide on test day. (See the section *To Type or Not to Type*.)

3. Do I have a choice of topics?
No, you will only be given one topic.

4. Will all test-takers have the same topic?
No. Not every test-taker will have the same topic.

5. What will happen if I don't understand the question?
If you study this book, that won't be a problem. You will understand all the possible

topics. On the day of the test, you will not receive any help with the topic.

6. What will happen if I don't understand how to work the computer?
There will be test administrators in the room who can answer your questions about using the computer. They will not answer any question about the use of English.

7. What kind of pencils should I bring?
None. Everything you need to write your essay will be given to you at the testing center. If you need extra pencils or paper, ask your test administrator.

8. Can I bring a clock with me?

No. Nothing can be brought into the test room. You can wear your watch or look at the clock on the computer screen. There will be a clock in the upper left corner that counts down the time remaining.

9. Can I bring a dictionary with me?

No. Nothing can be brought into the test room.

10. Can I bring paper with me?

No. Nothing can be brought into the test room. Scratch paper and paper on which to write your essay will be supplied.

11. What happens to the notes I take?

You can write your notes in English or your first language. They will be collected and discarded. They will not be seen by the raters.

12. Is there a spell checker or a grammar checker on the computer?

No. You will have to do your own proofreading. (See the section *To Type or Not to Type*.) Don't worry about a few spelling errors or a few mistakes with punctuation or grammar. A few small errors will not count against your score. Hint: If you are unsure how to spell a word, use a word you do know how to spell.

13. How long should the essay be?

It should be around 300 words. You should be able to address your topic completely in three to five short paragraphs.

14. What's more important in the essay: organization or grammar?

Both are important. A reader judges an essay on its organization, your use of details to support your opinions, and your facility with English. (See the section *Scoring the Essay*.)

15. Do I need a title?

No. However, a title helps the readers focus attention on your thesis. It helps them to understand your point of view.

16. Do I need an introduction?

You need something to introduce your readers to your topic. This will help them understand what you are going to say and how you plan to develop your ideas.

17. How many paragraphs do I need?

You need enough to cover your topic and show that you are proficient in English. A general rule is that you should have five paragraphs: the first paragraph is the introduction, the next three paragraphs are the body, and the fifth paragraph is the conclusion. In the three paragraphs of the body, you should have one paragraph for each topic sentence.

You will not be scored on how many paragraphs you write. You will be scored on how well you address your topic.

18. What happens if I don't finish?

You do not need to have an elegantly stated conclusion. What you do write should demonstrate your facility with English. Do not end with an apology. Do not apologize to the reader for what you did not do or for what you think should have been better.

19. Is there an extra fee for the essay?

No. The test fee covers all parts of the Computer-Based TOEFL.

20. Is the essay required?

Yes. All test-takers who take the Computer-Based TOEFL must write an essay.

21. How is my essay scored?

Your essay will be read by two readers. Neither reader will know the score the other reader gives your essay. If the scores are more than one point apart (one reader gives your essay a 6 and another reader gives it a 4), your essay will be read by a third person. If that reader gives your essay a 4.5, your score will be the approximate average of the three scores, 5.

22. Will I see my essay score immediately?

No. If you type your essay on the computer, your score will be mailed to you approximately two weeks after the test date. if you write your essay by hand, your score will be sent to you in five weeks. If you change your address, let the Educational Testing Service (ETS) know your new address.

23. Can I get my score by phone?

Yes. You can get your score report by phone on the day that the scores are mailed. See the latest edition of ETS' *Information Bulletin for the Computer-Based TOEFL* for precise instructions.

24. **What if I don't like my rating?**
    Take the test again.

25. **Can I cancel my essay score?**
    Yes. At the end of the test, you have the option to cancel your scores BEFORE you see them. If you choose this option, all of your scores, including your essay score, will be cancelled.

COMPUTER-BASED TOEFL ESSAY BASICS

TO TYPE OR NOT TO TYPE

When you sit down in front of the computer on test day, you will have to decide whether you will type your essay on the computer or whether you will write it out longhand. The following chart gives you some pros (+) and cons (–) for writing by computer or by hand.

	By Computer	By Hand
Input	+ Your essay will be legible, clear. – Readers may unconsciously expect more from a clean-looking essay.	+ Your essay will be as clear as your handwriting. – If your handwriting is illegible, your essay will be impossible to score. – Revisions/changes could make the essay look disorganized.
Speed	+ Faster if you are familiar with a computer or a keyboard. + If you are familiar with Windows, you will understand the functions. – Slow if you do not know how to type. – Potentially slow if you are used to standard word processing functions like tabs that are disabled on the Computer-Based TOEFL. You may waste time hitting these buttons by accident.	+ If you aren't familiar with a keyboard, you probably can write faster than you type. – If you have difficulty forming the letters, your brain will race ahead of you, causing you to skip letters and words. When you go back and revise, your essay may look messy.
Proofreading	– You have to scroll up and down to reread your essay.	+ You can see your entire essay at a glance.
Revising	+ You can easily cut/paste/delete words or sentences, and the essay will look clean. – No spell checker or grammar checker. It's all up to you.	+ You might be more careful when you write so that you won't need to revise so much. – Revisions/changes could make the essay look messy. – No spell checker or grammar checker. It's all up to you.

As part of your preparation, you should practice both ways. First write some practice essays out by hand. Then, if you have access to a computer, type the same essays without looking at the hand-written versions. Then switch the order. First type some essays and then write them out by hand without looking at the handwritten versions.

Ask yourself which was easier, which was more comfortable. Choose the option that was easier and more comfortable.

Get some other opinions. You might ask your teacher or a friend with good English skills to read your essays, both handwritten and typed. Which do they think are better essays? If your informal judges thought that the handwritten essays were better, you might want to consider writing your essay by hand.

A word of caution: opinions are subjective. When some readers read a perfectly typed essay, they have the expectation that the English will be perfect, too. Their expectations are high. The essay looks like a finished, proofed piece of writing. If there are mistakes in the essay, they are more evident. They stand out. A handwritten essay looks more like a draft and consequently the reader may not judge it so harshly.

TEST DAY

On the day of the test, you will have to make the decision: by computer or by hand. Even though you don't have to decide until test day, make your decision in advance. Don't waste time on test day making a decision. Spend that extra time on your essay.

You will be given paper and pencils to write your essay. If you type your essay, you can use the paper to make notes and to draw your concept maps. If you write your essay by hand, you will need to keep a few sheets clean for your essay; use the rest to make notes and draw your concept maps. You will have to turn in all paper at the end of the essay section.

If you write your essay by hand, write on the white areas only. Do not write on the shaded margins. Your handwritten essay will be scanned and sent over the Internet to the readers who score the essays. Words written in the gray, shaded margins will not appear.

THE TOPIC

The topic will be shown on the computer even though you choose to write by hand. The screen will look similar to this:

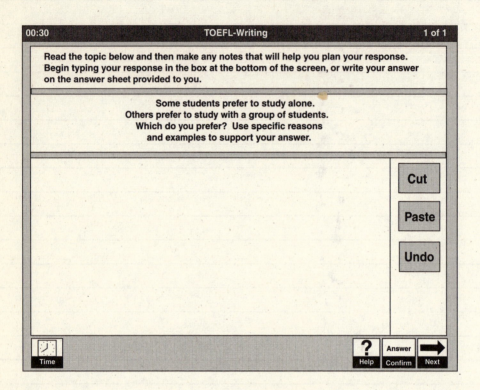

Notice the clock in the upper left corner. Use that to help you plan your essay. You can end the essay section at any time by clicking on Next and Confirm. Do NOT click on Next and Confirm until you have finished your essay. After you click on Next and Confirm, you will not be allowed to write or revise your essay.

   At the end of thirty minutes, the computer will automatically end the essay section.

TIME SCHEDULE

You only have thirty minutes to write your essay. Here is a plan to use that thirty minutes efficiently.

Time		Activity
30:00 – 25:00	PLAN	Read the topic and write your thesis statement. Create your concept map with supporting details.
25:00 – 05:00	WRITE	Write draft topic sentences for each of the supporting details on your scratch paper. Write your essay using your concept map as a guide.
05:00 – 00:00	REVISE	Reread and revise your essay.

COMPUTER TUTORIAL

The keyboard functions for the Computer-Based TOEFL are similar to that of any other word processing program. To perform standard tasks, follow the directions below.

Task	Operation
Start to type	The cursor will blink on the upper left corner of the screen. When you type on the keyboard, the letters will follow this cursor.
Move the cursor	You can reposition the cursor with the mouse or with the arrow keys. Use the arrow keys to move the cursor up, down, left, and right.
Scroll through the text	You can see the beginning of your essay by hitting the Page Up key. You can see the end of your essay by hitting the Page Down key.
Erase text	You can erase all characters to the left of your cursor by hitting the Backspace key.
Start a new paragraph	Hit the Return key twice.
Indent a paragraph	Hit the Space Bar three to five times to indent a paragraph.
Highlight Text	Move the cursor to the beginning of the word or sentence to be highlighted. Click and hold the mouse and move the cursor to the end of the word or sentence. Release the mouse.
Replace Text	Highlight text and type over it.
Delete text	Use the Backspace key or highlight the text to be deleted and click on the icon Cut.
Move text	Highlight the text to be moved. Click on the icon Cut. Move the cursor to the spot where you want the text. Click on the icon Paste.
Change your mind	If you cut text by accident, you can put it back by clicking on the icon Undo. Be careful. You must do this right away. You can't type or cut anything else between your accident and clicking on Undo.

KEYBOARD FOR THE ESSAY

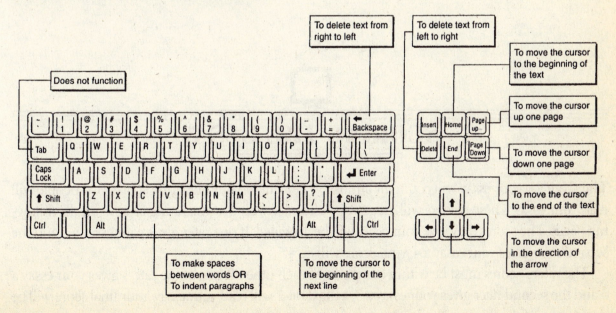

COMPUTER SCREEN FOR THE ESSAY

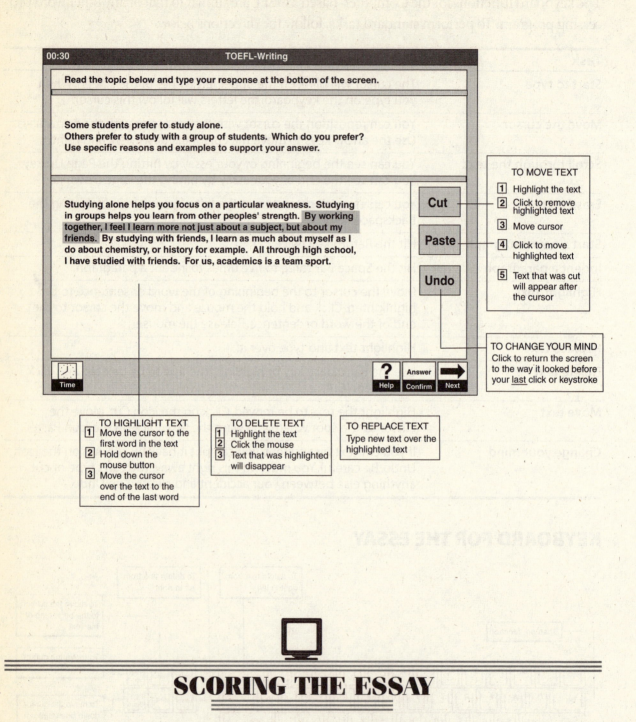

00:30   TOEFL-Writing

Read the topic below and type your response at the bottom of the screen.

Some students prefer to study alone.
Others prefer to study with a group of students. Which do you prefer?
Use specific reasons and examples to support your answer.

Studying alone helps you focus on a particular weakness. Studying in groups helps you learn from other peoples' strength. By working together, I feel I learn more not just about a subject, but about my friends. By studying with friends, I learn as much about myself as I do about chemistry, or history for example. All through high school, I have studied with friends. For us, academics is a team sport.

Cut

Paste

Undo

?
Help

Answer
Confirm

Next ➡

Time

TO MOVE TEXT
1 Highlight the text
2 Click to remove highlighted text
3 Move cursor
4 Click to move highlighted text
5 Text that was cut will appear after the cursor

TO CHANGE YOUR MIND
Click to return the screen to the way it looked before your last click or keystroke

TO HIGHLIGHT TEXT
1 Move the cursor to the first word in the text
2 Hold down the mouse button
3 Move the cursor over the text to the end of the last word

TO DELETE TEXT
1 Highlight the text
2 Click the mouse
3 Text that was highlighted will disappear

TO REPLACE TEXT
Type new text over the highlighted text

SCORING THE ESSAY

The score for your essay will count for almost 50 percent of your Structure score. Two people will read your essay. These readers will judge your essay according to the rating criteria on the following pages. The scores they give your essay will be averaged. If one rater gives your essay a 5 and the second rater gives your essay a 4, your score will be 4.5

The raters' scores must be within one point of each other. If one of the raters gives your essay a 5 and the second rater gives your essay a 3, a third rater will read your essay. Your final score will be the average of the three readers' ratings.

RATING SCALE

6 An essay at this level

____effectively addresses the writing task

____is well organized and well developed

____uses clearly appropriate details to support a thesis or illustrate ideas

____displays consistent facility in the use of language

____demonstrates syntactic variety and appropriate word choice

5 An essay at this level

____may address some parts of the task more effectively than others

____is generally well organized and developed

____uses details to support a thesis or illustrate an idea

____displays facility in the use of the language

____demonstrates some syntactic variety and range of vocabulary

4 An essay at this level

____addresses the writing topic adequately but may slight parts of the task

____is adequately organized and developed

____uses some details to support a thesis or illustrate an idea

____demonstrates adequate but possibly inconsistent facility with syntax and usage

____may contain some errors that occasionally obscure meaning

3 An essay at this level may reveal one or more of the following weaknesses:

____inadequate organization or development

____inappropriate or insufficient details to support or illustrate generalizations

____a noticeably inappropriate choice of words or word forms

____an accumulation of errors in sentence structure and/or usage

2 An essay at this level is seriously flawed by one or more of the following weaknesses:

____serious disorganization or under development

____little or no detail, or irrelevant specifics

____serious and frequent errors in sentence structure or usage

____serious problems with focus

1 An essay at this level

____may be incoherent

____may be undeveloped

____may contain severe and persistent writing errors

0 An essay will be rated 0 if it

____contains no response

____merely copies the topic

____is off-topic, is written in a foreign language, or consists only of keystroke characters

SCORED ESSAYS

Score 6

Topic 13

Some people prefer to eat at food stands or restaurants. Other people prefer to prepare and eat food at home. Which do you prefer? Use specific reasons and examples to support your answer.

Eating Out

Although many people prefer to cook at home, I prefer to eat out. Eating out allows me to spend time and effort on my academic studies instead of in the kitchen.

To begin with, I don't know how to cook. When you don't know how to cook, there is a good chance that what you cook will not be worth of eating. This results in a waste of food, as well as a waste of money and effort.

Also, cooking takes a lot of time. While the food might not actually be on the stove for very long, you also have to consider the time that is spent shopping for the food, cleaning and chopping it, and cleaning up the kitchen after it is cooked.

Finally, eating out is surprisingly economical. Of course going to elegant restaurants is expensive, but there are other ways to eat out. Food stands and some small, casual restaurants provides plenty of good food for very little cost. Many places of this type are located near the university and are very convenient for students.

As my life changes, my preferences about where to eat may change, too. For the life of a student, eating out is the only practical choice.

Proofing Checklist

✓	**CONTENT**
	This essay has a clear thesis in the beginning and is also very well organized. The first two of the three body paragraphs give reasons why the writer does not want to cook at home, while the third gives reasons why eating out is better. Although there is not a great deal of development, there are sufficient details to support the topic sentence in each paragraph. The conclusion paraphrases the main idea rather than simply repeating it.
✓	**CLARITY**
	There is good use of cohesive devices like repeating verbs, parallel structures, and rephrasing. This essay shows syntactic and semantic variety.
	There are very few grammar errors, and they do not interfere with comprehension. . . . there is a good chance that what you cook will not be <u>worth of </u>eating. . . . there is a good chance that what you cook will not be worth eating / worthy of eating. Food stands and some small, casual restaurants <u>provides</u> plenty of good food . . . Food stands and some small, casual restaurants <u>provide</u> plenty of good food . . .
✓	**PUNCTUATION**
	There are no punctuation errors.
✓	**SPELLING**
	There are no spelling errors.

Score 5

Topic 87

Some people think that the family is the most important influence on young adults. Other people think that friends are the most important influence on young adults. Which view do you agree with? Use examples to support your position.

The Important Influence

We are all influence by whomever we meet. We all stand as models to everyone in this world. However, our choice of a model is important especially when choosing a career. I believe that in the case concerning our future and our career, families have more influence on us than friends.

Friends are the ones we spend time having fun, enjoying, playing and so forth. Friends also teach good things and help us. Friends advice good things about life, but not like family. Family always thinks that their children will become superior ones in the future. They want their children be smarter than anyone else. However, friends are not such an influential adviser like family. Family feels that time is waste when their adult children have too much fun. However, friends influence us more to play or have fun rather than advising us about our career. Therefore, family puts their substantial impact on heir children in order to shape up their future career.

In the US, most young adults are usually influence by their friends rather than their parents. It depends upon what type of influence it is. Usually, people are busier in the US. They don't have time to give important influence to their children. Therefore, the children choose their own way to catch up their careers. Whatever they see around impacts these adult children, and they are influence by that. However, this impact might not better them for their future career.

Therefore, I'd say family influences their adult children more and better than friends and relatives.

Proofing Checklist

✓	CONTENT
	The thesis of this essay is very clear and easy to locate at the end of the introduction. This essay is generally well organized. The writer carefully compares and contrasts the level of influence one receives from one's parents with the influence one receives from one's friends. The writer is able to develop his/her thesis. There is a conclusion that restates the thesis.
✓	CLARITY
	The author displays facility in the use of language, but there are some repeated errors in usage and grammar that slow the reader down. S/he seems to be comfortable with expressing ideas in English. Word choice is not always ideal, but ideas are understandable.
	Friends <u>advice</u> good things about life, but not like family. Friends advise good things about life, but not like family. Therefore, <u>family puts their substantial impact on heir children</u> … Therefore, families have a substantial impact on their children… In the US, most young adults <u>are usually influence by</u> their friends… In the US, most young adults are usually influenced by their friends…
✓	PUNCTUATION
	There are no punctuation errors.
✓	SPELLING
	There is only one spelling error. Therefore, family puts their substantial impact on <u>heir</u> children… Therefore, family puts their substantial impact on their children…

Score 4

Topic 109

Do you agree or disagree with the following statement? Playing a game is fun only when you win. Use specific reasons and examples to support your answer.

Playing is Fun if We Win

Some would like to play the game such as, basketball, tennis, swimming, and riding bike for exercises and fun. But some, they play for their acheivement. I agree that playing game is fun when we win.

As a matter of fact, when I was in High school, I like to play basketball as my hobby. I was very excited when I won the game. All high schools in Cambodia, they required students to choose one kind of game such as, volleyball, soccer, basketball, tennis and swimming. By that time, I took basketball as my favorite hobby. My school gave me the best basketball coach. He had lot of experience of training basketball players. My teams and I were trained by him everyday for two months. After two monthes of training, My coach wanted us to compete with the other schools.

When the competition day came, our emotion was combined with happy and scare of losing the game. But our coach encourage us. He told us that "don't be afraid of your competitors, they are as same as you, so you have to have a confident in yourself." When time of competition of game started, our coach led us to basket-ball course to get to know our competitors. The result of competition was my team completely won. My coach and our team were very happy to win that game.

I believe that playing game is very difficult if we don't know a weakness of our competitors. We have to have a confident in ourselves. I agree that playing game is very fun when we win.

Proofing Checklist

✓	CONTENT
	This essay is adequately organized and developed. It shows development of ideas and some facility with English. In the first paragraph and in the conclusion, the writer states his/her opinion that playing a game is fun when one wins. He/She does not directly address the topic, which is more black and white: playing a game is fun ONLY when one wins. It is likely that the writer did not understand the question clearly.
	The writer uses a personal story to illustrate his/her thesis. This story seems to indicate that the writer also had a good time just playing basketball even when he/she didn't win.
✓	CLARITY
	Syntax and usage are inconsistent and distract the reader from the meaning. Everyone who is born into this world, <u>they have different idea of playing game</u>. Everyone who is born into this world has a different idea about playing games. . . . our emotion was <u>combined with happy and scare</u> of losing the game. . . . our emotion was a combination of happiness and fear of losing the game. We have to have <u>a confident</u> in ourselves. We have to have confidence in ourselves.
✓	PUNCTUATION
	There are some punctuation errors. After two month of training, <u>M</u>y coach wanted us to compete . . . After two month of training, my coach wanted us to compete . . . He told us that <u>"</u>don't be afraid of your competitors . . . He told us, "Don't be afraid of your competitors . . .
✓	SPELLING
	There are a couple of spelling errors. But some, they play for their <u>acheivement</u>. But some, they play for their achievement. After two <u>monthes</u> of training . . . After two months of training . . .

Score 3

Topic 84

Some people prefer to spend time with one or two close friends. Others choose to spend time with a large number of friends. Compare the advantages of each choice. Which of these two ways of spending time do you prefer? Use specific reasons to support your answer.

Friends

People need friends they include in a society. Some people try to find good people but some people just take any person who is around them. Which means first one is very serious to find friends and second people are not too serious to have friends. However, there are two types of character to make friends. Some people prefer to spend time with one or two friends. Others choose to spend time with a large number of friends.

First of all, some people want to spend time with one or two friends. Those people always take care of their friends very well. For example, when they have a party they can invite everyone their home even though her/his home is small. Also he/she can talk with each friend before party is over. Because he/she does not have many friends so he/she can be able to talk everyone. Therefore, his/her friends returns home very happy after party.

Secondly, some people want to spend time with a large number of friends. Those people love people also they can get a good advice from friends. For example, when they have a problem they can ask their many friends and then they can collect every answer. Therefore, they are figure it out to fix their problem easily.

Proofing Checklist

✓	**CONTENT**
	The organization and development of the topic is not fully adequate. The writer talks about each choice, but never accomplishes the task: to express a preference. There is no conclusion to this essay. There is a good attempt at addressing the task, discussing the topic in English, and demonstrating a basic level of competence as a writer in English. The writing is lively and earnest.
✓	**CLARITY**
	The writing is understandable, but syntax and usage are very inconsistent. Which means first one is very serious to find friends … This means the first one is very serious about finding friends … Because he/she does not have many friends so he/she can be able to talk everyone. Because he/she does not have many friends, he/she can talk to everyone / is able to talk to everyone. Those people love people also they can get a good advice from friends. Those people love people; also, they can get good advice from friends.
✓	**PUNCTUATION**
	There are a few punctuation errors. For example, when they have a problem they can ask their many friends… For example, when they have a problem, they can ask their many friends…
✓	**SPELLING**
	There are no spelling errors.

Score 2

Topic 101

Some people say that physical exercise should be a required part of every school day. Other people believe that students should spend the whole school day on academic studies. Which opinion do you agree with? Use specific reasons and details to support your answer.

Staying in School

I agree an opinion that students should spend the whole day on academic studies. Because there are have many opportunites for students to be a very good student, like, they have a lot time to spend studies, also, they will be effected by school when they are staying in school. Because of many people staying in library to spend their study, I think that, It will advise me to follow to them. Moreover, staying in school is good for students to enrolling to university. Because they don't have to think something of outside so they really have to think of their learning, this is a good idea for students to stay. Besides that, if they go home to study, it is ok. But when you are studying in your home, suddenly your father or someone call you at that time, I think, you are confusing about your study. Anyway, I still like to spend the whole school day on academic studies, Because there are have enough books and have many things to use in my knowledge. So I love staying in school day to increase my knowledge.

Proofing Checklist

✓	CONTENT
	This essay demonstrates "developing competence," but is flawed on several levels. It is possible that the writer does not fully understand the prompt. The writer seems to think the choice is between staying home or staying in school. S/he doesn't say why one should spend the day on academics and does not address why some physical education would be bad. The information is not organized into an essay, but is all one paragraph. There are insufficient details to support the author's opinions.
✓	CLARITY
	There is an accumulation of errors in sentence structure; in fact, there are errors in nearly every sentence. I agree an opinion that students should spend the whole day on academic studies. I agree that students should spend the whole day on academic studies. Because there are have many opportunites for students to be a very good student, Because there are many opportunities for them to be very good students, …they have a lot time to spend studies… …they have a lot of time to spend on their studies…
✓	PUNCTUATION
	There are a number of punctuation errors, mixed in with other errors. I think that, It will advise me to follow to them. I think that it will be advisable for me to follow to them.
✓	SPELLING
	There are a few spelling errors. …they will be effected by school… …they will be affected by school… Because there are have many opportunites for students to be a very good student,… Because there are have many opportunities for students to be a very good student,…

Score 1

Topic 117

Some people say that advertising encourages us to buy things we really do not need. Others say that advertisements tell us about new products that may improve our lives. Which viewpoint do you agree with? Use specific reasons and examples to support your answer.

Ads

Some people say that advertising encourages us to buy things we really do not need. Others say that advertisements tell us about new products that may improve our lives. Yes. It is. I buyed much, because TV ads.

Proofing Checklist

✓	**CONTENT**
	The student here simply rewrote the topic and added a few words. The essay is on topic, but there is no development of the topic. The author implies, but does not directly state, that s/he agrees with people who say that advertising encourages us to buy things we really do not need.
✓	**CLARITY**
	The few sentences or sentence fragments contain severe errors. The past tense of *buy* is *bought*. *Much* is not an appropriate word choice; *a lot* or *many things* would be better. *Because* should be *because of* or the phrase can be made into a sentence. *Because TV ads make me want to have everything.*

Essay Score 0

If the essay writer simply rewrites the topic question and doesn't add any additional words, the score will be 0.

If the essay writer creates a perfect essay or any essay on a topic that does not match the given topic, the score will be 0.

STRATEGIES AND TIPS

SPECIFIC COMPUTER-BASED TOEFL WRITING IMPROVEMENT STRATEGIES

1. Every day choose one TOEFL essay topic, study the concept map, and read the model essay.

2. Think about the essay topics you read. You may have never thought about a particular subject. After you read an essay topic, form an opinion about that subject. You need an opinion before you can write about one.

The general writing improvement strategies below will help you learn to think about a topic.

3. Once you have thought about a topic, write an essay on that topic. Follow the proposed time schedule to finish your essay in thirty minutes.

Time		Activity
30:00 – 25:00	PLAN	Read the topic and write your thesis statement. Create your concept map with supporting details.
25:00 – 05:00	WRITE	Write draft topic sentences for each of the supporting details on your scratch paper. Write your essay using your concept map as a guide.
05:00 – 00:00	REVISE	Reread and revise your essay.

GENERAL WRITING IMPROVEMENT STRATEGIES

Writing is a skill like playing tennis. You have to practice. There is a lot of extra work you can do on your own to help you become a better writer. Doing these activities, you'll practice your writing, practice your penmanship, and practice forming opinions.

1. To improve your writing, pay attention when you read. Notice how the author of your book organizes thoughts and expresses ideas. *Gone with the Wind* is a famous American novel by Margaret Mitchell. Many years after she died, a sequel was published. The author of that sequel wrote out, by hand, the entire 1037 pages of *Gone with the Wind* three times! She wanted to mimic the style of Margaret Mitchell. She wanted to get a feel for the way Mitchell put sentences together.

   You can do the same thing. Take the model essays in this book and write them out by hand. Write them several times until you get a feel for the use of transition phrases and other cohesive devices. Try to understand how the details support the topic sentences. Pay attention to the introductions and conclusions.

   Once you have copied the model essay several times, think about whether you agree or disagree with the opinion of the author. Then create your own essay on the same topic. Compare your essay with the model essay. Show your essay to a friend or teacher.

2. Read more. A lot of research has shown that reading improves your writing. Reading will build your vocabulary and your understanding of the way ideas are expressed. Read every chance you get.

3. An essay is made up of sentences. If you have some extra time, for example, while waiting for someone, don't just stare at the wall. Write!

   You don't have to write an essay; write just a sentence or two. Look around you. What do you see? Write what you see: *The wall is painted a light yellow.* Write what you think about it: *Yellow is too colorful for me; I'd prefer gray.* Write why you think so: *Yellow is too bright a color; it's hard to relax in a yellow room.*

4. Buy a notebook to record your thoughts and your writing. Don't use this notebook for anything but writing practice. This notebook will be your private classroom.

5. Keep a journal. Record the events of the day. Tell what happened and what you felt about the event. Record what you thought about the events and what conclusions you reached. This will give you practice in writing about your opinions. Review these notes periodically to see if any of these opinions can be used in your essays.

   Date every entry. Put the time of day you are writing. Dates will help you remember the event more clearly later on. A date is a detail, and details are important to good writing.

   Keep every other page blank. If you want to rewrite an entry or to expand on one, you will have the space. This will give you practice in revision.

   The journal does not have to be serious. It can be anything from words, to poems, to jokes, to a complete essay. It can be about your school, your family, or you. The important thing is to write.

6. When events happen, take notes. Later in the day reread your notes and turn them into sentences. Turn the sentences into paragraphs.

7. Write every day. Give yourself a gift of time. Spend five minutes a day writing, and do it faithfully everyday. Once a week, assign yourself a topic and write an essay in thirty minutes.

8. Go back over your writing frequently. The more you write, the better writer you will become. You may think of a better, or a different, way of expressing a thought. Use the blank page to experiment with different ways of expressing the same idea.

9. When you rewrite, imagine you are writing for a different audience. The first time you wrote for yourself. How would you change your writing if your friends were to read it? Your teacher? Your mother? A stranger?

TIPS ON TEST DAY

1. Decide before the test whether you will use the computer or whether you will write the essay by hand. (See section *To Type or Not to Type*.)

2. If you write by hand, your penmanship must be legible.

3. Take full advantage of the paper you are provided. Use it to draw your concept maps. Use it to plan your essay. Write in your first language if you want.

4. Don't be afraid to exaggerate. This essay does not have to be the truth. You do not have to give your real feelings. You can write whatever you want as long as it is on the topic and is grammatically and syntactically correct.

5. You may revise your essay. However, do not completely rewrite it. Think before you write. Try the sentence in your head before you put it on paper.

6. Try to save a few minutes to look over your essay. Look for errors and correct them. Do not do major rewrites here; correct only sentences that would make your essay difficult to understand.

Don't be tempted to memorize the essays in this book. The readers will be familiar with these essays. Use these essays as springboards for your own ideas. Develop your own concept maps and essays from the topics.

SELF-TEST ESSAY #1

Select a topic from the list in the *Appendix, Essay Topic Index*. Plan, write, and revise an essay on that topic within thirty minutes. Use the space on the pages following. Do NOT write in the shaded areas.

Divide your time like this.		
PLAN	5 minutes	30:00 – 25:00
WRITE	20 minutes	25:00 – 05:00
REVISE	5 minutes	05:00 – 00:00

Topic Number: _____

PLAN

Concept Map _____

Thesis Statement _____

General Ideas _____

Supporting Details _____

WRITE

REVISE

Proofing Checklist

Reread your essay. Use this checklist as a guide.

You will not be familiar with many of these items now. You will learn about them all as you study this book.

✓	CONTENT
	Is there a thesis statement or introduction?
	Is there a topic sentence for each paragraph?
	Are there supporting details for each topic statement?
	Is there a conclusion?
✓	CLARITY
	Are there run-on sentences or sentence fragments?
	Are there misplaced modifiers or dangling modifiers?
	Are the structures parallel?
	Are there transition words?
	Are the sentences and paragraphs cohesive?
✓	PUNCTUATION AND SPELLING
	Are the paragraphs indented?
	Are there punctuation marks such as periods at the end of each sentence?
	Do all sentences begin with capital letters?
	Are all the words spelled correctly?

Essay Writing in Twelve Steps

In this chapter you will learn a twelve-step program for writing an essay. You can follow these steps when writing any essay for any purpose. The only difference between writing the Computer-Based TOEFL essay and writing other essays is the time. You only have thirty minutes to write an essay. If you follow these twelve steps, you will be able to write a good essay for any purpose. You can find additional essays and topics, including new topics from ETS, on Dr. Lougheed's Web site: *www.lougheed.com.*

PLANNING THE ESSAY

There are two important parts to planning an essay:

addressing the writing task and

organizing the topic.

Here is an overview of the step-by-step process you will use to address the task and organize the topic.

Step 1	Read the essay topic.
Step 2	Identify the task.
Step 3	Write your thesis statement.
Step 4	Make notes about your general ideas.
Step 5	Expand your notes to include specific details.

The example that follows is a short introduction to the steps of planning an essay. Planning an essay will be discussed thoroughly in the chapter by the same name beginning on page 40. You will learn different ways to address a topic and different ways to organize a topic. You will learn different ways to plan your essay, but the steps remain the same. You must always follow these steps.

STEP 1: READ THE ESSAY TOPIC

(Topic 128) In the future, students may have the choice of studying at home by using technology such as computers or television or of studying at traditional schools. Which would you prefer? Use reasons and specific details to explain your choice.

STEP 2: IDENTIFY THE TASK

The topic wants you to state a preference. *Do you prefer to study at home using computers or study at school?* The instructions suggest you give reasons and specific details to support your answer.

Some people would just ID topic + focus at this stage or wait till eval ideas

STEP 3: WRITE YOUR THESIS STATEMENT

Thesis statement: _Studying at school would be best for me._

The thesis statement is the summation of your thoughts about the topic. In this case, it is the straightforward announcement of your preference.

STEP 4: MAKE NOTES ABOUT YOUR GENERAL IDEAS

These notes are the start of your concept map. The concept map, like a road map, will guide you as you write your essay.

As the writer, I need to plan the organization of the topic. I make two columns so that I can compare the quality of education at home with the quality of education at school.

home		school
	~~activities~~ ~~people~~ ~~day-to-day~~ interaction	
	subjects	
	~~future~~ technology	
	motivation	

I then make a list of all the general ideas that affect education at home and at school. As I write, I may change my mind and cross out a few ideas. I may not like them, or I may not think I could give any examples about them. If I can't give any examples, I shouldn't mention them. I must give reasons and specific details to support my ideas.

STEP 5: EXPAND YOUR NOTES TO INCLUDE SPECIFIC DETAILS

You started your concept map with general notes. Now expand your concept map with specific details.

home		school
isolation	~~activities~~ ~~people~~ ~~day-to-day~~ interaction	socialize
boring		learn from others
technology only source		technology plus teachers
	~~subjects~~ information	
limited	~~future~~ ~~technology~~	~~more au~~
hard to concentrate at home	motivation	work as team

In my first general idea, *interaction*, I added the specific details of *isolation* and *boredom* at home. I would find studying at home all by myself boring. At school, I would be able to socialize with other students and learn from them as well. Therefore, I put the specific details *socialize* and *learn from others* under school.

I crossed out *activities* and *day-to-day* because they weren't exactly the words I was looking for. Similarly *people* wasn't as precise a term as *interaction*.

In the third row for general ideas I thought more about what I wanted to say. I decided I had already talked about *technology* under *subjects* so I crossed it out.

In the second row for general ideas, the word *subjects* was not parallel with the other nouns. I needed a word that ended with *-tion*. I chose *information*.

WRITING THE ESSAY

There are two important parts to writing an essay:

developing the topic and

demonstrating facility with English.

We learned the five steps in planning the essay in the preceding section. Here is an overview of the step-by-step process that you will use to develop the topic and demonstrate your facility with English.

Step 6	Write the topic sentence for each paragraph.
Step 7	Write the introduction.
Step 8	Write the body of the essay.
Step 9	Write the conclusion.

The example that follows is a short introduction to the steps of writing an essay. Writing an essay will be discussed thoroughly in the chapter by the same name. You will learn different ways to develop a topic and demonstrate your facility with English. You will learn different ways to write your essay, but the steps remain the same. You must always follow these steps.

Now that we have planned the essay for Topic 128, let's write it.

Review: In Step 3 and Steps 4 and 5, we wrote a thesis statement and produced a concept map.

Step 3

Thesis statement: Studying at school would be best for me.

Steps 4 and 5
Concept map

home		school
isolation	~~activities~~ ~~people~~	socialize
boring	~~day-to-day~~ interaction	learn from others
technology only source	~~subjects~~ information	technology plus teachers
limited	~~future~~ ~~technology~~	~~more air~~
hard to concentrate at home	motivation	work as team

Now we must move on to Step 6, Write the Topic Sentence.

STEP 6: WRITE THE TOPIC SENTENCE FOR EACH PARAGRAPH

Each of the rows in the concept map could be a paragraph: one paragraph could be about interaction; one paragraph could be about course subjects; one paragraph could be about motivation.

Topic sentence for general idea: interaction

>   *You need interaction to get a good education.*

Topic sentence for general idea: information

>   *Both technology and teachers can give you a good education.*

Topic sentence for general idea: motivation

>   *If you are motivated to learn, you can get a good education.*

Once I have the topic sentences for my paragraphs, I can begin to write the essay.

STEP 7: WRITE THE INTRODUCTION

The introduction lets the reader know what my point of view is and how I plan to develop the essay.

>   *I could get a good education either at home or at school, but an education involves more than just studying. An education is not just getting information from a source. There is interaction with that source and motivation from that source. I need to interact and be motivated by humans not by a machine. Therefore, studying at school would be best for me.*

In this introduction, I have stated my opinion, *Studying at school would be best for me.* I have indicated that I will develop my topic by discussing *information*, *interaction*, and *motivation*.

STEP 8: WRITE THE BODY OF THE ESSAY

Paragraph 2

At home, I can only get information from technological sources like my computer, my DVD player, or my television. At school, I have access to these technological sources plus human ones as well. I have teachers and students who will share their knowledge with me. Both technology and teachers can give you a good education, but at home, I only have technology. I want both options to learn.

In this paragraph, I chose one of my topic sentences and developed it using the specific details in my concept map. I could pick any topic sentence I wanted. I did not have to follow any particular order.

Paragraph 3

You need interaction to get a good education. If no one ever challenges your opinion, you may never develop your ideas. At home, there would be no one to learn from, no one to socialize with. I'd be isolated and bored. The students at school always have new ideas. I want to learn from them.

In this paragraph, I chose another topic sentence and developed it using the specific details in my concept map.

Paragraph 4

If you are motivated to learn, you can get a good education. But how can you motivate yourself isolated at home? I like to work as a team. I want to do well so our class looks good. At home, I can't motivate myself. It's too easy to be distracted by unimportant things. I want the focus that a class goal can give me.

In this paragraph, I chose another topic sentence and developed it using the specific details in my concept map. I don't have to have a specific number of paragraphs. I can have three or I can have ten. I need enough paragraphs to develop my essay thoroughly.

STEP 9: WRITE THE CONCLUSION

If I could motivate myself to work harder, if I could sit all day in a room without interacting with anyone, and if I wouldn't mind getting information from limited sources, then I could study at home. But I can't. I need the stimulus of the classroom to motivate me; I need students to interact with; I need information from as many sources as possible. Give me the traditional school.

In this paragraph, I summarized why I preferred studying in school. I rephrased my ideas. I did not simply repeat them.

REVISING THE ESSAY

There are two important parts to revising an essay:

checking the content and clarity and

checking the punctuation and spelling.

Here is an overview of the step-by-step process that you will use to check the clarity and proof the essay. These steps parallel the Proofing Checklist (see page 27). Follow this checklist to help you proof all of your essays.

Step 10	Check the content.
Step 11	Check the clarity.
Step 12	Check the punctuation and spelling.

For this overview, we will proof the essay written on Topic 128. Since this is a model essay, there will be no major problems. Observe how the proofing checklist can help you review your own work.

Here is the essay on Topic 128 that we wrote following Steps 1 to 9.

I could get a good education either at home or at school, but an education involves more than just studying. An education is not just getting information from a source. There is interaction with that source and motivation from that source. I need to interact and be motivated by humans not by a machine. Therefore, studying at school would be best for me.

At home, I can only get information from technological sources like my computer, my DVD player, or my television. At school, I have access to these technological sources plus human ones as well. I have teachers and students who will share their knowledge with me. Both technology and teachers can give you a good education, but at home, I only have technology. I want both options to learn.

You need interaction to get a good education. If no one ever challenges your opinion, you may never develop your ideas. At home, there would be no one to learn from, no one to socialize with. I'd be isolated and bored. The students at school always have new ideas. I want to learn from them.

If you are motivated to learn, you can get a good education. But how can you motivate yourself isolated at home? I like to work as a team. I want to do well so our class looks good. At home, I can't motivate myself. It's too easy to be distracted by unimportant things. I want the focus that a class goal can give me.

If I could motivate myself to work harder, if I could sit all day in a room without interacting with anyone, and if I wouldn't mind getting information from limited sources, then I could study at home. But I can't. I need the stimulus of the classroom to motivate me; I need students to interact with; I need information from as many sources as possible. Give me the traditional school.

Let's proof this essay following Steps 10, 11, and 12.

STEP 10: CHECK THE CONTENT

Is there a thesis statement?	✔ Yes	Therefore, studying at school would be best for me.
Is there a topic sentence for each paragraph?	✔ Yes	**Paragraph 2** Both technology and teachers can give you a good education, but at school, I have both options to learn. **Paragraph 3** You need interaction to get a good education. **Paragraph 4** If you are motivated to learn, you can get a good education.
Are there supporting details for each paragraph?	✔ Yes	**Paragraph 2** At home, I can only get information from technological sources like my computer, my DVD player, or my television. At school, I have access to these technological sources plus human ones as well. I have teachers and students who will share their knowledge with me. **Paragraph 3** If no one ever challenges your opinion, you may never develop your ideas. At home, there would be no one to learn from, no one to socialize with. I'd be isolated and bored. **Paragraph 4** I like to work as a team. I want to do well so our class looks good. At home, I can't motivate myself. It's too easy to be distracted by unimportant things.
Is there a conclusion?	✔ Yes	I need the stimulus of the classroom to motivate me; I need students to interact with; I need information from as many sources as possible. Give me the traditional school.

STEP 11: CHECK THE CLARITY

Are there run-on sentences or sentence fragments?	✔ No	
Are there misplaced modifiers or dangling modifiers?	✔ No	
Are the structures parallel?	✔ Yes	**Introduction** either at home or at school *interaction with that source* and *motivation from that source*
		Paragraph 2 *at school, I have* both options to learn. *At home, I have* only technology.
		Paragraph 3 *no one to learn from, no one to socialize with*
		Last sentences of Paragraphs 2, 3, and 4 *I want* both options to learn. *I want* to learn from them. *I want* the focus that a class goal can give me.
		Conclusion *If I could motivate* myself to work harder, *if I could sit* all day in a room without interacting with anyone, and *if I wouldn't mind* getting information from limited sources…
		I need the stimulus of the classroom to motivate me; *I need* students to interact with; *I need* information from as many sources as possible.
Are there transition words?	✔ Yes	**Introduction** *Therefore*, studying at school…
		Paragraph 2 *But* used for contrast
		Paragraph 4 *But* used for contrast
		Conclusion *But* used for contrast
Are the sentences and paragraphs cohesive?	✔ Yes	Repetition of *at home, at school* in every paragraph
		Repetition of *information, interaction,* and *motivation* in introduction, body paragraphs, and conclusion

STEP 12: CHECK THE PUNCTUATION AND SPELLING

Are paragraphs indented?	✓ Yes
Are there punctuation marks such as periods at the end of each sentence?	✓ Yes
Do all sentences begin with capital letters?	✓ Yes
Are the words spelled correctly?	✓ Yes

Planning the Essay

ADDRESSING THE WRITING TASK

STEP 1: READ THE ESSAY TOPIC

The first thing to do is read the essay topic carefully. It will be given to you on the computer monitor.

To write a good essay, you must know what the topic asks you to do. You should know how to address the writing task. You must write on the topic. If you write on another subject, you will receive a 0. Pay attention to the task.

STEP 2: IDENTIFY THE TASK

There are four essay types on the Computer-Based TOEFL. The most common essay types are *agreeing or disagreeing* and *stating a preference*. It is more likely that you will get one of these essay topics to write, but you could also be given one of the others. You must know how to recognize the tasks in all four types.

Topic Type	Percentage of Topics on CBT
Agreeing or disagreeing	33%
Stating a preference	34%
Giving an explanation	22%
Making an argument	11%

Agreeing or disagreeing

In this essay, you must state an opinion and defend your point of view. You must give reasons for your thinking. You usually discuss only one side of the issue.

KEY WORDS OR PHRASES
Do you agree or disagree ...?
Do you support or oppose ...?
In your opinion, which is most effective?
Why or why not?

NOTE: Your opinion is an important part of every essay. You will see many different topics asking for your opinion. In determining the writing task, you must look at what the topic is asking you to do.

Examples

(**Topic 120**) Do you agree or disagree with the following statement? Playing games teaches us about life. Use specific reasons and examples to support your answer.

(**Topic 104**) Read and think about the following statement: Only people who earn a lot of money are successful. Use specific reasons and examples to support your answer.

Stating a preference

In this essay, you must discuss both sides of an issue. You will be asked to compare and contrast both sides. You may be asked to give the pros and cons, the advantages and disadvantages of something. You must also state your own personal preference and give reasons to support your choice. You may be asked to state what you think someone else's preference is.

KEY WORDS OR PHRASES
Some do this; others do that.
Some say this; others say that.
Which opinion do you agree with?
In your opinion, which is better?
Which would you prefer?
Would you prefer to …?
Compare the advantages and disadvantages.
Compare these views.
Which viewpoint do you agree with?
Discuss the advantages and disadvantages.
Which is best for you?
Compare these attitudes.
How is (something) different from (another thing)?

Examples

(**Topic 147**) A friend of yours has received some money and plans to use all of it either to:
• go on a vacation
• buy a car.
Your friend has asked you for advice. Compare your friend's two choices and explain which one you think you friend should choose. Use specific reasons and details to support your choice.

(**Topic 4**) It has been said, "Not everything that is learned is contained in books." Compare and contrast knowledge gained from experience with knowledge gained from books. In your opinion, which source is more important. Why?

Giving an explanation

In this essay, you must describe what something is, how it happened, why it occurs, or how it is different. You may have to tell why something is good or bad. You will have to establish criteria and use those criteria to make a judgement.

KEY WORDS OR PHRASES
Describe . . .
Explain . . .
What do you consider most important: (list)?
What have you learned by (doing something)?
Why do you think (something happens)?
What are the qualities of (something)?
Choose an event and tell why you enjoyed it.
How has (something) changed?
Why is (something) important?
How does (something) effect (something else)?
How is (something) different?

Examples

(**Topic 37**) Countries, businesses, and schools are three areas that need good leaders. Choose one of these three areas and describe the most important qualities of a leader in that area. Explain why these qualities are important, using specific examples and details.

(**Topic 1**) People attend college or university for many different reasons (for example, new experiences, career preparation, increased knowledge). Why do you think people attend college or university? Use specific reasons and examples to support your answer.

Making an argument

In this essay, you will be presented with a hypothetical situation. You will have to determine what needs to be done, make a choice, and support your hypothesis. In these essays, the topic is usually written in the future or conditional tense.

KEY WORDS OR PHRASES
If...
How...
In your opinion...
If you could change (something), what would you change?
What is the best way to (do something)?
What should be the main focus?
Which of the following should you do?
Which of the following is most important to you?
What would you give to help someone?
How would you do something?
How would you do something/choose between two things?
How will (something) affect (something else)?

Examples

(**Topic 113**) If you could make one important change in a school that you attended, what change would you make? Use reasons and specific examples to support your answer.

(**Topic 142**) When students move to a new school, they sometimes face problems. How can schools help these students with their problems? Use specific reasons and examples to explain your answer.

Practice 1

Read the following essay topics. Choose which task you are to do.

1. If you could change one important thing about your hometown, what would you change? Use reasons and specific examples to support your answer.

   (A) Make an argument   (B) Give an explanation

2. Some people say that physical exercise should be a required part of every school day. Other people believe that students should spend the whole school day on academic studies. Which opinion do you agree with? Give reasons to support your answer.

   (A) Make an argument   (B) State a preference

3. Do you agree or disagree with the following statement? Playing a game is fun only when you win. Use specific reasons and examples to support your answer.

   (A) Agree or disagree   (B) State a preference

4. Think of the most important class you have ever taken. Why did you enjoy this class so much? Use specific reasons and details to explain your answer.

   (A) Make an argument   (B) Give an explanation

5. Do you agree or disagree with the following statement? Books are not needed any more because people can read information on computers. Use specific reasons and details to explain your answer.

   (A) Make an argument   (B) Agree or disagree

6. In the twentieth century, food has become easier to prepare. Has this change improved the way people live? Use specific reasons and examples to support your answer.

   (A) State a preference   (B) Give an explanation

7. Some items (such as clothes or furniture) can be made by hand or by machine. Which do you prefer—items made by hand or items made by machine? Use reasons and specific examples to explain your choice.

    (A) State a preference   (B) Make an argument

8. A gift (such as a soccer ball, a camera, or an animal) can contribute to a child's development. What gift would you give to help a child develop? Why? Use reasons and specific examples to support your choice.

    (A) Make an argument   (B) Agree or disagree

9. Do you agree or disagree with the following statement? Universities should give the same amount of money to their students' sports activities as they give to their university libraries. Use specific reasons and examples to support your opinion.

    (A) Agree or disagree   (B) Make an argument

10. Some people prefer to spend most of their time alone. Others like to be with friends most of the time. Do you prefer to spend your time alone or with friends? Give reasons to support your answer.

    (A) State a preference   (B) Make an argument

STEP 3: WRITE YOUR THESIS STATEMENT

In order to write a good essay, you must clearly state your thesis. Every essay must have a thesis. The thesis is the main idea of your essay. A thesis statement focuses the direction of the topic and helps the reader understand what you want to say. It tells the reader what your topic is.

Look at these example topics to see how different thesis statements can come from the same topic.

Topic 72

You have been told that dormitory rooms at your university must be shared by two students. Would you rather have the university assign a student to share a room with you, or would you rather choose your own roommate? Use specific reasons and details to explain your answer.

Thesis statement A

Since I do not get along well with many people, I prefer to choose my own roommate.

From this statement, we can presume that the writer will discuss why s/he has difficulty having friendly relationships with people.

Thesis statement B

In the past, I've often been pleasantly surprised by chance encounters; therefore I would rather the university make my choice of a roommate.

From this statement, we can presume the writer will discuss why past encounters with strangers have been pleasant.

A thesis statement must be on the topic. Pay close attention to what the topic asks you to do.

Topic 68

Some people think governments should spend as much money as possible exploring outer space (for example, traveling to the moon and to other planets). Other people disagree and think governments should spend this money for our basic needs on Earth. Which of these two opinions do you agree with? Use specific reasons and details to support your answer.

Thesis statement A

> *The moon is a better place to explore because it is nearer than other planets.*

This thesis statement is NOT a good thesis statement for this topic. It takes two of the words from the topic and writes about exploration possibilities. The topic, though, is how best to spend limited resources: on space exploration or on needs on Earth. This thesis statement is off topic.

Thesis statement B

> *While there is still hunger, poverty, and illiteracy on Earth, our resources should be focused here not in outer space.*

From this statement, we can presume the writer will discuss why hunger, poverty, and illiteracy on earth are more worthy of attention than space exploration.

Thesis statement C

> *The psychological and scientific benefits of space exploration far outweigh chronic earthly problems.*

From this statement, we can presume the writer will discuss in detail the psychological and scientific benefits that we receive from space exploration.

Practice 2

Choose the thesis statements that are appropriate to the topic. There can be more than one possible answer.

1. What is one of the most important decisions you have made? Why was this decision important? Use specific reasons and details to explain your answer.

   (A) Decisions are important because without them nothing would get done.

   (B) Deciding to leave home to attend school in the US has been so far the most important decision I've made.

   (C) Although my parents wanted me to study medicine, I knew that I should follow my heart and get a degree in nuclear physics.

2. Someone who was considered an educated person in the past (for example, in your parents' or grandparents' generation) would not be considered an educated person today. Do you agree or disagree? Use specific reasons and examples to support your answer.

   (A) If you define education as earning degrees, than I would have to agree that today people are more educated than they were in the past.

   (B) It was more difficult to get an education in the past since there weren't as many schools.

   (C) Both my grandfather and my grandmother attended university which is where they met.

3. Many people visit museums when they travel to new places. Why do you think people visit museums? Use specific reasons and examples to support your answer.

   (A) New museums are opening in almost every city in the world.

   (B) Museums hold the historic and artistic record of a region, so visiting museums is the best way to understand a new place.

   (C) Travelers want to see in person famous works of art that they have only seen in books so they head to museums when in new cities.

4. In the future, students may have the choice of studying at home by using technology such as computers or television or of studying at traditional schools. Which would you prefer? Use reasons and specific details to explain your choice.

(A) Interaction with my fellow students is important to me so I would prefer to study in a more traditional setting.

(B) Computers and television are two examples of technology that will change a lot in the future.

(C) The advantages of studying what you want, when you want, and where you want do not, for me, outweigh the disadvantages of using technology for home education.

5. In general, people are living longer now. How will this change affect society? Use specific details and examples to develop your essay.

(A) People are living longer now because of improvements in medical care.

(B) As the majority of our population becomes older, our communities will have to shift their focus from providing services to the young, like schools, to services to aging adults, like medical care.

(C) Society has been around a long time and it is always changing.

Free Practice

Do any or all of the following activities on your own or in a group. There are no answers provided.

1. Write your own thesis statement for the five topics above.

2. Look at the Model Essays in the Appendix. Note whether each topic is an Argument (A), Preference (P), Explanation (E), or Problem Solving (PS) topic.

3. Write essays on the above topics.

ORGANIZING THE ESSAY

STEP 4: MAKE NOTES ABOUT YOUR GENERAL IDEA

To write a good essay, you must organize your thoughts before you write. First, of course, you must have some thoughts. You must have an opinion about a subject. Your opinion about a subject is the thesis of your essay.

Concept maps will help you organize the topic. Use a concept map to make notes. There are many different types of concept maps. We will discuss five in this chapter. Some of them are more appropriate for certain topics. Some are appropriate for all topics. Use the one that works best for you.

Concept Map	Topic
Web	All topics
Fish bone	All topics
Venn Diagram	Stating a preference
Matrix	Giving an explanation
NPR	Making an argument

STEP 5: EXPAND YOUR NOTES TO INCLUDE SPECIFIC DETAILS

Regardless of its shape, each concept map has three components: the thesis statement, some general ideas, and some supporting details. As a rule, you should try to have three general ideas per essay and at least two supporting details per general idea. This will vary according to your topic and the way you choose to organize your topic.

Web

The web concept map is like a spider web. Many ideas are linked by a common thread.

1. Read the topic. (Topic 130) The twentieth century saw great change. In your opinion, what is one change that should be remembered about the twentieth century? Use specific reasons and details to explain your choice.

2. Identify the task. Explanation

3. Write a thesis. Medical advances are the most important change.

4. Add general ideas.

5. Add supporting details.

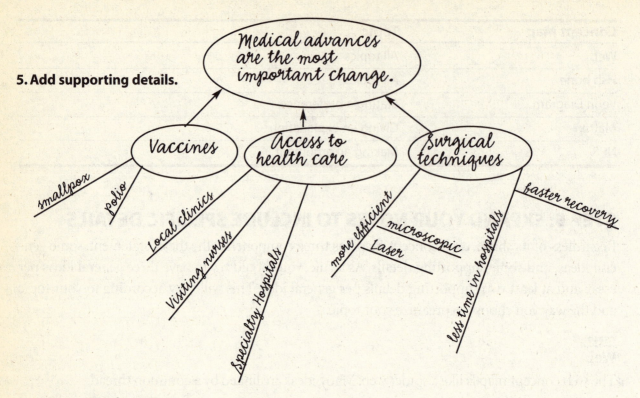

Essay Topic 130

Compare the web concept map with this essay.

Medical Advances: An Important Change
of the Twentieth Century

Although there were many changes, both technological and cultural, in the twentieth century, one stands out above the rest: advances in medical science. The changes in medical science cannot be isolated from the changes in technological and cultural areas. One can move ahead only with the help of the others.

We saw the results of medical advances in three areas: development of vaccines and antibiotics; expanded access to health care; and improved surgical techniques.

When medical researchers determined how to prevent disease and how to stop it from spreading, the quality of life for many people around the world improved. Today smallpox is a forgotten disease, and vaccinations are no longer required. Polio is under control and the vaccine is widely available. The development of penicillin has helped many people recover from serious illnesses.

Although health care is not universal even in developed countries, it is much better than it used to be. Local clinics, visiting nurses, and specialty hospitals have all improved the health care for our communities.

And if you should be unfortunate and require surgery, you are still more fortunate to have the surgery today than you would have been even ten years ago. Now with microscopic and laser surgery, operations are more efficient. You spend less time in the hospital and you recover faster.

I can't think of any other change that affected the lives of so many people. Our health is important to all of us. We all are thankful for advances in the area of medical science.

Fish bone

The fish bone concept map looks like a fish skeleton. The supporting reasons and specific examples point to the main idea.

1. Read the topic. Think of the most important class you have ever taken. Why did you enjoy this class so much? Use specific reasons and details to explain your answer.

2. Identify the task. Explanation

3. Write a thesis. Art History taught me a lot and it was fun.

4. Add general ideas.

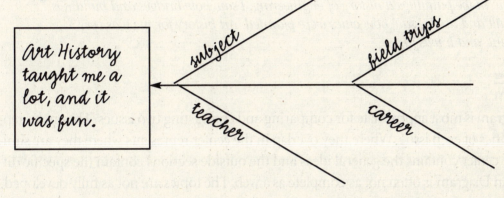

5. Add supporting details.

Essay

Compare the fish bone concept map with this essay.

Art History

As an engineering major, you may not think that I would choose an art history class as the most important class I've ever taken. "Most important" is a very big term to put on a subject that was fun since learning isn't supposed to be "fun." But for me it was fun, and it was important to my career as an engineer.

Art history should be a required subject for everyone. I learned a lot about his-

tory, religion, literature, and mythology during the course. This has been very useful. When I go to parties, no one wants to talk about building bridges. But if I tell someone she has a smile like the Mona Lisa, she is more interested in talking to me.

Of course, the most important part of any course is the teacher. A good teacher can make even a boring subject interesting and lively. I was very lucky to have a good teacher. She is very experienced and is very famous in the field. She's written a lot of books about art and has even curated museum shows.

We also took field trips during the course. We went to museums to see the paintings and sculpture we read about in class. We went to artists' studios to see how a painting was actually painted.

How did this help my career? Not only did it make me a more rounded person, but I saw in the paintings a history of engineering. I saw how bridges and buildings were built and used. I saw how cities were planned. Art history for me was very important, and it was fun.

Venn Diagram

The Venn Diagram is most appropriate for comparing and contrasting two issues. The circles represent the qualities of each issue. Where they overlap in the center represents where they are similar. Usually, the center contains the general ideas and the outside sections contain the specific differences. A Venn Diagram is often not as complete as a web. The topics are not as fully developed.

1. Read the topic.	**(Topic 85)** Some people think that children should begin their formal education at a very early age and should spend most of their time on school studies. Others believe that young children should spend most of their time playing. Compare these two views. Which view do you agree with? Why?
2. Identify the task.	Stating a preference
3. Write a thesis.	Children should play and learn.
4. Add general ideas.	Socialize and competition
5. Add supporting details.	

Learn · play

- learn facts, dates
- work together on projects
- compete for grades

socialize

competition

- watching TV alone
- playing with neighbors

Essay Topic 85

Compare the Venn Diagram with this essay.

Educating Children

Both sides of the argument, school or play, have one thing in common: the good of the child. The question is what will be better for the child. Should a young child spend his or her day playing with friends? Should a young child pass the time attending a formal school?

There are many things that could affect the outcome of the argument. What kind of a school is it? A school where the teacher makes every child sit at a desk all day long memorizing dates and facts? Or is it a school where the teacher helps the children learn what they want to learn?

And what kind of play are we talking about? Will the child be all by him or herself all day long watching television or kicking cans? Or will the child be involved in group activities with neighborhood children of the same age?

I would prefer to send my child to a school where there is a combination. Both school and play are an important way to learn to socialize. Children not only learn how to get along with one another when they play and study together, but they also learn to compete. They compete to win at sports and they compete to win good grades.

Matrix

The matrix is useful for categorizing and classifying qualities. It can be used for all topics.

1. Read the topic.	**(Topic 92)** Do you agree or disagree with the following statement? People behave differently when they wear different clothes. Do you agree that different clothes influence the way people behave? Use specific examples to support your answer.
2. Identify the task.	Agreeing or disagreeing
3. Write a thesis.	Your behavior changes by where you are, whom you interact with, and what you are wearing.

4. Add general ideas.

	Reaction	
	Friend	*Stranger*
Office Setting		
Non-office		

5. Add supporting details.

	Reaction	
	Friend	*Stranger*
Office Setting	*Casual clothes*	*Business dress*
Non-office	*Casual/uniform*	*Casual/uniform*

Essay Topic 92

Compare the matrix with this essay.

You Aren't What You Wear

People do behave differently depending on what they are wearing. The reason is not because they have changed, but people's reaction to them has changed.

Certain clothes are appropriate for certain situations. A man can wear a suit to work and a woman can wear something professional looking like a skirt and jacket. When everyone dresses the same, there is no problem. It is like a uniform.

Imagine going to a law office to hire a lawyer. One of the lawyers is wearing a suit; the other is wearing jeans. Which lawyer do you want to hire?

Similarly, a mechanic works on cars all day and wears clothes that can get dirty. It would be strange to find a mechanic wearing a coat and tie to repair an engine.

People will treat you differently depending on what you are wearing. It will depend on how well they know you and where you are. They will treat you with respect or with disrespect. I remember once I had an old army coat. I wore it into a fancy candy shop to buy some chocolates. The woman was very suspicious and a little afraid. I couldn't understand her reaction since it was still me underneath my big, old ugly green coat.

I was dressed like a bum and this caused the salesperson to react negatively to me. Consequently, I was even more polite than usual. So in this case, I did behave differently because of what I was wearing. I had to balance my appearance. But that doesn't mean that I'm rude if I dress up.

NPR

NPR is like a matrix and is also useful for categorizing and classifying qualities. It is most appropriate for making an argument. NPR stands for Now (topic the way things are now); Proposed (what we propose to change); and Reason (why we make this proposition).

1. Read the topic.   (Topic 119) Your school has received a gift of money. What do you think is the best way for your school to spend this money? Use specific reasons and details to support your choice.

2. Identify the task.   Making an argument

3. Write a thesis.   New equipment is needed.

	N – Now	P – Proposed	R – Reason
4. Add general ideas.	Old school	New Equipment	Better environment
5. Add supporting details.	Old classroom fixtures Shortage of teachers	More desks, chairs, chalkboards, bookshelves, cabinets	Improved learning Happier students Attractive for community

Essay Topic 119

Compare the NPR concept map with this essay.

> *A gift of money is generous and would be welcomed at our school. While there are many things that my school could use, first one must consider the amount of the gift and recognize the fact that a gift is, by nature, a one-time thing. Keeping this in mind, my school could most benefit from new classroom fixtures. While more teachers would be welcomed at our school, it would be misguided to hire new teachers without a way to continue paying their salary. If you were to look at our school, I'm sure that you would agree that nearly all of the classrooms could use new desks, chairs, chalkboards, bookshelves, and cabinets. Our school is old and the people who live here aren't very wealthy. Even though we value education highly, we are unable to provide our students with all that they need to learn.*
>
> *New equipment would provide students with the tools they need to learn. It is hard to write papers if there aren't enough desks and chairs in the classroom for all of the students. It is hard for students to learn when the blackboards are so old that they can't be erased properly. It is also difficult to keep school supplies organized without proper bookshelves and cabinets.*
>
> *Another plus that new equipment would provide is that it would make the school more attractive to the community. It is hard for a community to be proud of a school that is falling apart. If the community can feel that our school is important, perhaps others will give more money in the future, allowing us to further improve our school. Community members could come and help out in the school, making our school even better.*
>
> *Students would be happier with new equipment. It will make them want to come to school and learn. There will be fewer dropouts, and by continuing in their education, these students will be able to better contribute to our community in the future—perhaps even becoming future schoolteachers.*
>
> *While there are many things that can be purchased with a gift at our school, I believe that new equipment is the best choice. It would be a one-time expenditure of money, and new equipment will benefit the learning environment, the community's attitude and the students' feelings about their school.*

Practice 3

Look at the concept map. Read the essay. Complete the missing parts of the map.

1. Read the topic.   You have been asked to suggest improvements to a park that you have visited. This might be a city park, a regional park, or a national park. What improvements would you make? Why? Use specific reasons and examples to support your recommendations.

2. Identify the task.   Making an argument

3. Write a thesis.   Improve the city park to build a strong community feeling.

N — Now	P — Proposed	R — Reason
4. Add general ideas. Decay	Repair	Community feeling
5. Add supporting details. playground benches (5.1) _weeds_	new swings, picnic (5.2)_____, and benches new flowers	(5.3)_____ fun relaxing

Essay

Compare the NPR with this essay.

City Park for the City

Forty years ago people left the city and moved to the suburbs. They left behind what was once a green oasis in the center of the city, City Park. Where children used to play, there is now broken glass. Where their parents gossiped and watched their children play, there are now decayed benches. Where flowers bloomed every season, there are now just weeds. I want to bring this park back to life and encourage people to return to the city again to enjoy it.

The improvements I would propose are simple and relatively inexpensive. First, we have to clean up the park. Volunteer groups can bring rakes and brooms and pick up the trash that litters the playgrounds and the grass.

Second we have to add things that will make the park a place to come to. Swings and sandboxes for the children. Picnic tables and benches for families. Perhaps we can encourage food vendors to open a snack bar.

Third, we need to make the park beautiful again. Our volunteer groups can bring their trowels and their hoes. They can plant flowers and trim shrubs. They can cut the grass and pull the weeds. When more people return to use the park, the city can take over these chores.

People are returning to live in the city. We need to provide them a place that is safe, fun, and relaxing. We need the park to give us a sense of community.

Practice 4

Look at the concept map. Read the essay. Complete the missing parts of the map.

1. Read the topic.	(Topic 91) Some people enjoy change, and they look forward to new experiences. Others like their lives to stay the same, and they do not change their usual habits. Compare these two approaches to life. Which approach do you prefer? Explain why.
2. Identify the task.	Stating a preference
3. Write a thesis.	Your routine is determined by those around you.

	When I was young	Now I have a family	Advantages of routine
4. Add general ideas.	Enjoy change	Routine	Security
5. Add supporting details.	no responsibilities (5.1)_____ take off with friends day-to-day decisions	8 p.m.: bathe children put in pajamas (5.3)_____ 9 p.m.: put to sleep	friends know schedule; (5.4)_____ security
	(5.2)_____ meet new and interesting people, and learn a lot about life		

Essay Topic 91

Compare the matrix with this essay.

My Routine

It is true that there are those who prefer things to stay the same while there are others who prefer change. My personal preference is to establish a routine and stick to it, though this has not always been true of me.

When I was younger, I wasn't a creature of habit. I enjoyed change. When summers came and I was free from the responsibilities of school, I would travel, take off with friends at a moment's notice, and make decisions from day to day. In this way, I could have lots of new experiences, meet new and interesting people, and learn a lot about life.

These days, I enjoy sticking to a routine. This is partially due to the fact that I am a mother of two small children. I find that their lives are happier if I don't upset their schedules too much. For example, we give the children a bath every night at 8:00, put them in their pajamas, read them stories and put them to sleep by 9:00. There are times when this is inconvenient, but everyone in the household is happier if we stick to our routine. In addition, our friends know when to find us at home and when we are free which makes visiting easier.

In conclusion, the "type of person" I am has changed with the circumstances of my life. The obligations of my family force me to have a routine. When I was young, I enjoyed the suspense and adventure of living a crazy life, but now the stability of a household routine suits me better. I think that while, to some extent, all people need a minimum amount of security, those who depend on you often dictate your lifestyle.

Practice 5

Look at the concept map. Read the essay. Complete the missing parts of the maps.

1. Read the topic.   When choosing a place to live, what do you consider most important: location, size, style, number of rooms, types of rooms, or other features? Use reasons and specific examples to support your answer.

2. Identify the task.   Giving an explanation

3. Write a thesis.   The most important thing for me is location.

4. Add general ideas.

5. Add supporting details.

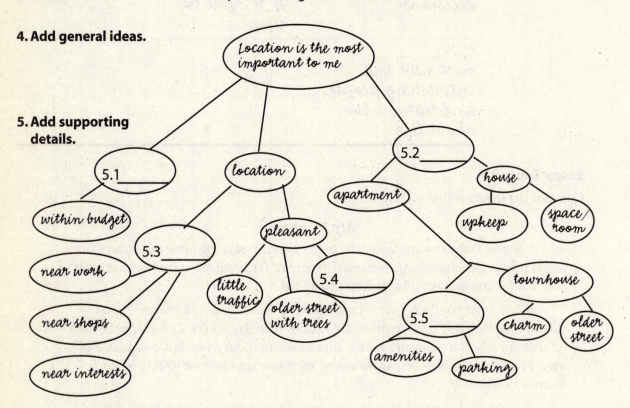

Essay

Compare the web concept map with this essay.

House Hunting

    When choosing a place to live, I look at three things: location, price, and type of housing. However, of the three the most important thing for me is location, location, location.

    The location must be convenient. I look for locations that are close to work, to shops, and to places I like to go. The location must also be pleasant. I like areas with tree-lined streets, away from heavy traffic and with an interesting mix of people. Of course, the price has to be within my budget.

    Once I've chosen my area that's within my budget, I decide what type of housing I want. Do I want to live in a house or an apartment? How much room am I going to need? A house will give me a lot more room for my furniture and clothes. However, will I have time to take care of a house, like mowing the lawn and cleaning out the gutters? I probably won't, so I decide to rent an apartment.

Then I think about whether I want to live in an apartment in a large apartment complex, or rent one in a renovated townhouse? A complex can be a lot of fun because it has amenities for its residents, like a swimming pool and a recreation center. There's also usually more parking available for me and my guests. In townhouses, there are only four or five apartments in one building, but these apartments have more charm. The townhouses are usually located on older streets where there are lots of trees.

Whether I have a swimming pool or parking doesn't matter. Whether I have a two-bedroom apartment or a studio doesn't matter. The location does matter. My new apartment has to be convenient to my office, my shops, and other places I like to go. Naturally, it has to be in a pleasant area, shady and quiet, with interesting neighbors. Aren't pleasant surroundings the most important thing in life?

Practice 6

Look at the concept map. Read the essay. Complete the missing parts of the maps.

1. Read the topic.	(**Topic 1**) People attend college or university for many different reasons (for example, new experiences, career preparation, increased knowledge). Why do you think people attend college or university? Use specific reasons and examples to support your answer.
2. Identify the task.	Giving an explanation
3. Write a thesis.	The three most common reasons are to prepare for a career, to have new experiences, and to increase their knowledge of themselves and the world around them.
4. Add general ideas.	
5. Add supporting details.	

Essay Topic 1

Compare the fish bone with this essay.

Three Reasons People Attend College

People attend colleges or universities for a lot of different reasons. I believe that the three most common reasons are to prepare for a career, to have new experiences, and to increase their knowledge of themselves and the world around them.

Career preparation is becoming more and more important to young people. For many, preparing for a career in a competitive job market is the primary reason to go to college. At college, it's possible to learn new skill for careers with a lot of opportunities. This means careers, such as information technology, that are expected to need a large workforce in the coming years.

Also students go to colleges and universities to have new experiences. This often means having the opportunity to meet people different from those in their home towns. For most students, going to college is the first time they're been away from home by themselves. Being independent like this means having to make decisions— decisions that they've never had to make before. Making these decisions increases their knowledge of themselves.

Besides looking for self-knowledge, people also attend a university or college to expand their knowledge in subjects they find interesting. For many, this will be their last chance for a long time to learn about something that doesn't have to do with their career.

I would recommend that people not be so focused on a career. They should go to college to have new experiences and learn as much as they can about themselves and the world they live in.

Practice 7

Look at the concept map. Read the essay. Complete the missing parts of the map.

1. Read the topic.	(Topic 80) Some people believe that a college or university education should be available to all students. Others believe that higher education should be available only to good students. Discuss these views. Which view do you agree with? Explain why.
2. Identify the task.	Stating a preference
3. Write a thesis.	Higher education should be available to all students.
4. Add general ideas.	*cost* *time*

5. Add supporting details.

not for poor   *Open to all*

- 5.1 _____
- *waste of time*

cost
5.2 _____

- 5.3 _____
- *time to learn about self*
- *meet new people*
- *separate from parents*

Essay Topic 80

Compare the Venn Diagram with this essay.

Higher Education: Open to All Students or Not?

An important goal of education is to learn about yourself. Once you are separated from your parents, you are on your own. You are forced to deal with all different kinds of people and issues. You make an investment in yourself and in your future.

I can understand why some people would think that a college or university education should be available only to good students. Higher education is very expensive. It might seem like a waste of money to send someone to college who might not be able to handle the course work. Higher education is also a big investment of time. Maybe it would make more sense for a mediocre student to use that time getting a job and starting to earn money. Also, there are trade schools for students who aren't academically inclined. Here they can learn a trade and a way to earn a living. Why should they go to college or university? Besides, if they go to college and fail, this will discourage them and make them feel inferior.

I don't agree with this position. I think a college or university education should be available to all students. I think every student should have the opportunity to at least try his hand at college classes. Yes, higher education is expensive, but it is worth it. Yes, higher education is a big investment of time, but it is a valuable investment. If a student finds out he or she can't handle the work, there's plenty of time after that to go to trade school or find a job. Failing at college or university might be hard on a student's self-image, but learning how to handle failure is one of the hard lessons of life.

I think every students should be given a chance to see how far she can go. Students who were got mediocre grades in secondary school might do very well in a different environment. College is more than just going to class. It's a time to meet different people, separate from parents, begin to define yourself as a person. I think that's an experience every student should have.

Practice 8

Look at the concept map. Read the essay. Complete the missing parts of the map.

1. Read the topic.   (Topic 109) Do you agree or disagree with the following statement? Playing a game is fun only when you win. Use specific reasons and examples to support your answer.

2. Identify the task.   Giving an explanation

3. Write a thesis.   I have fun playing all games because it gives me time to be with friends, learn new things, and work as a team.

4. Add general ideas.

5. Add supporting details.

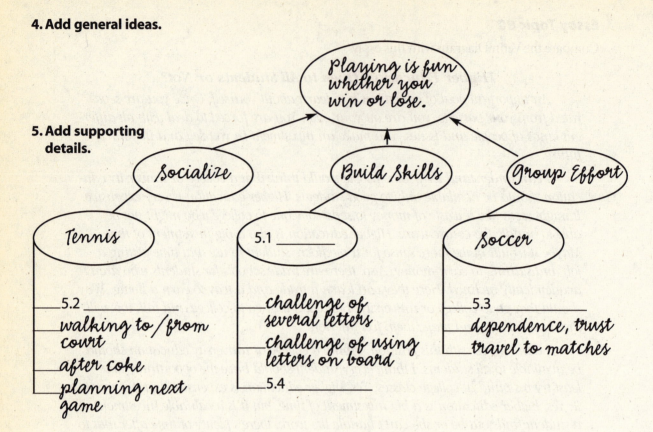

Essay Topic 109

Compare the web concept map with this essay.

Playing to Have Fun

I agree with the old saying, "It's not whether you win or lose, it's how you play the game." I have fun playing all games because it gives me time to be with friends, learn new things, and work as a team.

Tennis is one game that I enjoy. It's a great opportunity to socialize. Of course, you can't carry on a conversation while you're playing, but my tennis partner and I manage to talk a lot before the game. Since we have to reserve a court, we have to talk to one another to find a mutually convenient time. Then we have to make sure that the court is available at that time. This often takes many phone calls and, of course, we talk about many other things during the same conversation. Once we get to the court, we often have to wait so we have another opportunity to chat. After the game, we usually go out for a soda or something to eat and talk some more. We don't even talk about how well or how poorly we played. Tennis is just an excuse for us to get together.

The board game Scrabble, on the other hand, is a real skill builder. It's a challenge to try to form words from the letters you have in front of you or from those on the board. I always learn a new word from my opponents, although sometimes I'm suspicious whether the word really exists. Often we don't even keep score when we play Scrabble. We just do it because it's fun and we learn new English words.

Soccer is the most competitive sport I'm involved in. I do my best, but it doesn't matter to me if my team loses. I enjoy just being with my friends and travelling to different schools in different cities to play. I learn a lot about teamwork when we practice; our coach tells us the most important thing is to play well as a team. It seems she just wants us to have fun and not worry about winning.

All in all, I just enjoy having a good time. Presumably that's our purpose in life. Isn't that better than worrying about who wins and who loses all the time?

Free Practice

Identify the tasks for the following topics. Create a concept map for each. On a separate sheet of paper, write an essay using the concept map as your guide. Compare your essays with those essays in the Model Essay *section.*

1. **(Topic 11)** Do you agree or disagree with the following statement? Universities should give the same amount of money to their students' sports activities as they give to their university libraries. Use specific reasons and examples to support your opinion.

   Task: _____

   Thesis statement: _____

   Concept Map:

2. **(Topic 9)** Some people prefer to live in a small town. Others prefer to live in a big city. Which place would you prefer to live in? Use specific reasons and details to support your answer.

   Task: _____

   Thesis statement: _____

   Concept Map:

3. **(Topic 7)** How do movies or television influence people's behavior? Use reasons and specific examples to explain your answer.

   Task: _____

   Thesis statement: _____

Concept Map:

4. **(Topic 121)** Imagine that you have received some land to use as you wish. How would you use this land? Use specific details to explain your answer.

Task: _____

Thesis statement: _____

Concept Map:

5. **(Topic 97)** Do you agree or disagree with the following statement? It is more important for students to study history and literature than it is for them to study science and mathematics. Use specific reasons and examples to support your opinion.

Task: _____

Thesis statement: _____

Concept Map:

6. **(Topic 125)** In some countries, people are no longer allowed to smoke in many public places and office buildings. Do you think this is a good rule or a bad rule? Use specific reasons and details to support your position.

Task: _____

Thesis statement: _____

Concept Map:

SELF-TEST ESSAY #2

Write on the same topic from Self-test Essay #1. Plan, write, and revise an essay on that topic within 30 minutes. Use the space provided. Do NOT write in the shaded areas.

Divide your time like this.

PLAN	5 minutes	30:00 – 25:00
WRITE	20 minutes	25:00 – 05:00
REVISE	5 minutes	05:00 – 00:00

Topic Number: _____

PLAN

Concept Map

Thesis Statement

General Ideas

Supporting Details

WRITE

REVISE

Proofing Checklist

Reread your essay. Use this checklist as a guide.

✓	CONTENT
	Is there a thesis statement or introduction?
	Is there a topic sentence for each paragraph?
	Are there supporting details for each topic statement?
	Is there a conclusion?
✓	CLARITY
	Are there run-on sentences or sentence fragments?
	Are there misplaced modifiers or dangling modifiers?
	Are the structures parallel?
	Are there transition words?
	Are the sentences and paragraphs cohesive?
✓	PUNCTUATION AND SPELLING
	Are the paragraphs indented?
	Are there punctuation marks such as periods at the end of each sentence?
	Do all sentences begin with capital letters?
	Are all the words spelled correctly?

3

Writing the Essay

DEVELOPING THE TOPIC

STEP 6: WRITE THE TOPIC SENTENCE FOR EACH PARAGRAPH

In the chapter on *Planning Your Essay*, we learned about a thesis statement. A thesis statement tells the reader what the essay will be about. A topic sentence tells the reader what a paragraph will be about. A topic sentence can introduce the paragraph, or it can summarize what has been said in the paragraph. A topic sentence can be at the beginning, the middle, or the end of a paragraph.

When people start writing an essay without planning what they will say, the introduction usually has nothing to do with the essay. Some people write the body of an essay first; once they know what they have said, they go back and write the introduction. You don't have that time. You must plan in advance.

If you write a sentence for each of the general ideas in your concept map, you will have three to five topic sentences. These topic sentences will be used in the body of your essay and will be summarized in the introduction and conclusion. Learning to write a good topic sentence is important. If you think about the topic sentences that you want for each paragraph, your writing will be more coherent, and you will be able to write more quickly.

You must provide specific reasons to support the ideas in your essay. These phrases will often appear in the Computer-Based TOEFL topic.

KEY PHRASES
Use specific reasons and examples to support your answer.
Use specific reasons and examples to support your opinion.
Use specific reasons and examples to develop your essay.
Use specific reasons and examples to explain your choice.
Give specific details to support your position.

All paragraphs contain a topic sentence supported by specific details. A topic sentence is usually a generalization.

Topic sentence: Physical training is good for you.

Supporting details: Physical activity promotes blood circulation.

The brain needs oxygen to function.

You will be more alert in class.

The generalization is likely to be your opinion on the topic. You will need to support your opinion with details. Specific details give substance to your essay. They make it interesting and pertinent.

Topic sentence: I support the plan to build a new movie theater in my neighborhood.

Supporting details: The nearest movie theater is two miles away.

Restaurants will be built up around the theater.

Look at these examples.

Example from Topic 142

A school administrator should begin by giving students a complete orientation to their new school. She or he should take them on a tour of the school, showing them the classrooms, gym, computer lab, band room, and cafeteria. She or he should tell them about the history of the school, its academic achievements, its seven athletic and debating teams. The administrator can talk to the students about what's expected of them in the classroom and what rules the school has.

Topic sentence:	A school administrator should begin by giving students a complete orientation to their new school.
Supporting details:	take students on tour of school
	tell about history of school
	talk to them about what's expected

In the above paragraph the topic sentence is about the school administrator's job to give an orientation to new students. The orientation includes a tour of the school, its history, and a discussion of what is expected of students.

Example from Topic 152

Everyone, children as well as senior citizens, can have important relationships with pets. Children who have dogs have the opportunity to learn responsibility while caring for them. The elderly, who often feel lonely as they get older and have fewer living friends and relatives, are able to maintain a positive outlook and to feel needed because they are caring for a dog that needs them.

Topic sentence:	Everyone, children as well as senior citizens, can have important relationships with pets.
Supporting details:	teaches children responsibility
	elderly take care of dogs who, in turn, need them.

Example from Topic 94

One should spend time getting to know people before judging them. I know that I do not always make the best first impression, even when I truly like the person with whom I am interacting. We all have bad days, and I wouldn't want to lose a job or a potential friendship simply because I picked out the wrong clothing or said something wrong.

Topic sentence:	One should spend time getting to know people before judging them.
Supporting details:	I don't always make the best first impression.
	We all have bad days.
	We all pick out the wrong clothing or say something wrong.

Practice 1

Read the following paragraphs. Write the topic sentence and the supporting details for each paragraph. You may have more or fewer than three supporting details.

1. **Paragraph from Topic 120**
   Playing games also teaches us how to deal with other people. We learn about teamwork, if the game involves being on a team. We learn how to divide and assign tasks according to each person's skills. We learn how to get people to do what we want, and we learn that sometimes we have to do what other people want.

Topic sentence:	1.1
Supporting details:	1.2
	1.3
	1.4
	1.5

2. **Paragraph from Topic 13**
   Cooking takes a lot of time. While the food might not actually be on the stove for very long, you also have to consider the time that is spent shopping for the food, cleaning and chopping it, and cleaning up the kitchen after it is cooked.

Topic sentence:	2.1
Supporting details:	2.2
	2.3
	2.4

3. **Paragraph from Topic 7**

Watching movies and television can be good for us. One thing they do is give us a broader window on the world. For example, seeing movies can expose us to people of different races and cultures that we don't see often. We can then overcome some prejudices more easily. Recently there have been more handicapped people in films, and this also helps prevent prejudice.

Topic sentence:	3.1
Supporting details:	3.2
	3.3
	3.4

4. **Paragraph from Topic 30**

Our planet gives us everything we need, but natural resources are not endless. Strip mining devastates whole regions, leaving bare and useless ground. Deforestation removes old growth trees that can't be replaced. Too much fishing may harm fish populations to the point where they can't recover.

Topic sentence:	4.1
Supporting details:	4.2
	4.3
	4.4

5. **Paragraph from Topic 4**

The most important lessons can't be taught; they have to be experienced. No one can teach us how to get along with others or how to have self-respect. As we pass from childhood into adolescence, no one can teach us the judgement we need to decide on how to deal with peer pressure. As we leave adolescence behind and enter adult life, no one can teach us how to fall in love and get married, or how to raise our children.

Topic sentence:	5.1
Supporting details:	5.2
	5.3
	5.4

STEP 7: WRITE THE INTRODUCTION

You need two things to write a good introduction. You need to have an opinion on the topic and you need to have topic sentences for each of the paragraphs. Your opinion will tell the reader what you think about the subject; the summary of the topic sentences will guide your reader through your essay.

Stating Your Opinion

The introduction to your essay should tell the reader what your opinion is on the topic. The computer-based essay is a personal essay. Your ideas on a topic are important. The readers are interested in what you have to say. There is, however, no right or wrong opinion. The readers look to see how you express your opinion whatever it is.

You can express your opinion by using set phrases or by varying the verbs, adjectives, and adverbs you use. On the computer-based essay, you must show semantic and syntactic variety in your language to score high. This section will help you give your writing more variety.

Set Phrases

KEY WORDS	
In my opinion	It is my opinion that
According to me	I believe
To my way of thinking	I think
In my view	It seems to me that
To me	It appears that
From my point of view	To my mind

Examples

In my opinion, university students must attend classes.
According to me, one must change with the times.
To me, there is nothing more important than good health.

It is my opinion that one learns by example.
It seems to me that a good neighbor is one who respects your privacy.
It appears that all the information one needs is available on computer.

Practice 2

Give your opinion about these topics. Use the phrases suggested.

1. People's lives (are/are not) easier today.

    In my opinion *people's lives are easier today.*

2. Most people (prefer/do not prefer) to spend their leisure time outdoors.

    It seems to me that_____

3. An apartment building (is/is not) better than a house.

    To my mind _____

4. It (is/is not) good that English is becoming the world language.

From my point of view_____

Verbs

You can use different verbs to show how strongly you feel about something. *Believe* and *think* are the most common verbs used to express a personal opinion.

KEY WORDS	
Agree	Infer
Believe	Realize
Guess	Suppose
Hope	Think
Imagine	Understand

Examples

I agree that studying science is more important than studying literature.

I hope that people remember the special gifts I gave them.

I infer from their actions that most youth feel they have nothing to learn from older people.

I understand why people like to work with their hands.

Practice 3

Give your opinion about these topics. Use the verbs suggested.

1. High schools (should/should not) allow students to study what they want.

I believe that _____

2. It is better to be a (leader/member) of a group.

I guess that _____

3. People (should/should not) do things they do not enjoy doing.

I agree that _____

4. I would rather have the university (assign/not assign) me a roommate.

I suppose that _____

Adjectives

You can use different adjectives to show how strongly you feel about something.

KEY WORDS

Certain	Positive
Convinced	Sure

Examples

I am certain that movies influence people's behavior.
I am convinced that having a pet can contribute to a child's development.

Practice 4

Give your opinion about these topics. Use the adjectives suggested.

1. Children (should/should not) spend a great amount of time practicing sports.

   I am sure that _____

2. A shopping center in my neighborhood (will/will not) be a benefit to our community.

   I am positive that _____

Adverbials

You can use different adverbials to qualify your opinion. These adverbials show how strongly you feel about something.

KEY WORDS

Seemingly	Maybe	Almost
Conceivably	Probably	Doubtless
Possibly	Presumably	No doubt
Perhaps	Certainly	Definitely

Examples

Seemingly, playing games can teach us about life.
Daily exercise definitely should be a part of every school day.
Doubtless, helping a child to learn to read is important.
Individual sports are possibly better than team sports for some students.

Practice 5

Give your opinion about these topics. Use the adverbials suggested.

1. A zoo (has/does not have) a useful purpose.

   No doubt _____

2. Growing up in the countryside (is/is not) better than growing up in the city.

   Perhaps_____

3. Our generation (is/is not) different from that of our parents.

   Certainly, _____

4. A sense of humor can sometimes be (helpful/detrimental) in a difficult situation.

   Conceivably_____

You can use different adverbials to make a general statement about how you feel about something.

KEY WORDS		
All in all	Basically	Generally
All things considered	By and large	In general
Altogether	Essentially	On the whole
As a rule	For the most part	Overall

Examples

All in all, it is better to learn from a teacher than on your own.
As a rule, it is better for students to wear uniforms to school.
For the most part, countries are more alike than different.
On the whole, higher education should be available to all.

Practice 6

Give your opinion about these topics. Use the adverbials suggested to make a general statement.

1. The family (is/is not) the most important influence on young adults.

   All things considered,_____

2. Parents (are/are not) the best teachers.

   In general, _____

3. People (are never/are sometimes) too old to attend college.

   By and large, _____

You can use different adverbials to qualify your opinion. These adverbials show an idea is not completely true.

KEY WORDS	
Almost	So to speak
In a way	For all intents and purposes
More or less	To some extent
practically	Up to a point

Examples

> Up to a point, people succeed because of hard work, not because of luck.
> For all intents and purposes, television has destroyed communication among family members.

Practice 7

Give your opinion about these topics. Use the adverbials suggested to show an idea is not completely true.

1. It is better to make a wrong decision than to make no decision.

   or

   It is better to make no decision than to make a wrong decision.

   In a way, _____

2. Watching movies (is/is not) more enjoyable than reading.

   To some extent, _____

3. You (can/cannot) learn as much by losing as winning.

   More or less, _____

GUIDING THE READER

The introduction to your essay should also tell the reader how you plan to develop your topic. The topic sentences that you developed from your concept maps can be summarized in the introduction.

Compare these introductions.

Introduction to Topic 1

Version A

> *I believe that people attend college for many different reasons. These reasons are personal to them.*

Version B

> *People attend colleges or universities for a lot of different reasons. I believe that the three most common reasons are to prepare for a career, to have new experiences, and to increase their knowledge of themselves and the world around them.*

Comment

Version A starts with the writer's opinion, but it does not tell us much. What are these reasons? We need to know the basic reasons so we can prepare ourselves to find supporting details in the body of the essay.

Version B gives three specific reasons that the writer believes are the most important ones: to prepare for a career, to have new experiences, and to increase their knowledge of themselves and the world around them. From this introduction I will expect to see three paragraphs on each of these reasons.

Introduction to Topic 6

Version A

> *I think there are changes necessary in my hometown. It is always the same. There has to be something different.*

Version B

> *If I could change one thing about my hometown I think it would be the fact that there's no sense of community here. People don't feel connected, they don't look out for each other, and they don't get to know their neighbors.*

Comment

Version A starts with the writer's opinion but doesn't say what changes are necessary. We need some guidance.

Version B narrows in on the topic and talks about the sense of community. The writer says that "People don't feel connected, they don't look out for each other, and they don't get to know their neighbors." From this introduction, I will expect to see three paragraphs on each of these reasons.

Introduction to Topic 13

Version A

> *I believe that some people like to eat at food stands, and some like to eat in restaurants. There are different reasons for this.*

Version B

> *Some people like to eat out at food stands and restaurants, while others like to prepare food at home. Often it depends on the kind of lifestyle people have. Those with very busy jobs outside the house don't always have time to cook. They like the convenience of eating out. Overall, though, I think it is cheaper and healthier to eat at home.*

Comment

In *Version A*, the writer does not share what these reasons are. There are no general statements.

In *Version B*, the writer tells us that the choice depends on a person's lifestyle. The writer will probably give us more details about the reasons of convenience, costs, and health.

Practice 8

Read the following introductions and tell us what the writer believes and the focus of each paragraph. You may not have three paragraphs for all introductions.

1. **Introduction to Topic 84**

   We all need to have friends, and I think the more friends we have the better. Friendship helps us learn how to trust others, it helps us know what to expect from others, and it helps us profit from experiences. I want to have a lot of friends around me so I can learn more about myself from different people.

   Opinion: *I think the more friends we have the better*

   Paragraph focus: *learn how to trust others*

   Paragraph focus: *learn what to expect from others*

   Paragraph focus: *helps us profit from experiences*

2. **Introduction to Topic 120**

   Almost everyone, from little children to adults, loves games. The types of games may change and get more complex as we grow up, but our enjoyment never changes. I believe that playing games is both fun and useful, because it teaches us the skills we need in life. Games teach us there is a cause-effect relationship; teach us about teamwork; and teach us to follow rules.

   Opinion: _____

   Paragraph focus: _____

   Paragraph focus: _____

   Paragraph focus: _____

3. **Introduction to Topic 87**

   Although friends make an impression on your life, they do not have the same influence that your family has. Nothing is as important to me as my family. From them, I learned everything that is important. I learned about trust, ambition, and love.

   Opinion: _____

   Paragraph focus: _____

   Paragraph focus: _____

   Paragraph focus: _____

4. **Introduction to Topic 83**

If I had to choose between spending time alone or spending time with my friends, I'd rather be alone. I need this time alone to "recharge my batteries," to re-energize my mind and spirit. Being with friends can be fun and can help you get through the rough spots in life, but it's the time alone, I think, that forms you as a person.

Opinion: _____

Paragraph focus: _____

Paragraph focus: _____

Paragraph focus: _____

5. **Introduction to Topic 52**

Traveling alone is the only way to travel. If you take someone with you, you take your home with you. When you travel alone, you meet new people, have new experiences, and learn more about yourself.

Opinion: _____

Paragraph focus: _____

Paragraph focus: _____

Paragraph focus: _____

DEMONSTRATING FACILITY WITH ENGLISH

STEP 8: WRITE THE BODY PARAGRAPHS

Once you have stated your opinion and shown the reader how you plan to develop your essay, the rest is easy. You simply turn the supporting details in your concept maps into sentences. Of course, you must make sure your sentences have semantic and syntactic variety. Look how these concept maps turned into paragraphs.

Examples

Paragraph 3 from Topic 113

> *The foreign language program should be staffed with well-trained instructors. The current teachers in the program lack proficiency in the language. In our classes teachers frequently made errors that the students repeat. If the teachers were well-trained, they would be good models for the students.*

Now	Proposed	Result
Lack proficiency in language	well-trained teachers	teachers provide good model

Paragraph 2 from Topic 101

> *Another issue is economic. Many schools simply do not have the money to provide gym facilities, playing fields, and athletic equipment for their students. Other schools are located in cities where that kind of space just isn't available. A few schools would rather keep money for academic purposes.*

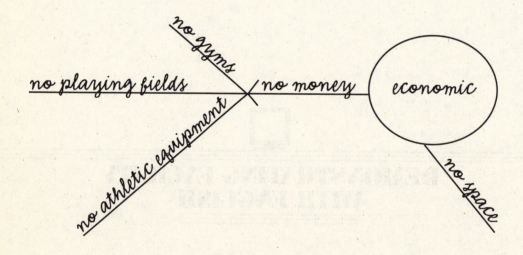

Practice 9

Read the following paragraphs and complete the concept maps for the paragraphs.

1. **Paragraph 3 from Topic 13**
   Eating at home is better for you. Meals at restaurants are often high in fat and calories, and they serve big plates of food—much more food than you need to eat at one meal. If you cook food at home, you have more control over the ingredients. You can use margarine instead of butter on your potatoes, or not put so much cheese on top of your pizza. At home, you can control your portion size. You can serve yourself as little as you want, instead of having in a restaurant a full plate of food that you eat "because you paid for it."

Restaurant   Healthier   Home

High in fat
and calories
1.1 _____

ingredients
portions

1.2 _____

1.3 _____

2. Paragraph 2 from Topic 42

The internet and the world wide web have opened every major library and database to students around the world. Information comes not only in print form, but also in multimedia. You can get audio and video data. You can get information about events in the past as well as events that unfold as you watch your computer monitor.

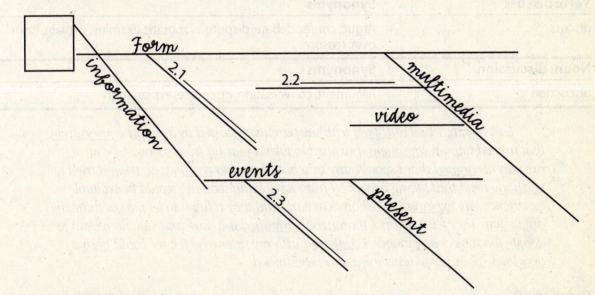

Form

information

2.1

2.2 _____

multimedia

video

events

2.3

present

3. Paragraph 5 from Topic 14

In class, students receive the benefit of a teacher's knowledge. The best teachers do more than just go over the material in the class textbook. They draw their students into discussion of the material. They present opposing points of view. They schedule guest speakers to come, give the students additional information, or show documentary films on the subject.

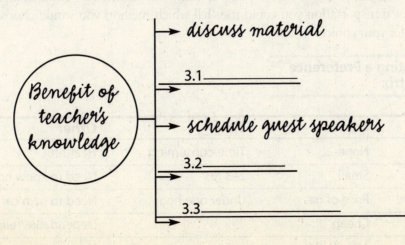

→ discuss material

3.1 _____
→

Benefit of
teacher's
knowledge

→ schedule guest speakers

3.2 _____
→

3.3 _____
→

Using Semantic Variety

In order to be a good essay, your essay must interest the reader. One way to do this is to vary your vocabulary. Learning different ways to express similar ideas (synonyms) and different ways to help the reader move from one idea to the next will help you develop semantic variety.

Synonyms

When you are writing on one topic, you don't want to repeat the same verb or adverb, noun or adjective in every sentence. You should try to use words that are similar in meaning, and that will carry the meaning of the sentence. Synonyms are important because they help you link closely related words or ideas. Synonyms provide coherence in your essay.

Read the paragraph below. Look for these synonyms of *discuss* and *discussion*.

Verb: discuss	Synonyms
discuss	Argue, confer, debate, dispute, elaborate, examine, explain, hash over, reason

Noun: discussion	Synonyms
discussion	Argument, conversation, discourse, explanation

Last month, I had a <u>dispute</u> with my parents. It started as a simple <u>conversation</u> that turned into an <u>argument</u>. I wanted to take a year off from school. Of course, my parents <u>argued</u> that I should stay in school. I tried to <u>reason</u> with them; I tried to <u>persuade</u> them that taking a year off from school and working would be valuable experience. My <u>explanation</u> fell on deaf ears, and they refused to let me continue the <u>discussion</u>. They felt I had not thoroughly <u>examined</u> the issue and saw no reason to <u>debate</u> the subject any longer. I <u>conferred</u> with my sister who felt we could <u>hash</u> it <u>over</u> later when my parents were in a better mood.

Practice 10

Read the following topic and study the concept map. Then read the essay.

Topic 79

You need to travel from your home to a place 40 miles (64 kilometers) away. Compare the different kinds of transportation you could use. Tell which method you would choose. Give specific reasons for your choice.

Task: Stating a Preference
Concept Map: Matrix

Transportation	Cost	Time	Other
Walking	None	Time-consuming	Healthful
Horse	Small	2–3 hrs	Need to know how to ride
Car	Price of gas	Under one hour	Need to own car
Mass transportation	Cheap		Dependable/reliable
Shared taxi	Affordable		Need people

Essay (Topic 79)

There are many different types of transportation that vary depending on numerous factors, including speed and cost. Which type of transportation one chooses depends on an individual's time constraints, financial situation, and the distance to be covered. While the question states that I need to travel 40 miles, it does not say how long I have to travel, so I will outline the various choices.

The most economical choice is walking. It costs nothing and is healthful, but it is time-consuming. The average person can walk about four to five miles per hour, so this trip would take at least ten hours to complete, which would probably necessitate sleeping somewhere along the way. After walking comes animal transportation. In my country, horses are not common, but are available for travel in the countryside. I believe that a 40-mile trip would take 2 or 3 hours on a horse. If one has access to a horse, the cost is minimal. Of course, you have to know how to ride!

If one is lucky enough to own a car, then the time is minimal (under one hour), with only the cost of gasoline to consider. However, many people don't own cars, so they must depend on mass or public transportation. Shared taxis are one form of affordable transportation, with four or five people sharing the cost of a car trip to a common destination. The only downside is finding people to share the fare with. In urban areas, there are buses, subways, and trains to consider, if these forms of transportation service your destination.

In short, the kind of transportation depends on how fast I need to get to my destination and how much money I have. If I need to get there fast, and money isn't important, I can hire a private taxi. Since I don't own my own car, I don't have that option, and I have never walked 40 miles in one trip. I usually depend on the bus and trains, and would do so in this circumstance. They are cheap, dependable, and reliable.

The highlighted words in the essay could be replaced with a word from this synonym list. Write the synonym that matches the highlighted word.

Synonym List

passengers	form	transit	insignificant
quickly	turn to	going on foot	traveled
require	take you where you want to go.	options	typical

Highlighted Words in Essay (Topic 79)

covered	1	Traveled
choices	2	
walking	3	
average	4	
necessitate	5	
minimal	6	
transportation	7	

people	8	_____
service your destination	9	_____
kind	10	_____
fast	11	_____
depend on	12	_____

Practice 11

Read the following topic and study the concept map. Then read the essay.

Topic 90

Some people choose friends who are different from themselves. Others choose friends who are similar to themselves. Compare the advantages of having friends who are different from you with the advantages of having friends who are similar to you. Which kind of friend do you prefer for yourself? Why?

Task: **Giving an Explanation**
Concept Map: Stating a Preference

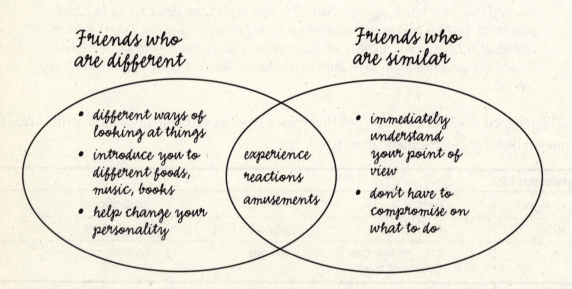

Essay Topic 90

My Friends

There are a lot of advantages to having friends who are different from you. For one thing, they will present you with a different way of looking at the world. If you're a very liberal person, then a friend who tends to be more conservative can give you a different perspective on politics. Friends who are different can introduce you to new foods, music, and books. If you're a spontaneous kind of person, someone who is more scheduled can help you get yourself better organized. And you can help them loosen up a little bit, do things on the spur of the moment.

Someone who is different from you won't have the same reaction to situations, and this can be a big help. If you're the kind of person who gets very impatient waiting for your meal in a restaurant, it helps to have someone with you who can calm you down before you lose your temper. On the other hand, if you're a bit timid about standing up for yourself, a more assertive friend can help you develop a little more self-respect.

There can be some disadvantages to a friendship of opposites. If you don't enjoy doing the same things, that can mean that one of you is always having to compromise on what you want to do. Sometimes it's fun experiencing new things; other times, it's more fun doing what you know you'll enjoy.

All things considered, I think I'd like to have a lot of acquaintances who are different and a few close friends who are similar to me. That seems the best of both worlds.

The highlighted words in the essay could be replaced with a word from this synonym list. Write the synonym that matches the highlighted word.

Synonym List

is apt	a number of	relax	trade off
benefits	shy	restless	becomes
introduce to	impulsive	response	confident

Highlighted Words in Essay (Topic 90)

a lot of	1	_____
advantages	2	_____
present with	3	_____
tends	4	_____
spontaneous	5	_____
loosen up	6	_____
reaction	7	_____
gets	8	_____
impatient	9	_____
timid	10	_____
assertive	11	_____
compromise	12	_____

Transition Words

Transitional words and phrases will help your reader follow your ideas from sentence to sentence and from paragraph to paragraph. Without transitional words and phrases, your ideas will stand alone, unrelated to the thesis of your essay.

In this section, you will learn to use transition words that show time; degree; comparison and contrast; and cause and effect. You will also learn transition words that let you add more information and transition words like pronouns that let you make connections to previously mentioned subjects.

Time

When you are explaining the sequence of events, you may want to use these expressions.

before	next	then	often
after	during	always	sometime
since	at the same time	while	meanwhile

Example

The school counselors should help students who are new to a school. *Before the first day* of school, they should give an orientation to the building. *On the opening day*, they should introduce the students to the teachers. *After* the students have gotten used to their classes, the counselors should find out about any hobbies that the students might have and recommend some extracurricular clubs. *Sometime during* the first month, the counselor should invite the parents to visit the school so they can meet the teachers and administrators.

Degree

When you are explaining why one thing is more or less important than another thing, you may want to use these expressions.

most important	first	primarily	essentially
less important	second	secondary	principally
basically	subordinate	lesser	chiefly

Example

One of the *most important* gifts we can give to a child is an animal. *Above all*, an animal will help a child learn responsibility. A *lesser* reason, but an important one, is that a pet, especially a dog, will return the child's love. But *essentially*, a child needs to learn how to take care of something that is dependent on the child.

Comparison and Contrast

When you are explaining how two or more things are similar or how they are different, you may want to use these expressions.

To compare

similar to	similarly	like, alike	either/or
correspondingly	resemble	almost the same as	at the same time as
as	just as	in a like manner	in the same way
common in	than	also	neither/nor

To contrast

differ from	however	otherwise	still
nevertheless	even do	different from	less than
more than	unlike	in contrast to	on the other hand
although	while yet	but	instead

Example

Although my friend chose to buy a car with his gift, I would have gone on vacation. He said he needed the car to go to work, *but* I think he should take the bus. He also wanted the car for convenience. *However*, a taxi is *just as* convenient and doesn't have to be serviced. We are *both alike* in that *neither* of us knows how to drive. *Otherwise*, I might have bought a car, *too*.

Cause and Effect

When you are explaining how something caused a change in something else, you may want to use these expressions.

so	thus	consequently	therefore
for this reason	as a result	because, because of	owing to
since	due to	although	so that

Example

Effective advertising wants to change people's behaviors. Some public service ads show coffins of people who died of lung cancer; *as a result* many people have quit smoking. Other ads show glamorous people smoking; *consequently* young people start to smoke. *Owing to* the susceptibility of youth to advertising, many cigarette ads are not allowed near schools or on TV. *Although* these rules have been in effect a long time, the number of young smokers has increased. If this is not *due to* advertising, what is the reason?

Explanation

If you are explaining what something is by giving an example or if you are restating something for emphasis, you may want to use these expressions.

in other words	to clarify	to explain	to paraphrase
as	like	that is	for example
such as	for instance	to illustrate	namely

Example

People are never to old to attend college. *For example*, there are many women who stayed at home to raise their families and now have time to return to school. There are other examples *such as* retired people who move to a college town just so they can take occasional classes or even working people in their sixties, *for instance*, who want to take some night classes. *In other words*, you are never to old to learn.

Adding More Information

If you are adding more information to make your point stronger, you may want to use these expressions.

in addition	besides	furthermore	as well as
moreover	similarly	also	what's more

Example

Besides the fact that English is the international language of business, it is *also* becoming the language of social interaction. Because of the Internet, many people correspond in English by e-mail. *Moreover*, much of the information on the World Wide Web is in English *as well as* in the language of the web host. *In addition*, English is the language of diplomacy.

Pronouns

If you are describing someone or something, you may use some of these pronouns to refer to the person or thing you are describing.

Pronouns that replace a subject			
he	she	it	they
this	that	those	

Pronouns that replace an object

his	her	them
this	that	those

Pronouns that replace a possessive

his	her	its	their

Example

My community should hire a health worker. I worked in a rural area one summer with a community health worker and saw the wonderful ways *she* helped the people in the area. She worked with mothers teaching *them* how to keep *their* children healthy. She worked with school teachers helping *them* recognize early signs of illness. She worked with restaurant personnel showing *them* proper food handling techniques. A community needs help in many ways. *This* is one way *its* citizens can make *it* healthier.

NOTE: *This* in the last sentence refers to the whole paragraph. *This* equals *hiring a health worker*.

Practice 12

Read the paragraphs below. Choose the appropriate transition words or phrases to complete the thought.

1. **Paragraph from Topic 17**
   If I did want to chose my own roommate, I'd __(1)___ pick some candidates from the list supplied by the university. ___(2)__ I'd write to them and they'd write back. Through our letters, we'd find out if __(3)___ shared common interests, __(4)___ sports or movies. __(5)___, we'd find out if we liked doing the same things in our free time. __(6)___ my investigation, I'd more likely get someone compatible with my personality and likes and dislikes.

   1.1 Time
   (A) first
   (B) often
   (C) seldom

   1.2 Time
   (A) After
   (B) Next
   (C) When

   1.3 Pronoun
   (A) we
   (B) they
   (C) you

   1.4 Explanation
   (A) to explain
   (B) to paraphrase
   (C) such as

   1.5 Degree
   (A) Most importantly
   (B) Lesser
   (C) Essential

   1.6 Cause and effect
   (A) For this reason
   (B) As a result of
   (C) Although

2. **Paragraph from Topic 31**
   __(1)__ the traffic immediately __(2)___ and __(3)___ after the school day, there also would be traffic __(4)___ there was a sporting event__(5)___ a basketball or football game, or activities at the school. Would there be enough parking in the school lot for everyone attending those events? Probably not. __(6)___, those extra cars would end up in __(7)___ neighborhood.

2.1 Adding more information

(A) Furthermore

(B) In addition to

(C) What's more

2.2 Time

(A) before

(B) when

(C) next

2.3 Time

(A) meanwhile

(B) immediately

(C) during

2.4 Time

(A) often

(B) sometime

(C) whenever

2.5 Explanation

(A) such as

(B) to paraphrase

(C) to clarify

2.6 Cause and effect

(A) Due to

(B) Since

(C) Consequently

2.7 Pronoun

(A) our

(B) its

(C) her

3. **Paragraph from Topic 82**

___(1)___ of adapting to the customs of a new country is learning that country's language. Children learn the language in school, and use it all day ___(2)___ going to class and playing with other children. ___(3)___ many times adults coming to a new country don't have time for formal language classes. Their ___(4)___ is getting a job. ___(5)___, they have contacts in the new country—family or friends—who help them find employment. ___(6)___ they're working with people from their own country who speak their language, they don't have occasion to use the new language. This means even if they're trying to learn it, they don't have a lot of opportunities to practice it.

3.1 Degree

(A) A majority

(B) A major part

(C) A major

3.2 Time

(A) while

(B) during

(C) anytime

3.3 Contrast

(A) Unlike

(B) But

(C) Instead

3.4 Degree

(A) principally

(B) primary

(C) first priority

3.5 Time

(A) Usually

(B) Never

(C) Meanwhile

3.6 Cause and effect

(A) If

(B) Consequently

(C) Owing to

4. **Paragraph from Topic 107**

In the past in America, children were valuable workers. ___(1)___, they helped on the farm or in the family business ___(2)___ bring in money. Just a couple of generations ___(3)___, attitudes have changed. Now children are ___(4)___ expected to work at all. Modern children often don't ___(5)___ do household chores. This is sad, because I think that ___(6)___ are missing something if they don't help out at home. Sharing in household tasks benefits children of all ages.

4.1 Explanation

(A) For example

(B) Likely

(C) Namely

4.2 Cause and effect

(A) in order to

(B) as a result

(C) thus

4.3 Time

(A) while

(B) during

(C) later

4.4 Degree

(A) merely

(B) hardly

(C) secondarily

4.5 Adding more information

(A) moreover

(B) even

(C) furthermore

4.6 Pronoun

(A) they

(B) its

(C) their

5. Paragraph from Topic 102

__(1)__, an agricultural research center would help all people. No country can survive without adequate means of food production. __(2)__ the U.S. is able to produce or import enough food now, that may not remain the case. __(3)__ trends in the erosion of natural resources __(4)__ the closing of more and more American farms may reduce its food supply. Farmers' problems could be remedied __(5)__ they were able to build stronger networks across the country and internationally, __(6)__ businessmen already have.

5.1 Contrast	**5.3 Time**	**5.5 Cause and effect**
(A) Different from	(A) Current	(A) if
(B) While yet	(B) Always	(B) because of
(C) On the contrary	(C) Now	(C) owing to

5.2 Contrast	**5.4 Compare**	**5.6 Compare**
(A) Unlike	(A) resemble	(A) similar to
(B) Even though	(B) as well as	(B) common in
(C) In contrast to	(C) similarly	(C) much as

Using Syntactic Variety

On the Computer-Based TOEFL you must not only demonstrate your command of vocabulary; you must also show your command of grammar. You cannot write only simple sentences. Your essay must show syntactic variety.

- **Paragraph with simple sentences**

  Television is bad for children. Television shows are too violent. Children are influenced by television. Television shows should not be so violent.

- **Paragraph with syntactic variety**

  Since many television shows are violent, many child psychologists believe that watching television is not good for children. As children are easily influenced, we should limit violence on television.

You will develop variety in your prose by using parallel structures, making your paragraphs cohesive, and writing sentences that vary in type, length, subject, and voice.

Parallel Structures

Parallelism gives your essay rhythm. It makes it easier to read and understand. Your structures, however, must be parallel. That is, the subjects, verbs, adjectives, adverbs, and gerunds must be parallel. Look at these examples of parallelism.

Parallel Subjects

Work and play should be more evenly divided in my day.

Both *work* and *play* are the same kind of nouns. The subjects are parallel.

> *Working* and *play* should be more evenly divided in my day.

Here *working* is a gerund. It is not incorrect to use it here, but it sounds awkward. The subjects are not parallel.

> *Working* and *playing* should be more evenly divided in my day.

Here both *working* and *playing* are gerunds. The subjects are parallel.

Parallel Verbs

> We *press* a button, *wait* a short time, and *remove* the food from the microwave.

All three verbs are in the present tense. The verbs are parallel.

> We *press* a button, *wait* a short time, and *can remove* the food from the microwave.

The third verb uses the auxiliary *can*. It is not incorrect, but it sounds awkward. The verbs are not parallel.

> We *can press* a button, *wait* a short time, and *remove* the food from the microwave.

Here *can* precedes the first verb. This makes all three verbs parallel.

Parallel Adjectives

> I found the movie *long* and *boring*.

The adjectives are both parallel.

> I found the movie *long* and *it bored me*.

The sentence is not wrong, but it is not parallel.

Parallel Adverbs

> Athletes often move *gracefully*, *easily*, and *powerfully*.

The three adverbs all end in *-ly*. They are all parallel.

> Athletes often move with *grace*, *easily* and *powerfully*.

The first description is a prepositional phrase. The adverbs are not parallel.

> Athletes often move *gracefully*, *carefully*, and *powerfully*.

The second adverb *easily* was replaced with another adverb *carefully*. The meanings of *easily* and *carefully* are not the same, but *carefully* could be used to describe how an athlete moves. In this sentence, *carefully* adds to the rhythm of the sentence since the suffix *-fully* is used three times.

> *Athletes move with <u>grace</u>, <u>ease</u>, and <u>power</u>.*

This sentence can also be made parallel by using three prepositional phrases. The objects of the preposition *with* are all parallel nouns: *grace*, *ease*, and *power*.

Parallel Gerunds

> *I enjoy <u>shopping</u> and <u>keeping</u> up with the latest styles, but not <u>paying</u> the bills.*

Shopping, keeping up, and *paying* are gerunds. The gerunds are parallel.

> *I enjoy <u>shopping</u> and to <u>keep up</u> with the latest styles, but not t<u>o pay</u> the bills.*

To keep up and *to pay* not only are not parallel with *shopping*, they are incorrect. The verb *enjoy* must be followed by a gerund, not an infinitive.

Parallel Sentences

> <u>*While*</u> *there are advantages and disadvantages to both machine-made, and hand-made products, <u>I</u> prefer machine-made products. <u>While</u> hand-made products are generally high quality, <u>I</u> find them expensive. <u>While</u> I appreciate high-quality products, <u>I</u> can't afford them.*

These three sentences are parallel. They all begin with an adverb clause introduced by *While*. The subject of the independent clause in all three sentences is *I*. Each sentence after the first one takes an idea from the previous sentence and carries it forward using the same construction. There is a nice rhythm to these sentences. Be careful though. There is a narrow line between rhythmic parallels and boring repetitions.

> *While there are advantages and disadvantages to both, given my type of personality, I prefer machine-made products. While hand-made products are generally high quality, they are also very expensive. While I do appreciate high quality, my status as a student makes me appreciate low cost as well.*

In this version, the basic parallel construction remains. The last two sentences have been changed. In these two sentences, the parallelism is within the sentences as well as between the sentences.

> *Hand-made products are high quality.*

> *Hand-made products are very expensive.*

> *I appreciate high quality.*

> *I appreciate low cost.*

The writer draws a similarity between adjectives *high quality* and *very expensive*, and contrasts the products with the adjectives *high quality* and *low cost*.

Practice 13

Read the sentences and decide if the underlined word or phrase should be changed. Some underlined words are incorrect; others are grammatically correct, but not well written. If the word should be changed, rewrite it.

1. Dogs provide older people an important chance to learn or *maintain* <u>maintaining</u> social skills.

2. My parents didn't have time to analyze their feelings or <u>thinking</u> about themselves.

3. I believe zoos are useful both in terms of educating the general public as well as <u>they can advance</u> scientific research.

4. I prefer a combination of living <u>at</u> a small, suburban town and working in a big city,

5. Agricultural research improves individual citizens' lives, whereas successful businesses <u>to improve</u> a country's economy.

6. Heated debate is interesting, and <u>interest</u> things are easier to learn about.

7. <u>One</u> might think that it is a waste of time getting to know people you probably won't like when there are many others you would like and could spend time getting to know.

8. Teachers can instruct tomorrow's leaders; doctors can make those leaders healthier; and <u>engineering</u> can guarantee that future generations have good housing.

9. I could see the house where my grandmother grew up and my cousins still live in that <u>house</u>.

10. Novels are translated into English to reach a large segment of the international market; scholarly texts, too, are often translated into English <u>so that they can</u> reach the largest number of professionals in a particular field.

Coherence

Transition words help the reader see the relationship between sentences and ideas. They are one way to provide coherence in an essay. There are two other ways to provide coherence, repeating words and rephrasing ideas.

Repeating

Repeating words can provide a rhythm to a paragraph. In the example on page 95, notice how the phrase *She worked with* is repeated three times to show ways a community health worker helped people.

Example

She *worked with* mothers teaching *them* how to keep *their* children healthy. She *worked with* school teachers helping *them* recognize early signs of illness. She *worked with* restaurant personnel showing *them* proper food handling techniques.

Repeating words can also link ideas that may be several sentences apart. Again look at the Pronoun example. The second sentence in the example above ends with *she helped the people in the area*. The next to the last sentence, *A community needs help in many ways*, emphasizes the need of the community for *help*.

Rephrasing

We learned the words to use to introduce a statement that has been restated or rephrased for emphasis. We can also rephrase words to provide coherence in the essay. Rephrasing gives the reader a second chance to understand your thesis. Synonyms are one way to rephrase.

Example

The countryside where I grew up is very *isolated*. You can drive for miles without seeing another car. It seems in all directions you look at a *breathtaking vista*. The *scenery near the ocean* is especially *dramatic, with giant dark* cliffs rising out of the water.

Such a *secluded, remote* environment is a perfect place to relax. The *spectacular views* bring out the artist in me. I often take my paints and a canvas and try to capture the exciting *feel of the shoreline*.

Notice the ideas that are rephrased:

The countryside where I grew up is very *isolated*. You can drive for miles without seeing another car.

Such a *secluded, remote* environment is a perfect place to relax.

It seems in all directions you look at a *breathtaking vista*.

The *spectacular views* bring out the artist in me.

The *scenery near the ocean* is especially *dramatic, with giant dark* cliffs rising out of the water.

I often take my paints and a canvas and try to capture the exciting *feel of the shoreline*.

Practice 14

Choose which phrase or sentence best completes the thought and makes the paragraph cohesive.

1. An effective advertisement matches images and background music to its product and ___(1)__. For instance, if it's selling cars to young men, it uses the image of speed and aggressive rock music. If it's selling cars to families, it uses the image of practicality and wholesome melodies. _____(2)_____.

1.1
   (A) its market
   (B) the market it wants to reach
   (C) to those who will buy the product

1.2
   (A) If it's trying to sell a more expensive car, it uses classical music to suggest elegance and comfort.
   (B) If the car is for the rich, advertisers will want to emphasize elegance and affluence.
   (C) If it's selling cars to affluent executives, it uses the image of affluence and classical music.

2. Our parents were taught grammar, a subject that a lot of schools don't teach today. They were taught penmanship, a skill that few today have mastered. _____(1)_____ _____. And when they learned that language, they had to learn all about the culture of the people who used it, too. They didn't have to learn advanced mathematics, such as physics and trigonometry, but _____(2)_____ how to do basic math and algebra without the help of a calculator.

2.1
   (A) A foreign language which is optional today was a required subject.
   (B) They were taught to communicate in a foreign language.
   (C) They were taught a foreign language, something that's an option in many schools today.

2.2
   (A) they had to learn
   (B) it was important to learn
   (C) they felt they should know

3. The contributions scientists make to society are more obvious. The cars we drive, the computers we use at home and at work,_____(1)_____—all of these come from the ideas and hard work of scientists. Because of scientific contributions, we're living longer and more healthful lives. Scientists also _____(2)_____ the arts. Movies are the result of science, as are television, radio, and compact discs.

3.1
   (A) and the stove and cleaning machine
   (B) the appliances we have to help us cook our meals and clean our houses
   (C) the cooking and cleaning inventions

3.2
   (A) contribute to
   (B) help fund
   (C) support

Practice 15

Which option rephrases the word, phrase, or sentence taken from the paragraph. There may be more than one correct answer.

1. Zoos are also important for the research opportunities they provide. Because zoos are controlled environments, research is safer and easier to conduct. Scientists can feel safe in the confined area of the zoo. They may not be as safe in the wild. For example, while conducting a medical experiment in an open field, scientists have to worry about both the animal they are working with, and also other animals nearby in the bush. In zoos, however, they need only worry about the research subject.

1.1 zoos are controlled environments

(A) Zoos are also important for the research opportunities they provide.

(B) Scientists can feel safe in the confined area of the zoo.

(C) ...while conducting a medical experiment in an open field

1.2 in the wild

(A) in an open field

(B) in the bush

(C) In zoos

2. Teachers bring with them a varied and useful background. They've been trained to teach their students in whatever way helps students learn the most about the subject. For instance, some students learn better by discussing a topic; others by writing about it. Teachers can help students learn in the way that's best for each student. A textbook or a manual can only give you one way of learning something. And they're only as helpful as your ability to understand them. But a teacher can adapt her teaching to your needs as a student.

2.1 whatever way helps students learn

(A) some students learn better by discussing a topic

(B) others by writing about it

(C) in the way that's best for each student

3. Both art and music feed students' imaginations and help them express themselves. Students who've never drawn a sketch or even thought about sculpting will find themselves pleasantly surprised once they get their hands in the clay or start handling the pencils. Trying something new is always satisfying, even if you find you don't like it.

3.1 express themselves

(A) get their hands in the clay

(B) handling a pencil

(C) find themselves surprised

Sentences

The Computer-Based TOEFL wants you to demonstrate syntactic variety. You can vary the types of sentences you use, the length of the sentences, the subject of the sentences, and the voice of the sentences.

Type

There are four types of sentences: simple, compound, complex, and compound-complex.

- **Simple sentence**

  A simple sentence has one subject and one verb.

  Television <u>commercials</u> <u>are</u> the most effective form of advertising.
  $\quad\quad\quad$ subject $\quad$ verb

- **Compound sentence**

  A compound sentence has two or more simple sentences linked by the conjunctions *and*, *or*, and *but*.

  <u>Newspaper ads are often ignored</u>, and <u>radio ads are quickly forgotten.</u>
  $\quad$ simple sentence 1 $\quad\quad\quad$ conjunction $\quad$ simple sentence 2

- **Complex sentence**

  A complex sentence is made up of a simple sentence (independent clause) and one or more subordinate clauses.

  <u>Most people listen to radio</u> <u>when they're driving to work.</u>
  $\quad$ simple sentence $\quad\quad\quad\quad$ subordinate clause

- **Compound-complex sentences**

  A compound-complex sentence has two or more simple sentences (independent clauses) and one or more subordinate clauses.

  <u>Although families may listen to a radio during the day</u>, <u>the parents listen only for news reports</u>, and <u>the children use it for background noise.</u>

Length

Some students think they have to use compound-complex sentences to show they are very proficient in English. This makes the essay very heavy and very difficult to read. It is better to mix up the type of sentences you use. For example, a complex sentence followed by several simple sentences can be very effective.

Example

As the number of pets increase, the amount of money being spend on pets is also increasing. Pet owners buy special toys for their pets. They order them special clothes. They put them in day care centers. They treat them like children.

Practice 16

Label the sentences by their type in the following essay.

Simple = S	Complex = Cx
Compound = C	Compound-Complex = C-Cx

Topic 12

1. *Cx*	**Why People Visit Museums**
2. ___	I think people visit museums when traveling to new places because a museum tells them a lot about the culture of those places. They also go to museums to enjoy themselves. It's almost impossible to get bored in a museum. Every museum will have at least one thing of interest to somebody. It's always interesting to see what other cultures find interesting.
3. ___	
4. ___	
5. ___	
6. ___	When visiting someplace new, you can find out about the culture of that place by going to a movie or a place of worship or a nightclub. Another option is to sit in the park and listen to the people around you. The easiest way to learn about a place's culture, though, is by visiting its museums. Museums will show you the history of the place you're visiting. They will show you what art the locals think is important. If there aren't any museums, that tells you something, too.
7. ___	
8. ___	
9. ___	
10. ___	
11. ___	
12. ___	
13. ___	Museums are fun. Even if you're not interested in art or history, there is always something to get your attention. Many museums now have what they call "hands-on" exhibits. These were originally designed to keep children occupied while their parents were looking at exhibits. However, museums have found that adults enjoy hands-on opportunities just as much as children. These exhibits usually involve activities like pushing a button and hearing more about what you're looking at, or using similar materials to create your own work of art, or trying on clothes like those on the models in the museum.
14. ___	
15. ___	
16. ___	
17. ___	

18. _____	*People also enjoy visiting museums about unusual subjects. For instance, in my hometown there's a museum devoted to the potato. This museum has art made out of potatoes, tells all about the history of the potato, and sells potato mementos, like key chains and potato dolls. People enjoy visiting this museum because it's not something they'd find in their hometown and the museum's curators enjoy talking about the Great Potato.*
19. _____	
20. _____	
21. _____	
22. _____	*Museums are popular because they are about us. They reflect our creations, our values, and our dreams. No matter who you are or what you like, somewhere there is a museum that will amaze and interest you.*
23. _____	
24. _____	
25. _____	

Subject

Not all sentences should have the same subject. You will want to vary the subjects that you use. Notice in the example in the section *Sentence Length*, the subject of the last four sentences is the same: *Pet owners* and the pronoun *they*. In this case, there is a rhythm to the paragraph, and the sentences do not seem monotonous. These last four sentences are essentially a list; they tell you on what four things pet owners are spending money.

Compare these two versions of the same paragraph from Topic 144.

Version A

My parents' generation has strict standards about acceptable behavior. My parent's generation has a difficult time accepting other standards of behavior. My parents' generation is still very concerned about what other people think of them. My parent's generation grew up in small communities where everyone knew everybody.

Version B

My parent's generation has strict standards about acceptable behavior. Consequently, they have a difficult time accepting other standards of behavior. Since my parents' generation grew up in small communities where everyone knew everybody, they are still very concerned about what other people think of them.

By combining sentences and rearranging the order, you can provide variety to the paragraph and not repeat the same subject in every sentence.

Practice 17

Choose the subject that best completes the blank.

1. High school students aren't always the best judges of what they will find useful in the years ahead. __(1)__ need the guidance of experts in the field of education. However, they also need the freedom to follow their curiosity and individual interests. __(2)__ should be given the freedom to choose some courses, while being required to take others.

   1.1

   (A) They

   (B) We

   (C) Secondary school attendees

   1.2

   (A) One

   (B) You

   (C) They

2. English is a difficult language to learn. Its pronunciation is erratic and so is its spelling. Try explaining the logic in the differences in pronunciation between "though," "through," and "thought." And try understanding why so many English words are acceptable with two different spellings. __(1)__ is very idiomatic, too. No matter where you travel in an English-speaking country. __(2)__ find different expressions for the same thing, and different pronunciations for the same word.

   2.1

   (A) Spelling

   (B) Logic

   (C) English

   2.2

   (A) you'll

   (B) travelers

   (C) there'll

3. A good neighbor is respectful of your property and asks your permission before doing anything that interferes with what's yours. This means __(1)__ wouldn't put in a driveway that would take up part of your lawn. Or build a fence that would cut you off from part of your back yard. A good __(2)__ would work with you to decide where a fence should be placed and maybe the two of you could split the cost.

   3.1

   (A) he or she

   (B) they

   (C) it

   3.2

   (A) fence builder

   (B) friend

   (C) neighbor

Voice

There are two voices in English: active and passive. The active emphasizes the doer of the action; the passive emphasizes the action itself.

- **Active voice**

  <u>Parents</u> must teach their children computer skills.
    doer

- **Passive voice**

  Children must be <u>taught</u> computer skills by their parents.
        action

Some students think they should write only in the passive voice because it sounds more impressive. The active voice is a very direct way of writing and is often clearer and easier to read than the passive voice. Again, you should vary the use of voice in your essay.

Practice 18

Underline the verbs in the following essay and tell whether they are active or passive.

Topic 5

1. *active*	**No Factory!**
2. _____	
3.1. _____	*New factories often <u>bring</u> many good things to a community, such as jobs and increased prosperity. However, in my opinion, the benefits of having a factory*
3.2. _____	*are outweighed by the risks. That is why I oppose the plan to build a factory near my community.*
4.1. _____	
4.2. _____	*I believe that this city would be harmed by a large factory. In particular, a factory would destroy the quality of the air and water in town. Factories bring*
5. _____	*smog and pollution. In the long run, the environment will be hurt and people's*
6. _____	*health will be affected. Having a factory is not worth that risk.*
7.1. _____	
7.2. _____	
8. _____	

9.1. _____	
9.2. _____	
10. _____	*Of course, some will say that more jobs will be created by the factory. Our population will grow. To accommodate more workers, more homes and stores*
11. _____	*will be needed. Do we really want this much growth, so fast? If our town is*
12.1. _____	*going to grow, I would prefer slow growth with good planning. I don't want to*
12.2. _____	*see rows of cheaply constructed townhouses. Our quality of life must be considered.*
13. _____	
14. _____	
15. _____	

16.1. _____	*I believe that this growth will change our city too much. I love my home-*
16.2. _____	*town, because it is a safe, small town. It is also easy to travel here. If we must*
17.1. _____	*expand to accommodate new citizens, the small-town feel will be gone. I would*
17.2. _____	*miss that greatly.*
18. _____	
19.1 _____	
19.2. _____	
20. _____	

21. _____	*A factory would be helpful in some ways. After careful consideration,*
22.1. _____	*however, I feel that the dangers outweigh the benefits. I simply cannot support a*
22.2. _____	*plan to build a factory here, and hope that others feel the same way.*
23.1. _____	
23.2. _____	

Practice 19

Choose the active sentence that correctly carries the meaning of the passive sentence.

1. Our lives have been dramatically improved by changes in food preparation.

(A) Changes in food preparation have dramatically improved our lives.

(B) Our lives are changing dramatically and so have changes in food preparation.

(C) Our food preparation improvements have been dramatic changes.

2. Young people will be helped to overcome the fear of aging by associating with older people.

(A) Our fear of associating with older people can overcome young people.

(B) Young people can associate with older people who fear aging.

(C) Associating with older people will help young people overcome the fear of aging.

3. I do not like the fact that these products are made by machines.

(A) I do not like the fact that these are machine-made products.

(B) Products made by machine are not liked; it's a fact.

(C) It's not a fact that these products were made by machines.

4. Large sums of money are earned by entertainers who do little to contribute to society.

(A) Society earns a little from entertainers' contributions.

(B) Entertainers earn large sums of money yet contribute little to society.

(C) Money is contributed to society by entertainers who earn a lot.

5. If an agricultural research station were established, our community would profit.

(A) The agricultural research station would profit from our community.

(B) The community would be profitable if an agricultural research station were established.

(C) We would benefit from the establishment of an agricultural research station.

Free Practice

Do either or both of the following activities on your own or in a group. There are no answers provided.

1. Read the essays in the Model Essay section. Identify the use of syntactic and semantic variety.

2. In the essays in the Model Essay section, underline and label all parallel structures, transition words, and examples of coherence. Identify the types of sentences, the subjects of the sentences, and the voice of the sentences.

CONCLUDING THE TOPIC

STEP 9: WRITE THE CONCLUSION

A good essay should have a good conclusion. A conclusion is a few sentences that support your thesis and remind the reader of your intentions. There are a few different ways to write a conclusion. Look at these conclusions from the essays in this book. You can review the complete essay in the Model Essay section.

Restatement

You can end your essay by restating your thesis and/or restating your topic sentences.

Conclusion from Topic 107

Children should not work all the time. A happy life needs balance. If children can successfully handle tasks at home, they will handle life better, too. They will know the satisfaction of doing a good job, be involved in family life, and become more confident and responsible adults.

Generalization

You can use all the information you provided and make a generalization about it.

Conclusion from Topic 90

All things considered, I think I'd like to have a lot of acquaintances who are different and a few close friends who are similar to me. That seems to be the best of both worlds.

Prediction

You can summarize the information you provided and point the reader toward the next logical step.

Conclusion from Topic 27

I believe that a new movie theater is a fine idea. I support it fully because of the changes it will bring to our citizens and our town. I anticipate the reduction in crime, the increase in employment, and the improved infrastructure will make our town a nicer place to live.

Question

You can conclude with a question that does not need an answer. This is called a rhetorical question. The answer is contained in the question.

Conclusion from Topic 2

The most important thing to realize is that we all have many teachers in our lives. Where we would be without our parents, teachers, and our peers to guide us? What would we do without books, newspapers, and television to inform us? All of them are very valuable.

Recommendation

You can urge your readers to do something with the information you provided.

Conclusion from Topic 13

Both eating at restaurants and cooking at home can be satisfying. Both can taste good and be enjoyed with family and friends. I prefer cooking at home, because of the money and health issues. I encourage my friends to eat out less, but it's up to them to make the choice that fits their lifestyles best.

Practice 20

What kind of a conclusion is each of these sentences or paragraphs? Refer to the whole essay, given at the end of the book, to help you decide.

1. **Conclusion from Topic 20**
    If you give up you might as well die. My advice is to always look for another opportunity, another goal, or another option. There is always something else. Don't give up.

    (A) Restatement   (D) Question
    (B) Generalization   (E) Recommendation
    (C) Prediction

2. **Conclusion from Topic 41**
    Of course, not every wrong decision is going to be a disaster. We all make decisions we regret, and we can all learn from them. But I don't think there's anything wrong with deciding not to decide, at least for the moment. If a decision can't wait to be made, then maybe you shouldn't make it at all.

    (A) Restatement   (D) Question
    (B) Generalization   (E) Recommendation
    (C) Prediction

3. **Conclusion from Topic 26**

On the whole, though, I think my neighborhood should support having a shopping center built here. It would bring more variety to our shopping, give us the opportunity to amuse ourselves at movie theaters and restaurants, and bring more jobs into the area.

(A) Restatement

(B) Generalization

(C) Prediction

(D) Question

(E) Recommendation

4. **Conclusion from Topic 94**

Further, if we all based our final opinion of others on first impressions, it would be hard to get to know anyone. There is always more to people than meets the eye, and if we don't give them a chance, we may be missing out on meeting a lifelong friend. That would truly be a shame.

(A) Restatement

(B) Generalization

(C) Prediction

(D) Question

(E) Recommendation

5. **Conclusion from Topic 32**

The more I move the more I experience change. I would meet new people in every place I lived; I could move to sample countries with four seasons or even a continent like Antarctica which only has two. Wherever I lived, I would experience living in housing particular to that area. I would then be a citizen of the world, wouldn't I? Could you call me a foreigner if I called everyplace my home?

(A) Restatement

(B) Generalization

(C) Prediction

(D) Question

(E) Recommendation

Practice 21

Read the essay. Underline the topic sentences. Double underline the words in the introduction that guide the reader. Circle the nine words or phrases that indicate a personal opinion.

Topic 40

Learning about the past has no value for those of us living in the present. Do you agree or disagree? Use specific reasons and examples to support your answer.

People often say "Those who don't understand history will repeat the mistakes of the past." I totally disagree. I don't see any evidence that people have made smart decisions based on their knowledge of the past. To me, the present is what is important, not the past. I think that people, the weather, and politics determine what happens, not the past.

People can change. We can't assume that people will continue to hate one another just because they have had hated one another for years. Look at Turkey and Greece. When Turkey had an earthquake, Greece sent aid. When Greece had an earthquake, Turkey sent aid. Now, these two countries are cooperating and looking forward to improved relations. No doubt, if we looked at the past, we would have thought this was a lost cause. But people change.

The weather can change. Farmers think that they can plant certain crops because these crops have always grown well in their fields before. But the weather can change. There can be a long drought. The crops that have always worked well, will die. A drought-resistant crop needs to be tried. If we looked at the past, we would not have changed our crop and we would have lost our farm. Weather changes.

Politics can change. According to my way of thinking, politicians must be responsive to changes in the people. If politicians looked only at the past, they would always say the same thing. People change. On the whole, people today care about human rights. They want all people to have the equal rights. If we looked at the past in the United States, we would see a lot of discrimination against races, women, and sexual orientation. Now, that is changing. Politicians change, too.

As a rule what is important today is to follow the mood of the moment. We can't be locked into the past. It doesn't do us any good to think about the past. People, the weather, and politics can change in any direction. The direction of this change, in my opinion, can not be predicted by studying the past.

Practice 22

Read the essay. Underline the topic sentences. Double underline the words in the introduction that guide the reader. Circle the nine words or phrases that indicate a personal opinion.

Topic 106

Do you agree or disagree with the following statement? A person's childhood years (the time from birth to 12 years of age) are the most important years of a person's life. Use specific reasons and examples to support your answer.

I think I'd have to agree that a person's childhood years, the time from birth until twelve years of age, are the most important. I say "have to" because all the information I've read about the early years of life states that these are the years that form us. These years determine what kind of a person the child will become. During these years we learn about relationships, begin our formal education, and develop our moral sense of right and wrong.

No doubt, the early years are the time when we learn about relationships, first with our parents and siblings, then with the rest of the world. We learn how to respond to others based on the treatment we're given. If we're loved, then we know how to love others. If we're treated harshly, then, seemingly, that's all we know of how to deal with other people. We also form our ideas about our own self-worth from the way others treat us during these years. They can convince us we're worthless, or they can teach us we deserve love and respect.

These are the years when we begin our formal education. We acquire the basic skills—reading, writing, working with numbers—that we'll use throughout our lives, no matter what we end up doing for a living. If we're not given a good foundation in these subjects, anything we try to do later will be undermined by our lack of skills. Perhaps the most important thing we can learn during these years is how to learn, how to analyze information and use it. Presumably, these are skills that will always be useful.

Most importantly, from my point of view, these are the years when we develop our moral sense of what's right and wrong. We're taught by others about good and bad, but it's during the latter part of these early years that we begin to decide for ourselves. It's also during this time that we begin to develop the self-discipline to live according to our morals.

I believe a person grows and changes for the better throughout the many stages of life. However, the foundation is laid, by and large, in those first few years of life.

Practice 23

Read the essay. Underline the topic sentences. Double underline the words in the introduction that guide the reader. Circle the nine words or phrases that indicate a personal opinion.

Topic 104

Do you agree or disagree with the following statement? Only people who earn a lot of money are successful. Use specific reasons and examples to support your answer.

Many people believe that a large income equals success. I believe, however, that success is more than how much money you make. Some of those measures of success definitely include fame, respect, and knowledge.

Most people assume that famous people are rich people, but that isn't always true. For example, some day I would like to be famous in my field as a professor of English. I will still only make a professor's salary, which by U.S. standards will not mean that I am rich. Still, I will feel myself to be successful if I am well known. Additionally, there are many famous humanitarians who are not rich. Mother Theresa was one. Certainly, no one would say she was not successful.

I also believe that being respected by coworkers indicates success. Without that respect, money means little. For example, I once did some work for a top attorney in a law firm. He made a very good salary, but he wasn't a nice man. No one ever did work for him willingly. He ordered everyone around, and we didn't respect him. In contrast, however, I had a band director in high school who had to take extra jobs just to make enough money to support his family. His students had great respect for him and always listened to what he said. As a result, we were a very good band. In my opinion, my band director was more successful than the attorney was.

Finally, I think one of the most important indicators of success is knowledge. Wealthy people don't always know all the answers, and sometimes pay others to do work they can't do. Similarly, in the movie Good Will Hunting, *the only person who could solve some complex problems was the janitor. He knew a lot, and decided what he wanted to do with that knowledge rather than just think about money. In my opinion, he was extremely successful.*

When we think of history, there are few people that we remember simply because they were rich. Overall, we remember people who did something with their lives—they were influential in politics, or contributed to science or art or religion. If history is the ultimate judge of success, then money surely isn't everything.

Free Practice

Do either or both of the following activities on your own or in a group. There are no answers provided.

1. Read the essays in the Model Essay section. Identify the type of conclusion each contains.

2. Change the conclusion in any or all of the essays to another type of conclusion.

SELF-TEST ESSAY #3

Write on the same topic from Self-test Essay #1. Plan, write, and revise an essay on that topic within 30 minutes. Use the space on the following pages. Do NOT write in the shaded areas.

Divide your time like this.		
PLAN	5 minutes	30:00 – 25:00
WRITE	20 minutes	25:00 – 05:00
REVISE	5 minutes	05:00 – 00:00

Topic Number: _____

PLAN

Concept Map

Thesis Statement

General Ideas

Supporting Details

WRITE

REVISE

Proofing Checklist

Reread your essay. Use this checklist as a guide.

✓	**CONTENT**
	Is there a thesis statement or introduction?
	Is there a topic sentence for each paragraph?
	Are there supporting details for each topic statement?
	Is there a conclusion?
✓	**CLARITY**
	Are there run-on sentences or sentence fragments?
	Are there misplaced modifiers or dangling modifiers?
	Are the structures parallel?
	Are there transition words?
	Are the sentences and paragraphs cohesive?
✓	**PUNCTUATION AND SPELLING**
	Are the paragraphs indented?
	Are there punctuation marks such as periods at the end of each sentence?
	Do all sentences begin with capital letters?
	Are all the words spelled correctly?

Revising the Essay

CHECKING THE CONTENT
AND CLARITY

STEP 10: CHECK THE CONTENT

The Proofing Checklist advises you to check four things in your essay.

Is there a thesis statement or introduction?
Is there a topic sentence for each paragraph?
Are there supporting details for each topic statement?
Is there a conclusion?

These content items have been fully explained in the chapters on planning and writing your essay. You will get more practice in checking the content in the section on proofing that follows.

STEP 11: CHECK THE CLARITY

On the Computer-Based TOEFL essay your computer will not have a grammar checker. Whether you type your essay or write by hand, you will have to proofread carefully to find your errors. Of course, it is better not to make errors. By thinking before you write, you can avoid common errors with sentences and modifiers.

Sentences

A sentence must have a subject and a verb. If a sentence is missing a subject or verb or both, it is called a sentence fragment. If a sentence has extra subjects and/or verbs (for example, two sentences written as one), it is called a run-on sentence.

Recognizing Sentence Fragments

The following examples of sentence fragments show how a subject and/or verb can be forgotten.

Example 1

Fragment   Gives us the big picture.

This sentence fragment is missing a subject. A possible subject is *History*.

Corrected   History gives us the big picture.

116

Example 2

Fragment   What they did learn, much more completely.

This sentence fragment *much more completely* is missing both a subject and a verb in the independent clause. The noun clause *What they did learn* is complete. The independent clause needs a subject and a verb such as *they learned*.

Corrected   What they did learn, they learned much more completely.

Example 3

Fragment   Means more than drawing or sculpting.

The verb *means* has no subject. A possible subject is *Studying art*.

Sentence   Studying art means more than drawing or sculpting.

Example 4

Fragment   A major part of adapting to the customs of a new country learning that country's language.

The sentence fragment is missing a verb. A possible verb is *is*.

Corrected   A major part of adapting to the customs of a new country is learning that country's language.

Practice 1

Tell which of the following from Topic 98 are sentence fragments. There are 8 sentence fragments. Choose a possible subject and/or verb from this box to complete the sentence.

study	who	you	It
help	that's	is	am

1. I agree that all students should study art and music in high school.

2. Young children who study those subjects in grade school do better in other subjects.

3. I assuming this would be true of teenagers.

4. All high school students must take physical education because it good for their physical health.

5. Well, studying art and music is good for their mental health.

6. Both art and music feed students' imaginations and them express themselves.

7. Students have never drawn a sketch will be surprised once they start to draw.

8. Trying something new is always satisfying, even if you find don't like it.

9. There's a reason cave dwellers drew on the walls and made music with drums.

10. Wanting to express ourselves that way is a natural human inclination.

11. Gives us an avenue for our emotions and fears.

12. It may not always be music other people want to hear or art others will appreciate, but it's the doing enjoyable.

13. It shouldn't matter if the end result is mediocre.

Recognizing Run-on Sentences

The following examples of run-on sentences show how two sentences can be incorrectly written together.

Example 1

Run-on sentence	We all make decisions we can learn from them.
	We all make decisions.
	We can learn from them.
Corrected	We all make decisions that we can learn from.

Example 2

Run-on sentence	A movie is more vivid you're seeing it on a large screen.
	A movie is more vivid.
	You're seeing it on a large screen.
Corrected	A movie is more vivid because you're seeing it on a large screen.

Example 3

Run-on sentence	We can conduct research on Earth this is less costly than in space.
	We can conduct research on Earth.
	This is less costly than in space.
Corrected	Conducting research on Earth is less costly than in space.

Example 4

Run-on sentence	English is a difficult language to learn its spelling is irregular.
	English is a difficult language to learn.
	Its spelling is irregular.
Corrected	English is a difficult language to learn because its spelling is irregular.

Practice 2

Decide if these sentences are run-on sentences. There are six run-on sentences. In these six, underline the first sentence and double underline the second sentence in the run-on sentences below.

1. The most important decisions I made in my life was to major in computer science.

2. This enabled me to get in on the ground floor of computer technology this ensured that I would have a successful and rewarding career.

3. I was in college, computer science was relatively new.

4. None of my friends understood what I was doing all day.

5. They were learning how to be teachers, journalists, and economists I was learning how to write computer programs.

6. I graduated I had eight very good job offers.

7. My choice of college major not gave me a lucrative career it helped in my married life.

8. I married a Naval officer through the years we've moved six times.

9. Each time, no matter where we've lived, I've been able to find a job with my computer programming skills.

10. In fact, by moving I learned about various computer technologies that I wouldn't have learned by staying with one company.

Correcting Sentences

Both sentence fragments and run-on sentences can be fixed by combining them correctly. Some of the ways sentences can be combined are shown below. For more practice, you should study the Grammar Review section in Pamela Sharpe's *How to Prepare for the TOEFL*, Barron's Educational Series, 9ed.

You can combine two simple sentences to make a compound sentence.

> *I want to buy a house, but I don't have enough money.*

You can add a dependent clause to a simple sentence to make a complex sentence.

> *I want to buy a house that has three bedrooms.*

You can add an independent clause to a complex sentence to make a compound-complex sentence.

> *I want to buy a house that has three bedrooms, but I don't have enough money.*

To combine two simple sentences, you can use coordinating conjunctions.

and	but	or
nor	then	yet

Sentence Fragment	I prefer to study in the morning. My sister to study in the evening.
Combination	I prefer to study in the morning, *and* my sister prefers to study in the evening.
Run-on Sentence	People exercised more years ago they called it work, not exercise.
Combination	People exercised more years ago, *but* they called it work, not exercise.

To combine a dependent clause with a sentence, you need subordinating conjunctions. There are a variety of subordinating conjunctions with different purposes. The following conjunctions are used to indicate contrast, manner, time, relationship, and reason.

CONTRAST			
although	even though	though	much as
while	in spite of	despite	whereas

Sentence Fragment   Teenagers should have jobs. While they are students.

Combination   Teenagers should have jobs *while* they are students.

Run-on Sentence   Not everyone can get the best health care everyone can get basic health care and advice.

Combination   *Although* not everyone can get the best health care, everyone can get basic health care and advice.

MANNER				
as	as if	as though	like	the way

Sentence Fragment   We can understand other cultures through their music. As we can through their art.

Combination   We can understand other cultures through their music *as* we can through their art.

Run-on Sentence   The Spanish-speaking population is increasing, the English-speaking population is remaining at the same level.

Combination   The Spanish-speaking population is increasing, *even as* the English-speaking population is remaining at the same level.

TIME			
after	as	as soon as	before
once	since	the minute	until
when	while	the moment	the second

Sentence Fragment   We should earn money. Before we spend it.

Combination   We should earn money *before* we spend it.

Run-on Sentence   Poor people need help they can manage on their own.

Combination   Poor people need help *until* they can manage on their own.

RELATIONSHIP		
that	which	who
whom	whose	where

Sentence Fragment   We should eat more fruits. Now available year-around

Combination   We should eat more fruits, *which* are now available year-around

Run-on Sentence   Food contains a lot of preservatives they aren't good for us.

Combination   Food contains a lot of preservatives, *which* aren't good for us.

REASON		
what	why	how

Sentence Fragment   The teacher asked me. Why he wasn't here.

Combination   The teacher asked me *why* he wasn't here.

Run-on Sentence   Doctors know more now about reasons what causes disease and how to cure it.

Combination   Doctors know more now about *what* causes disease and *how* to cure it.

Practice 3

Combine the following to avoid sentence fragments or run-on sentences. Use the subordinate conjunctions suggested.

1. **Reason *why***
   Students wonder. Teachers are critical.
   Students wonder why teachers are critical.

2. **Time *when***
   A birdbath is a source of water for birds the weather is hot.

3. **Relationship *where***
   I'd like to have a garden I could grow vegetables.

4. **Contrast *Even though***
   We have all we need, want more.

5. **Manner *As***
   Our population ages we will need more services for the elderly.

Modifiers

Earlier we saw how you can combine sentences using conjunctions. You can combine sentences by taking words or phrases from the second sentence and inserting them in the first as modifiers.

Original

Sentence 1　　I want to live in a townhouse.

Sentence 2　　The townhouse should be <u>renovated.</u>

Revised

Sentence 1+2　I want to live in a <u>renovated</u> townhouse.

This is a simple, straightforward combination. An adjective *renovated* describing *townhouse* in the second sentence is placed in front of the noun *townhouse* in the first.

You must be careful when you combine participial phrases or prepositional phrases in other sentences. There are two problems that can occur here: a misplaced modifier and a dangling modifier. Look at these examples.

Misplaced modifier

Sentence　　　I had difficulty finding a parking space <u>searching for an apartment.</u>

Original

Sentence 1　　I had difficulty finding a parking space.

Sentence 2　　I was searching for an apartment.

Revision

Sentence 1+2　<u>Searching for an apartment,</u> I had difficulty finding a parking space.

The parking space is NOT searching for an apartment. A person is searching. You must place the participial phrase *near* the noun it modifies.

Dangling modifier

Sentence　　　<u>To live within my budget,</u> a place should be convenient.

Original

Sentence 1　　I need to live within my budget.

Sentence 2　　I need a convenient place.

Revision

Sentence 1+2　<u>To live within my budget,</u> I need a place that is convenient.

A place cannot "live within a budget." The person *I* that the prepositional phrase modifies is missing.

Practice 4

Combine these sentences as directed.

1. There would be more money for schools.

   There would be more money for libraries.

   There would be more money for other community needs.

Combine with *and*

_____

_____

2. Once the buildings were completed, the jobs would be those on the campus itself. The jobs would include teachers, office workers, custodians, and librarians.

   Combine with *and*

   _____

   _____

3. Our community is a place.
   It is a place where everyone knows everyone else.

   Combine by deleting *It is a place.*

   _____

   _____

4. Playing sports is a wonderful way to learn discipline.
   Playing sports should not be the focus of a university education.

   Combine by adding *Although* to the first sentence. Use a pronoun as the subject for cohesion.

   _____

   _____

5. Emigrant children learn their new language while playing with other children.
   They also learn while going to school.

   Combine with *and*

   _____

   _____

Practice 5

Rewrite these sentences to place the modifiers correctly.

1. A child has exciting places to visit in the city growing up.

   _____

   _____

2. Children do better in all subjects who study art.

   _____

   _____

3. Reading fiction is more enjoyable than watching a movie such as novels and short stories.

_____

_____

4. English is the language of diplomacy which is very idiomatic.

_____

_____

5. Looking for a rewarding career computer science attracts many young people.

_____

_____

CHECKING THE PUNCTUATION
AND SPELLING

STEP 12: CHECK THE PUNCTUATION AND SPELLING

It is beyond the scope of this book to provide activities to improve your spelling. Remember that there is no spell checker on the computer that you use with the Computer-Based TOEFL. When you read, pay close attention to words. This will help you understand English spelling patterns.

Also when you read, pay attention to punctuation. This will help you when writing your essay. There are four important things to remember about punctuation on the Computer-Based TOEFL essay.

- **Indent each paragraph.**
  This will help the reader determine when you are starting a new idea.

- **Capitalize the first word of a sentence.**
  This will help the reader determine when you are starting a new sentence.

- **Put a period or question mark at the end of a sentence or question.**
  This will help the reader determine when you are ending a sentence or question.

- **Start each paragraph on a new line.**
  This will help the reader determine when you are starting a new topic.

Here are some other forms of punctuation that will make your essay easier to read.

Comma

Use a comma in a list of three or more things. It is optional to put a comma before the *and*.

> *I want to have a kitchen, living room and bedroom.*
>
> *I want a large, airy, inexpensive house.*

Use a comma between a noun and any following descriptions.

> *My favorite area, Orchard Hill, was developed by John Bartle, an entrepreneur.*

Use a comma to separate adjectives or participles that are not part of the sentence or were added for emphasis.

> *The apartment was expensive, very expensive.*
>
> *Excited, I signed the lease without reading the fine print.*

Use a comma to separate a non-restrictive relative clause.

> *All the neighbors, who are very friendly, keep their houses very tidy.*

Use a comma after a subordinate clause at the start of the sentence.

> *Once I've chosen an area, I decide whether I want to live in a house or an apartment.*

Semicolon

Use a semicolon to separate closely related sentences.

> *I wanted a renovated townhouse; none was available.*

Colon or Dash

Use a colon or dash in front of a list or explanation.

> *I looked at these kinds of apartments: studio, one-bedroom, and two-bedroom.*
>
> *My needs are simple—a swimming pool and a two-car garage.*

Practice 6

Punctuate the following essay. Check Essay Model 21 for your answers.

Topic 21

Why People are Living Longer

today people are living to be much older than ever before. some of the main reasons for this are the improved health care and better nutrition available to everyone

medical care is more available to people Although not everyone can get the best health care everyone can get basic health care and advice. when someone is seriously ill they can go to a public hospital and be taken care of Years ago, health care wasn't available to everyone. some people didn't live near a doctor or a hospital, and others couldnt pay for the care they needed. they made do with herbal medicines or folk remedies Of course, some of these worked, but not for the more serious diseases

the quality of medical care has improved, and thats also a factor in longevity. doctors know more now about what causes disease and how to cure it. years ago, doctors only knew about the most basic diseases and cures Medicine was very rudimentary. many people didnt live to adulthood because of something as simple as an infection from a cut or a virus. now we have antibiotics and other medicines to help cure infections

people are also living longer now because of better nutrition Were eating better and more healthfully than we used to, and thats reduced the number of people with heart disease and cancer. we try to eat low-fat foods and eat more vegetables and fruits, which are now available year-round.

improved medical care and healthy eating habits has greatly expanded our life spans What we need to do now is make sure that everyone in the world has these benefits

Free Practice

Do any or all of the following activities on your own or in a group. There are no answers provided.

1. Read the essays in the Model Essay section. Identify all the subjects and verbs.

2. Read the essays in the Model Essay section. Identify the coordinate and subordinate conjunctions.

3. Read the essays in the Model Essay section. Underline all modifying expressions.

4. Read the essays in the Model Essay section. Circle all the punctuation.

5. Review all of the essays you have written. Check the sentences, clauses, modifiers, and punctuation.

USING THE PROOFING CHECKLIST

HOW TO REVISE

It is very easy to make clean, precise revisions when you use the computer. If you make corrections on your handwritten essay, you must do so very neatly. Here are some ways to make your revisions clear to your reader.

Delete a word or phrase.   Cross out the word completely.

Insert a word or phrase.   Use the caret (^) symbol to indicate where something should be inserted.

> $\overset{also}{}$ Student evaluations of teachers $_\wedge$ makes students feel $_\wedge$ ~~like~~ $\overset{as\ if}{}$
> they have a say in what happens in $\overset{their}{_\wedge}$ schools.

If you write your essay by hand, you might want to leave extra space between the lines in case you need to insert a change.

Proofing Checklist

You will not be able to take this list into the testing room, but soon it will be second nature to you. As you proof the practice essays in this book and proof your own practice essays, you will become familiar with the four areas of this checklist.

✓	**CONTENT**
	Is there a thesis statement or introduction?
	Is there a topic sentence for each paragraph?
	Are there supporting details for each topic statement?
	Is there a conclusion?
✓	**CLARITY**
	Are there run-on sentences or sentence fragments?
	Are there misplaced modifiers or dangling modifiers?
	Are the structures parallel?
	Are there transition words?
	Are the sentences and paragraphs cohesive?
✓	**PUNCTUATION AND SPELLING**
	Are the paragraphs indented?
	Are there punctuation marks such as periods at the end of each sentence?
	Do all sentences begin with capital letters?
	Are all the words spelled correctly?

Practice 7

Proof the following essay by answering the questions that follow.

Which activity is most important?
• reducing pollution in your neighborhood
• helping a child learn to read
• visiting an elderly person regularly

Explain your choice using reasons and details.

Helping a child learn to read is important.

opens up new world

forms a child's personality

feeds a child's creativity

- *other times, cultures*
- *other ways to view situation*
- *leaves options*

- *logical or fanciful*
- *sympathetic or judgmental*

- *how to "draw" with words*
- *increases vocabulary*

Helping a Child to Read

To say that children are the future has become trite, but it's true nonetheless. The children of today will be the citizens of tomorrow. They will control the world we live in. For that reason, they must have the best education possible. We must prepare them for their role in our future. I think the most important preparation is helping a child learn to read.

Reading opens up a whole new world to a child. It takes them away from their daily lives and, through books, lets them travel to other countries, other centuries, and to cultures that are different. It teaches them about the way people different from themselves think about things. They learn that there are another ways to view situations.

Reading helps to form a child's personality. The way a child figures out what all the words mean can develop that child's way of thinking. Will the child be strictly logical or will he be a dreamer. will she be sympathetic with the characters' shortcomings, or will she decide what happens to them is there own fault? Children learn how to make judgements when they're reading.

A childs creativity is fed by reading. It helps them see all the different shapes and patterns there are in the world. It shows them there are many ways to "draw" the same image with words. It increases their vocabulary which will help them learn subjects in school more quickly.

Many ways to make a difference in a community. Learning to read, I believe that the activity brings hope to the future.

Answer the questions.

1. Which of the following sentences is the thesis statement for this essay?

   (A) They learn that there are other ways to view situations.

   (B) I think the most important preparation is helping a child learn to read.

   (C) They will control the world we live in.

   (D) None of the above.

2. Which of the following sentences is the topic sentence for paragraph 3?

   (A) Will the child be strictly logical or will he be a dreamer?

   (B) Children learn how to make judgements when they're reading.

   (C) Reading helps to form a child's personality.

   (D) None of the above.

3. Which of the following sentences supports this statement: Reading opens up a whole new world to a child.

   (A) There are many way to make a difference in a community

   (B) We must prepare them for their role in our future.

   (C) It teaches them about the way people different from themselves think about things.

   (D) None of the above.

4. In which paragraph is there a sentence fragment? Correct it.

   (A) Paragraph   1 (B) Paragraph 3   (C) Paragraph 5

   _____

   _____

5. In which sentence is there a dangling participle? Correct it.

   (A) Sentence 4, paragraph 1   (B) Sentence 1, paragraph 4   (C) Sentence 2, paragraph 5

   _____

   _____

6. Which sentence is not parallel with the others in paragraph 2? Correct it.

   (A) Sentence 2   (B) Sentence 3   (C) Sentence 4

   _____

   _____

7. Which topic sentence is not parallel with the others? Correct it.

   (A) Sentence 1, paragraph 1   (B) Sentence 1, paragraph 2   (C) Sentence 1, paragraph 3

   _____

   _____

8. Which object in sentence 2, paragraph 2 is not parallel with the others? Correct it.

   (A) other countries   (B) other centuries   (C) to cultures that are different.

   _____

   _____

9. In paragraph 1, the transition phrase *For that reason* connects which two ideas?

(A) control of world and education

(B) trite and true

(C) children and preparation

_____

_____

10. In paragraph 4 , which words provides cohesion?

(A) different shapes and patterns/draw the same image

(B) same image/vocabulary

(C) increases/quickly

11. Which paragraph is not indented?

(A) Paragraph 1   (B) Paragraph 3   (C) Paragraph 4

12. Which sentence does not end with the correct punctuation? Correct it.

(A) Sentence 2, paragraph 2   (B) Sentence 3, paragraph 3   (C) Sentence 1, paragraph 4

_____

_____

13. Which sentence does not begin with a capital letter?

(A) Sentence 5, paragraph 1   (B) Sentence 2, paragraph 2   (C) Sentence 4, paragraph 3

14. Which word is not spelled correctly in this essay? Correct it.

(A) *lives* in sentence 2, paragraph 2

(B) *there* in sentence 4, paragraph 3

(C) *see* in sentence 2, paragraph 4

_____

_____

15. Which word is not used correctly in this essay? Correct it.

(A) *say* in sentence 1, paragraph 1

(B) *another* in sentence 4, paragraph 2

(C) *learn* in sentence 4, paragraph 4

_____

_____

Practice 8

Proof the following essay by answering the questions that follow.

Your community has enough money to hire one new employee. Which one of the following (three choices will be presented in the actual test) should your community hire? • a community health worker • a counselor • an emergency medical technician • a firefighter • a judge • a landscaper • a police officer • a recreation center director • a teacher. Use specific reasons and details to develop your essay.

Now	Proposed	Reason
poor recreation areas	more park areas	bring community together socially
areas not useful	more bicycle paths/hiking	encourage exercise
not enough shade	plant trees	cooler, better appearance
entrance to community poorly defined	plantings around entranceway	recognition as community pride

A Landscaper for Our Community

Since our community has only enough money to hire one new employee, the townspeople have been debating which specialty would be the best. After considering alot of possibilities, I believe that hiring a landscaper would be most beneficial to us.

Right now, we don't really have a community recreation area but we have empty land that is barely used. A landscaper could come up with design ideas and make these areas more attractive and useful. For example, they could be made more like a park, with more bike and walking paths. both kids and adults would enjoy this. It would encourage healthy activity and bring the community together socially.

Our community doesn't have enough shade. A landscaper suitable to the area could plant trees and take care of them. Trees would improve the appearance of our community right away and help property values. Every year our community will become shadier, cooler, and it will be more attractive as the trees grow.

The entrance to our community poorly defined. guests and delivery people drive right by all the time, even though there is a sign there with the name of our development. A landscaper could help by planting bushes and flowers around the entranceway. A good design up front would get us noticed and create pride in our neighborhood.

We all want a community that is a safe, pleasant place four families and children to live. Our next step should be to make our neighborhood more beautifully and functional by hiring a professional landscaper.

Answer the questions.

1. Which of the following sentences is the thesis statement for this essay?

   (A) I believe that hiring a landscaper would be most beneficial to us.

   (B) Everyone has been debating which specialty would be the best.

   (C)) Our community has only enough money to hire one new employee.

   (D) None of the above.

2. Which of the following sentences is the topic sentence for paragraph 4?

   (A) The entrance to our community is poorly defined.

   (B) There is a sign there with the name of our development.

   (C) A landscaper could help by planting bushes and flowers.

   (D) None of the above.

3. Which of the following sentences supports this statement: A landscaper could come up with design ideas and make these areas more attractive and useful.

    (A) Our community doesn't have enough shade.

    (B) They could be made more like a park, with more bike and walking paths.

    (C) We have empty land that is barely used.

    (D) None of the above.

4. In which paragraph is there a run-on sentence? Correct it.

    (A) Paragraph 1   (B) Paragraph 2   (C) Paragraph 4

    _____

    _____

5. In which sentence is there a misplaced modifier? Correct it.

    (A) Sentence 2, paragraph 1   (B) Sentence 1, paragraph 2   (C) Sentence 2, paragraph 3

    _____

    _____

6. Which modifier is not parallel in paragraph 5? Correct it.

    (A) safe   (B) beautifully   (C) professional

    _____

    _____

7. Which adjective in sentence 4, paragraph 3 is not parallel with the others? Correct it.

    (A) shadier   (B) cooler   (C) it will be more attractive

    _____

    _____

8. In paragraph 4, the transition phrase *Our next step* connects which two ideas?

    (A) We don't have a recreation area./We should hire a landscaper.

    (B) We don't have shade./We don't have trees.

    (C) We need defined entrance./Our neighborhood is safe.

9. In paragraph 2, which words provide cohesion?

    (A) shade/shadier

    (B) community/landscaper

    (C) appearance/values

10. Which words provide cohesion?

    (A) In paragraph 1, *Since*

    (B) In paragraph 2, *For example*

    (C) In paragraph 4, *all the time*

11. Which paragraph is not indented?

    (A) Paragraph 1   (B) Paragraph 2   (C) Paragraph 5

12. Which sentence is not correctly punctuated? Correct it.

(A) Sentence 1, paragraph 2   (B) Sentence 2, paragraph 3   (C) Sentence 3, paragraph 4

_____

_____

13. Which sentences do not begin with a capital letter?

(A) Sentence 2, paragraph 1
(B) Sentence 4, paragraph 2
(C) Sentence 2, paragraph 4

14. Which word is not spelled correctly in this essay? Correct it.

(A) *be* in sentence 2, paragraph 1
(B) *by* in sentence 2, paragraph 4
(C) *four* in sentence 1, paragraph 5

_____

_____

15. Which word is not used correctly in this essay? Correct it.

(A) *enough* in sentence 1, paragraph 1
(B) *alot* in sentence 2, paragraph 1
(C) *get us* in sentence 3, paragraph 4

_____

_____

Practice 9

Proof the following essay by answering the questions that follow.

Topic 137

Your school has enough money to purchase either computers for students or books for the library. Which should your school choose to buy—computers or books? Use specific reasons and examples to support your recommendation.

Now	Proposed	Reason
out-of date reference material	use Internet	get current information
not enough computers	computer for every students	buy more computers
slow access to info	get information instantaneously	find information quickly on Internet

Buy Computers

Our school has been given a grant to make necessary improvements in the its facilities. we can spend it on new books for the library or on more computers. Our school already books in its library and it already has computers. Since we have more books than computers, I think that new computers will benefit the students more.

Computers, unlike books, can access up-to-date information on the Internet. Right now, the books reference in our library are very outdated. Our encyclopedia set is eight years old. Give every student access to a computer. We all can have the latest facts and figures on everything.

Unfortunately, giving every student a computer means we need a lot of computers. Right now, the ratio of computers to students is one to twelve. This means students only get to work on the computers three or four times a week. But if every student had a computer, we could use it whenever we wanted.

"Information on demand" should be our slogan. Students today need whatever they want, and they want it whenever. Life goes by to quickly to wait. It takes forever to identify a book that you think might have the information you need? then you have to go to the library and look for the book; usually it's not even there. We need information now.

With a computer, information searches are instantaneous. If we all had computers, we could access more information and access it faster by computer. If we all had computers, we could have all the information we needed for our school work. Give all of us a computer and look our grades go up. For these reasons, I feel that purchasing more computers will benefit us more than buying more books.

Answer the questions.

1. Which of the following sentences is the thesis statement for Topic 137?

   (A) Our school has been given a grant to make necessary improvements in the its facilities.

   (B) Our encyclopedia set is eight years old.

   (C) "Information on demand" should be our slogan.

   (D) None of the above.

2. Which of the following sentences is the topic sentence for paragraph 2?

   (A) The reference books in our library are very outdated.

   (B) Give every student access to a computer.

   (C) Computers, unlike books, can access up-to-date information on the Internet

   (D) None of the above.

3. Which of the following sentences supports this statement: "Information on demand" should be our slogan

   (A) Watch their grades go up.

   (B) Right now, the ratio of computers to students is one to twelve

   (C) We need information now.

   (D) None of the above.

4. In which paragraph is there a sentence fragment? Correct it.

   (A) Paragraph 1   (B) Paragraph 4   (C) Paragraph 5

5. In which sentence is there a misplaced modifier? Correct it.

(A) Sentence 4, paragraph 1

(B) Sentence 2, paragraph 2

(C) Sentence 3, paragraph 4

_____

_____

6. In which sentence in paragraph 4 could parts be made parallel? Correct it.

(A) Sentence 2   (B) Sentence 3   (C) Sentence 4

_____

_____

7. Which sentence in paragraph 5 could be made parallel with the others? Correct it.

(A) Sentence 1   (B) Sentence 4   (C) Sentence 5

_____

_____

8. In paragraph 2, sentence 4, the pronoun *We* provides cohesion with which antecedent?

(A) Our teachers   (B) Our community   (C) Our students

9. Which words provide cohesion between paragraphs 2 and 3?

(A) Right now   (B) Access   (C) Work on

10. Which words provide cohesion?

(A) In paragraph 2, *up-to-date* and *latest*

(B) In paragraph 3, *a lot* and *whenever*

(C) In paragraph 4, *forever* and *not there*

11. Which paragraph is not indented?

(A) Paragraph 1   (B) Paragraph 3   (C) Paragraph 5

12. Which sentence does not begin with a capital letter?

(A) Sentence 2, paragraph 1

(B) Sentence 3, paragraph 3

(C) Sentence 2, paragraph 5

13. Which sentence should end in a semicolon?

(A) Sentence 1, paragraph 3

(B) Sentence 1, paragraph 4

(C) Sentence 4, paragraph 4

14. Which word is not spelled correctly in this essay? Correct it.

    (A) *already* in sentence 3, paragraph 1

    (B) *to* in sentence 3, paragraph 4

    (C) *than* in sentence 5, paragraph 5

_____

_____

15. Which word is not used correctly in this essay? Correct it.

    (A) *unlike* in sentence 1, paragraph 2

    (B) *look* in sentence 4, paragraph 1

    (C) *go up* in sentence 4, paragraph 5

_____

_____

Practice 10

Proof the following essay. Use the Proofing Checklist as a guide. Use the concept map to help you iden-tify the content.

    The type and number of errors are identified.

Proofing Checklist

✓	CONTENT
1	Is there a thesis statement or introduction?
✓	Is there a topic sentence for each paragraph?
✓	Are there supporting details for each topic statement?
✓	Is there a conclusion?
✓	**CLARITY**
2	Are there run-on sentences or sentence fragments?
1	Are there misplaced modifiers or dangling modifiers?
1	Are the structures parallel?
✓	Are there transition words?
✓	Are the sentences and paragraphs cohesive?
✓	**PUNCTUATION AND SPELLING**
✓	Are the paragraphs indented?
2	Are there punctuation marks such as periods at the end of each sentence?
1	Do all sentences begin with capital letters?
1	Are all the words spelled correctly?

Topic 2

Do you agree or disagree with the following statement? Parents are the best teachers. Use specific reasons and examples to support your answer.

Not the Best Teachers

Throughout my life, I have been lucky enough to have a very good relationship with my parents. They have supported me, given me necessary criticism, and taught me a great deal about how to live my life. Parents can be very important teachers in our lives;

Parents may be too close to their children emotionally. Sometimes they can only see their children through their eyes, the eyes of a parent. For example, limit a child's freedom in the name of safety. What a teacher sees as a valuable new experience, like travelling to a big city, might seem too dangerous to a parent.

Another problem that parents may expect their children's interests to be similar to their own. They can't seem to separate from their children in their mind. if they love science, they may try to force their child to love science, too. But what if their child's true love is art, or writing, or car repair?

Parents are usually eager to pass on there values to their children. But should children always believe what their parents do. Maybe different generations need different ways of thinking. When children are young, they believe that their parents are always right. But when they get older, they realize there are other views. Sometimes parents can't keep up with rapid social or technological changes, especially older ones. A student who has friends of all different races and backgrounds at school may find that his parents have narrower views, or a student who loves computers may find that her parents don't really understand or value the digital revolution. Sometimes kids have to find their own ways to what they believe in.

The most important thing to realize is that we all have many teachers in our lives. Our parents teach us, our teachers teach us, and we learn from our peers. Books and newspapers and television also teach us. All of them are valuable

Write the error, its location (sentence/paragraph), and its correction.

ERROR	LOCATION	CORRECTION
CONTENT		
1. Thesis statement	paragraph 1 sentence 3+	Parents can be very important teachers in our lives; however, they are not always the best teachers.
GRAMMAR		
2.		
3.		
4.		

5.

_____

PUNCTUATION

6.

_____

7.

_____

8.

_____

SPELLING

9.

_____

Practice 11

Proof the following essay. Use the Proofing Checklist as a guide. Use the concept map to help you iden-tify the content.

The type and number of errors are identified.

Proofing Checklist

✓	**CONTENT**
1	Is there a thesis statement or introduction?
✓	Is there a topic sentence for each paragraph?
1	Are there supporting details for each topic statement?
✓	Is there a conclusion?
✓	**CLARITY**
1	Are there run-on sentences or sentence fragments?
1	Are there misplaced modifiers or dangling modifiers?
1	Are the structures parallel?
✓	Are there transition words?
✓	Are the sentences and paragraphs cohesive?
✓	**PUNCTUATION AND SPELLING**
5	Are the paragraphs indented?
1	Are there punctuation marks such as periods at the end of each sentence?
1	Do all sentences begin with capital letters?
1	Are all the words spelled correctly?

Topic

Is it better for children to participate in team sports or individual sports? Why? Use specific reasons and examples to support your answer.

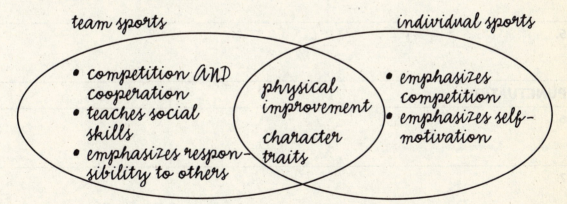

team sports

individual sports

- competition AND cooperation
- teaches social skills
- emphasizes responsibility to others

physical improvement

character traits

- emphasizes competition
- emphasizes self-motivation

Learning to be a Team Player

Both individual and team sports are meant to help children to improve physically. Both types of sports build important character traits in children, too.

Both individual sports and team sports emphasize competition, and children must learn to be competitors. Team sports have an added benefit, however They also emphasize cooperation with teammates. For example, one great player will not make a baseball team win. Everyone must work hard, and more important, work together.

For example, timing is important when throwing and to catch are involved. Only a cooperative effort will make the team a winner.

Team sports teach social skills better than individual sports. Players must learn to communicate with other players to succeed that is not true for individual sports, of course. Often you focus more on beating a score or a time clock than on another person. Sometimes the idea is to fool an opponent. that seems to be the opposite of good communication to me.

Finally, teem sports help children learn to be responsible to others.

All sports teach traits important, but I believe that a good team player has learned skills that will make him or her successful and happy throughout life. Thus, I always encourage young people that I know to try a team sport.

Write the error, its location (sentence/paragraph), and its correction.

ERROR	LOCATION	CORRECTION
CONTENT		
1.		
2.		
GRAMMAR		
3.		
4.		
5.		
PUNCTUATION		
6.		
7.		
8.		
9.		

10. _____

_____

11. _____

_____

12. _____

_____

SPELLING

13. _____

_____

Practice 12

Proof the following essay. Use the Proofing Checklist as a guide. Use the concept map to help you iden-tify the content.

The type and number of errors are identified.

Proofing Checklist

✓	**CONTENT**
✓	**Is there a thesis statement or introduction?**
✓	**Is there a topic sentence for each paragraph?**
✓	**Are there supporting details for each topic statement?**
1	**Is there a conclusion?**
✓	**CLARITY**
1	**Are there run-on sentences or sentence fragments?**
1	**Are there misplaced modifiers or dangling modifiers?**
3	**Are the structures parallel?**
✓	**Are there transition words?**
1	**Are the sentences and paragraphs cohesive?**
✓	**PUNCTUATION AND SPELLING**
1	**Are the paragraphs indented?**
✓	**Are there punctuation marks such as periods at the end of each sentence?**
1	**Do all sentences begin with capital letters?**
✓	**Are all the words spelled correctly?**

Topic 98

Do you agree or disagree with the following statement? All students should be required to study art and music in secondary school. Use specific reasons to support your answer.

All students should be required to study art and music in secondary school

Express themselves to learn ourselves

Learn what Society Values

Ancestors drew on walls, Made music with drums

Avenue for emotions and fears

Museums

concerts

Learn about other cultures

Similarities

differences

Yes to Music and Art in High School

I agree that all students should be required to study art and music in high school. I've read that young children who study art and music in grade school do better in their other studies. That argument aside, we should study art and music for its sake alone. We should study art and music to learn more about ourselves, our culture, and the world we live in.

Both art and music feed students' imaginations and help them express themselves. There's a reason our ancestors in caves drew on the walls and made music with drums. Wanting to express ourselves that way is natural. It gives us an avenue for our emotions and fears. It may not always be music other people want to hear or art others will appreciate, but it's the activity itself that's enjoyable. It shouldn't matter if the end result isn't perfect. In the process, we learn what we ourselves like and dislike.

Studying art and music means more than drawing or playing an instrument. Students usually go to art galleries and concerts, too. By studying the pictures on the museums' walls or by reading the program notes at a recital, students will learn what society has decided is worthy of praise. They learn what is important in their own culture.

Students may also learn about other cultures by looking at art and listening to music from other countries. When they study the art and music of other cultures, they will see similarities and differences with their own. They will learn about what is important in other societies. Students will also learn how the art and music of other cultures affect our own.

Write the error, its location (sentence/paragraph), and its correction.

ERROR	LOCATION	CORRECTION
CONTENT		
1.		
GRAMMAR		
2.		
3.		
4.		
5.		
6.		
PUNCTUATION		
7.		
8.		

Free Practice

Do the following on your own or in a group. There are no answers provided.

1. Exchange essays with your friends and proof them following the Proofing Checklist.

SELF-TEST ESSAY #4

Write on the same topic from Self-Test Essay #4. Plan, write, and revise an essay on that topic within 30 minutes. Use the space on the following pages. Do NOT write in the shaded areas.

Divide your time like this.

PLAN	5 minutes	30:00 – 25:00
WRITE	20 minutes	25:00 – 05:00
REVISE	5 minutes	05:00 – 00:00

Topic Number: _____

PLAN

Concept Map

Thesis Statement

General Ideas

Supporting Details

WRITE

REVISE

Proofing Checklist

Reread your essay. Use this checklist as a guide.

✓	**CONTENT**
	Is there a thesis statement or introduction?
	Is there a topic sentence for each paragraph?
	Are there supporting details for each topic statement?
	Is there a conclusion?
✓	**CLARITY**
	Are there run-on sentences or sentence fragments?
	Are there misplaced modifiers or dangling modifiers?
	Are the structures parallel?
	Are there transition words?
	Are the sentences and paragraphs cohesive?
✓	**PUNCTUATION AND SPELLING**
	Are the paragraphs indented?
	Are there punctuation marks such as periods at the end of each sentence?
	Do all sentences begin with capital letters?
	Are all the words spelled correctly?

Appendix

MODEL ESSAYS

Topics in the following list may appear in your actual test. You should become familiar with this list before you take the computer-based TOEFL test. Remember that when you take the test you will not have a choice of topics. You must write only on the topic that is assigned to you.

Computer-Based Essay Topics		
AD Agreeing or Disagreeing	51	33%
PR Stating a Preference	52	34%
EX Giving an Explanation	34	22%
MA Making an Argument	18	11%

1	EX	People attend college or university for many different reasons (for example, new experiences, career preparation, increased knowledge). Why do you think people attend college or university? Use specific reasons and examples to support your answer.

People attend colleges or universities for a lot of different reasons. I believe that the three most common reasons are to prepare for a career, to have new experiences, and to increase their knowledge of themselves and the world around them.

Career preparation is becoming more and more important to young people. For many, this is the primary reason to go to college. They know that the job market is competitive. At college, they can learn new skill for careers with a lot of opportunities. This means careers, such as information technology, that are expected to need a large workforce in the coming years.

Also, students go to colleges and universities to have new experiences. This often means having the opportunity to meet people different from those in their hometowns. For most students, going to college is the first time they've been away from home by themselves. In addition, this is the first time they've had to make decisions on their own. Making these decisions increases their knowledge of themselves.

Besides looking for self-knowledge, people also attend a university or college to expand their knowledge in subjects they find interesting. For many, this will be their last chance for a long time to learn about something that doesn't relate to their career.

I would recommend that people not be so focused on a career. They should go to college to have new experiences and learn about themselves and the world they live in.

▶

| 2 | AD | Do you agree or disagree with the following statement? Parents are the best teachers. Use specific reasons and examples to support your answer. |

Throughout my life, I have been lucky enough to have a very good relationship with my parents. They have supported me, given me necessary criticism, and taught me a great deal about how to live my life. Parents can be very important teachers in our lives; however, they are not always the best teachers.

Parents may be too close to their children emotionally. Sometimes they can only see their children through the eyes of a protector. For example, they may limit a child's freedom in the name of safety. A teacher might see a trip to a big city as a valuable new experience. However, it might seem too dangerous to a parent.

Another problem is that parents may expect their children's interests to be similar to their own. They can't seem to separate from their children in their mind. If they love science, they may try to force their child to love science too. But what if their child's true love is art, or writing, or car repair?

Parents are usually eager to pass on their values to their children. But should children always believe what their parents do? Maybe different generations need different ways of thinking. When children are young, they believe that their parents are always right. But when they get older, they realize there are other views. Sometimes parents, especially older ones, can't keep up with rapid social or technological changes. A student who has friends of all different races and backgrounds at school may find that his parents have narrower views. A student who loves computers may find that her parents don't really understand or value the digital revolution. Sometimes kids have to find their own ways to what they believe in.

The most important thing to realize is that we all have many teachers in our lives. Our parents teach us, our teachers teach us, and our peers teach us. Books and newspapers and television also teach us. All of them are valuable.

▶

| 3 | EX | Nowadays, food has become easier to prepare. Has this change improved the way people live? Use specific reasons and examples to support your answer. |

The twentieth century has brought with it many advances. With those advances, human lives have changed dramatically. In some ways life is worse, but mostly it is better. Changes in food preparation methods, for example, have improved our lives greatly.

The convenience of preparing food today is amazing. Even stoves have gotten too slow for us. Microwave cooking is much easier. We can press a few buttons and a meal is completely cooked in just a short time. People used to spend hours preparing an oven-cooked meal, and now they can use that time for other, better things. Plus, there are all kinds of portable, prepackaged foods we can buy. Heat them in the office microwave, and lunch at work is quick and easy.

Food preparation today allows for more variety. With refrigerators and freezers, we can preserve a lot of different foods in our homes. Since technology makes cooking so much faster, people are willing to make several dishes for even a small meal. Parents are more likely to let children be picky, now that they can easily heat them up some prepackaged macaroni and cheese on the side. Needless to say, adults living in the same house may have very different eating habits as well. If they don't want to cook a lot of different dishes, it's common now to eat out at restaurants several times a week.

Healthful eating is also easier than ever now. When people cook, they can use new fat substitutes and cooking sprays to cut fat and calories. This reduces the risk of heart disease and high cholesterol. Additionally, we can buy fruits and vegetables fresh, frozen or canned. They're easy to prepare, so many of us eat more of those nutritious items daily. A hundred years ago, you couldn't imagine the process of taking some frozen fruit and ice from the freezer, adding some low-fat yogurt from a plastic cup and some juice from a can in the refrigerator, and whipping up a low-fat smoothie in the blender!

Our lifestyle is fast, but people still like good food. What new food preparation technology has given us is more choices. Today, we can prepare food that is more convenient, healthier, and of greater variety than ever before in history.

▼

4	PR	It has been said, "Not everything that is learned is contained in books." Compare and contrast knowledge gained from experience with knowledge gained from books. In your opinion, which source is more important? Why?

"Experience is the best teacher" is an old cliche, but I agree with it. The most important, and sometimes the hardest, lessons we learn in life come from our participation in situations. You can't learn everything from a book.

Of course, learning from books in a formal educational setting is also valuable. It's in school that we learn the information we need to function in our society. We learn how to speak and write and understand mathematical equations. This is all information that we need to live in our communities and earn a living.

Nevertheless, I think that the most important lessons can't be taught; they have to be experienced. No one can teach us how to get along with others or how to have self-respect. As we grow from children into teenagers, no one can teach us how to deal with peer pressure. As we leave adolescence behind and enter adult life, no one can teach us how to fall in love and get married.

This shouldn't stop us from looking for guidelines along the way. Teachers and parents are valuable sources of advice when we're young. As we enter into new stages in our lives, the advice we receive from them is very helpful because they have already had similar experiences. But experiencing our own triumphs and disasters is really the only way to learn how to deal with life.

▼

5	PR	A company has announced that it wishes to build a large factory near your community. Discuss the advantages and disadvantages of this new influence on your community. Do you support or oppose the factory? Explain your position.

New factories often bring many good things to a community, such as jobs and increased prosperity. However, in my opinion, the benefits of having a factory are outweighed by the risks. That is why I oppose the plan to build a factory near my community.

I believe that this city would be harmed by a large factory. In particular, a factory would destroy the quality of the air and water in town. Factories bring smog and pollution. In the long run, the environment will be hurt and people's health will be affected. Having a factory is not worth that risk.

Of course, more jobs will be created by the factory. Our population will grow. To accommodate more workers, more homes and stores will be needed. Do we really want this much growth, so fast? If our town is going to grow, I would prefer slow growth with good planning. I don't want to see rows of cheaply constructed townhouses. Our quality of life must be considered.

I believe that this growth will change our city too much. I love my hometown because it is a safe, small town. It is also easy to travel here. If we must expand to hold new citizens, the small-town feel will be gone. I would miss that greatly.

A factory would be helpful in some ways. However, I feel that the dangers are greater than the benefits. I cannot support a plan to build a factory here, and hope that others feel the same way.

▼

6	MA	If you could change one important thing about your hometown, what would you change? Use reasons and specific examples to support your answer.

If I could change one thing about my hometown I think it would be the fact that there's no sense of community here. People don't feel connected, they don't look out for each other, and they don't get to know their neighbors.

People come and go a lot here. They change jobs frequently and move on. This means that they don't put down roots in the community. They don't join community organizations, and they're not willing to get involved in trying to improve the quality of life. If someone has a petition to put in a new street light, she has a very hard time getting a lot of people to sign. They don't feel it has anything to do with them. They don't get involved in improving the schools because they don't think the quality of education is important to their lives. They don't see the connection between themselves and the rest of their community.

People don't try to support others around them. They don't keep a friendly eye on their children, or check in on older folks if they don't see them for a few days. They're not aware when people around them may be going through a hard time. For example, they may not know if a neighbor loses a loved one. There's not a lot of community support for individuals.

Neighbors don't get to know each other. Again, this is because people come and go within a few years. So when neighbors go on vacation, no one is keeping an eye on their house. No one is making sure nothing suspicious is going on there, like lights in the middle of the night. When neighbors' children are cutting across someone's lawn on their bikes, there's no friendly way of casually mentioning the problem. People immediately act as if it's a major property disagreement.

My hometown is a nice place to live in many ways, but it would be much nicer if we had that sense of community.

▼

7	EX	How do movies or television influence people's behavior? Use reasons and specific examples to support your answer.

Do movies and television affect our behavior? A special concern is whether movies and television make children and society more violent. I believe that movies and television do influence our behavior, both for the better and for the worse.

Movies do make people more violent. The more we see violent acts on television, the less sensitive we become to them. Eventually violence doesn't seem wrong. We may even commit violent acts ourselves. This is especially true because we don't always realize that violence has consequences. Actors can be killed and come back for another movie. Sometimes we confuse that with reality. We forget that killing someone is permanent.

Movies and television also influence our behavior because they make us less active. Looking at films is a passive activity. If we watch too much, we become unhealthy, both mentally and physically. We stop using our own imagination when we see things acted out for us. Mental laziness becomes physical laziness; we'd rather watch sports on tv than play sports ourselves. We'd rather visit with the characters on "Seinfeld" or "Friends" than go chat with our own neighbors. Imaginary people have exciting lives. Is it any wonder that some people would rather live a fantasy life than their own?

Of course, watching movies and television can also be good for us. It can give us a broader window on the world. For example, seeing movies can expose us to people of different races and cultures. We can then overcome some prejudices more easily. Recently there have been more handicapped people in films, and this also helps reduce prejudice.

The best influence on our behavior is that movies and television reduce stress. Watching films, we can escape our own problems for a little while. Also, sometime movies show positive ways to resolve problems we all face. While tv and movies shouldn't be a way to hide from life, sometimes they can help us cope.

It is true that movies and television can influence our behavior negatively. However, I also believe that they influence our behavior in positive ways. How they affect you depends on how much you watch, what you watch, and how you respond to what you watch.

▼

| 8 | AD | Do you agree or disagree with the following statement? Television has destroyed communication among friends and family. Use specific reasons and examples to support your opinion. |

Some people believe that television has destroyed communication among friends and family. I think this is an exaggeration. In my opinion, whether or not television hurts communication depends on what type of program is being viewed. More importantly, it depends on the type of viewer.

There are empty programs and educational programs. Empty programs do not challenge people. They have just enough storyline to keep them from switching channels. There are also passive and active viewers. A passive viewer will just watch television without thinking about what he or she is seeing. The combination of an empty program and a passive viewer makes communication unlikely. Passive viewers just continue to watch, actually enjoying the fact that they don't have to think. They won't break away to talk about programming with friends and family. Even with better programming, passive viewers still won't think or communicate much. They'll probably even prefer the empty programs because the better programming is too much work.

On the other hand, active viewers watching educational programming always want to share what they see with friends and family. "Educational" doesn't necessarily mean documentaries on PBS. They could be dramas with realistic relationships or action shows with clever plotlines. When active viewers watch programs, they have ideas and talk about them with others. Good programming inspires them to change their thinking and their lives. Unlike passive viewers, they don't want to watch more and more without thinking.

Television may destroy communication among passive viewers. Those viewers probably don't want to communicate with friends and family much anyway. For active viewers who already enjoy communicating, television is actually helpful!

▼

| 9 | PR | Some people prefer to live in a small town. Others prefer to live in a big city. Which place would you prefer to live in? Use specific reasons and details to support your answer. |

I grew up in a small town and then moved to a big city, so I have experienced the good and bad sides of both. I never thought that I would like living in a big city, but I was wrong. After ten years of living in one, I can't imagine ever living in a small town again.

Small towns and big cities both have some problems in terms of transportation. In a small town, you have to own a car to ensure a comfortable living. You can't get around without one because there isn't any kind of public transportation. Big cities generally have heavy traffic and expensive parking, but there you have a choice of taking public transportation. It's not free, but it's often cheaper than driving when you consider gas and time. Especially if you don't have a car, you're better off in the city.

I love the excitement of big cities. Small towns have a slow pace. Large cities mean you have to adapt to a variety of situations, like finding a new route to work or trying a new restaurant. I enjoy that challenge very much. Another part of the excitement of city living is the variety of cultural activities available. There is a wide assortment of theatre, music and dance performances available in big cities. These things are rare in small ones.

The final thing I like about large cities is the diversity of the people. The United States is made up of people of different races, religions, abilities, and interests. However, you seldom find such a variety of people in a smaller town. I think that living in an area where everyone was just like me would quickly become boring.

Of course, security is a concern, and that's one area where small towns are superior to big cities. Still, I would rather be a bit more cautious and live in a large city than to feel secure but bored.

▼

10	AD	"When people succeed, it is because of hard work. Luck has nothing to do with success." Do you agree or disagree with the quotation above? Use specific reasons and examples to explain your position.

When people succeed, it is because of hard work, but luck has a lot to do with it, too. Success without some luck is almost impossible. The French emperor Napoleon said of one of his generals, "I know he's good. But is he lucky?" Napoleon knew that all the hard work and talent in the world can't make up for bad luck. However, hard work can invite good luck.

When it comes to success, luck can mean being in the right place to meet someone, or having the right skills to get a job done. It might mean turning down an offer and then having a better offer come along. Nothing can replace hard work, but working hard also means you're preparing yourself for opportunity. Opportunity very often depends on luck.

How many of the great inventions and discoveries came about through a lucky mistake or a lucky chance? One of the biggest lucky mistakes in history is Columbus' so-called discovery of America. He enriched his sponsors and changed history, but he was really looking for India. However, Columbus' chance discovery wasn't pure luck. It was backed up by years of studying and calculating. He worked hard to prove his theory that the world was round.

Success that comes from pure luck and no hard work can be a real problem. For example, consider a teenage girl who becomes a movie star. Imagine she's been picked from nowhere because of her looks. She is going to feel very insecure, because she knows she didn't do anything to earn her stardom. On the other hand, think about an actress who's spent years learning and working at her craft. When she finally has good luck and becomes a success, she will handle stardom better. She knows she earned it.

People who work hard help make their own luck by being ready when opportunity knocks. When it comes to success, I think that hard work and luck go hand in hand.

▼

11	AD	Do you agree or disagree with the following statement? Universities should give the same amount of money to their students' sports activities as they give to their university libraries. Use specific reasons and examples to support your opinion.

I disagree strongly with the idea that the same amount of money should go to university sports activities as to university libraries. Although playing sports is a wonderful way to learn about teamwork, strategy and reaching your goals, it should not be the principal focus of a university education.

Students need the most up-to-date library facilities available to get the best education. Many of those facilities are very expensive to buy and maintain. These include computerized programs and access to Internet research databases that students can use to find information all around the world. If a university is only offering its students resources of a decade ago, it's depriving those students of a tremendous amount of information.

Even the book and magazine budget of universities has gone up tremendously in the last decade. More is being published on every subject, and every university wants to have this information available to its students.

It also costs money for universities to keep their libraries open. Students need to have access to all the libraries' research tools as much of the time as possible. Because students are young and can stay up all night studying, many universities are starting to leave their libraries open all night during exam periods. This costs money, because the staff has to be paid extra to be there. It also costs money to run the building (electricity, heat) during that time.

Students at universities are only going to benefit from their education if they can get to all the tools they need to learn. Sports are secondary to the resources that students need from university libraries. For this reason, libraries should always be better funded than sports activities.

▼

12	EX	Many people visit museums when they travel to new places. Why do you think people visit museums? Use specific reasons and examples to support your answer.

People love to visit museums when traveling to new places. I think this is because museums tell them a lot about the culture of those places. Museums are also fun. It's almost impossible to get bored in a museum. Every museum will have at least one thing of interest to somebody.

When visiting someplace new, you can find out about the culture of that place in many ways. You can go to a movie or a place of worship or a nightclub. Another option is to sit in the park and listen to the people around you. The easiest way to learn about a place's culture, though, is by visiting its museums. Museums will show you the history of the place you're visiting. They'll show you what art the locals think is important. If there aren't any museums, that tells you something, too.

Museums are fun. Even if you're not interested in art or history, there is always something to get your attention. Many museums now have what they call "hands-on" exhibits. These were originally designed to keep children occupied while their parents were looking at exhibits. However, museums have found that adults enjoy hands-on opportunities just as much as children. These exhibits have activities like pushing a button to hear more about what you're looking at, creating your own work of art, or trying on clothes like those on the models in the museum.

People also enjoy visiting museums about unusual subjects. For instance, in my hometown there's a museum devoted to the potato. This museum has art made out of potatoes. It also tells all about the history of the potato, and sells potato mementos like key chains and potato dolls. People enjoy visiting this museum because it's different. It's not something they'd find in their hometown and the museum's curators enjoy talking about the Great Potato.

Museums are popular because they are about us. They reflect our creations, our values, and our dreams. No matter who you are or what you like, somewhere there is a museum that will amaze and interest you.

▼

13	PR	Some people prefer to eat at food stands or restaurants. Other people prefer to prepare and eat food at home. Which do you prefer? Use specific reasons and examples to support your answer.

Some people like to eat out at food stands and restaurants, while others like to prepare food at home. Often it depends on the kind of lifestyle people have. Those with very busy jobs outside the house don't always have time to cook. They like the convenience of eating out. Overall, though, it is cheaper and healthier to eat at home.

While eating in restaurants is fast, the money you spend can add up. When I have dinner at a restaurant with a friend, the bill is usually over twenty dollars. I can buy a lot of groceries with that much money. Even lunch at a fast-food stand usually costs five or six dollars for one person. That's enough to feed the whole family at home.

Eating at home is better for you, too. Meals at restaurants are often high in fat and calories, and they serve big plates of food—much more food than you need to eat at one meal. If you cook food at home, you have more control over the ingredients. You can use margarine instead of butter on your potatoes, or not put so much cheese on top of your pizza. At home, you can control your portion size. You can serve yourself as little as you want. In a restaurant, you may eat a full plate of food "because you paid for it."

It's true that eating out is convenient. You don't have to shop, or cook, or clean up. But real home cooking doesn't have to take up a lot of time. There are lots of simple meals that don't take long to make. In fact, they're faster than eating out, especially if you think of the time you spend driving to a restaurant, parking, waiting for a table, waiting for service, and driving home.

Both eating at restaurants and cooking at home can be satisfying. Both can taste good and be enjoyed with family and friends. I prefer cooking at home because of the money and health issues, but people will make the choice that fits their lifestyle best.

| 14 | PR | Some people believe that university students should be required to attend classes. Others believe that going to classes should be optional for students. Which point of view do you agree with? Use specific reasons and details to explain your answer. |

Some people may believe that going to classes should be optional, but I disagree. I don't understand how university students can expect to learn anything if they don't attend classes. Personal experience can help people learn about themselves and the world outside the classroom, but when it comes to learning about academic subjects, students need to be in class.

In class they receive the benefit of the teacher's knowledge. The best teachers do more than just go over the material in the class textbook. They draw their students into discussion of the material. They present opposing points of view. They schedule guest speakers to come, give the students additional information, or show documentary films on the subject.

Also, attending classes on any subject teaches more than just facts. It teaches students how to learn, how to absorb information and then apply what they've learned to other situations. Their teacher is the best one to help them with these skills. They can't learn them just by reading the textbook.

Going to class also teaches students how to work with the other members of the class. Many times students will be given group assignments. This is different from what they did in secondary school. Here they're with people from different backgrounds and experiences. In this situation, they learn how to handle working with people different from themselves to achieve a common goal.

Going to class also teaches students responsibility and discipline. Having to be at a particular place at a particular time prepares them for getting a job. Being at that place on time with an assignment completed prepares them for a career.

In short, by going to class students learn more than just information from the teacher. They also learn how to learn, how to work with others, and how to work responsibly. These are not optional skills in life, so attending classes should not be optional in college.

| 15 | EX | Neighbors are the people who live near us. In your opinion, what are the qualities of a good neighbor? Use specific details and examples in your answer. |

If you have a good neighbor, you are a lucky person. You have someone who cares about your needs and your property, who is helpful in the little day-to-day situations that come up, and who is supportive in times of crisis.

A good neighbor is someone who, for instance, understands that your children may occasionally run across his lawn, even though you tell them not to. He'll realize that children can be careless about things like that, and he won't make a big fuss about it unless it becomes a regular thing. In the same vein, he knows that you'll understand if some of the trash from his trash cans blows across into your yard. In other words, he is sensitive to the unintentional things that can happen. He doesn't make a big deal about them.

A good neighbor is also respectful of your property. For example, she asks your permission before doing anything that interferes with what's yours. This means she wouldn't plant a huge tree in between your houses without asking how you felt about it. If she wanted to put up a fence, she would let you know first. She might work with you to decide where it should be placed. Maybe the two of you would even split the cost.

A good neighbor would lend you some milk if you ran out. She'd give you a ride to work if your car was broken, and let your children stay at her house in the evening if you got stuck working overtime. You would do the same for her. Both of you would help make the other's life easier.

When something really awful happens to you, like a death in the family, a good neighbor will volunteer to help in any way he can. This could mean something small, like making some casseroles to put in your freezer to feed visiting relatives. Or it could mean something big, like helping you get through the sadness of the funeral.

I think only someone who has experienced a bad neighbor can really appreciate a good one! A good neighbor can be a good friend. He or she can make all the difference in the world to your life.

▼

| 16 | AD | It has recently been announced that a new restaurant may be built in your neighborhood. Do you support or oppose this plan? Why? Use specific reasons and details to support your answer. |

I can see both advantages and disadvantages to having a new restaurant built in our neighborhood. I'm worried about traffic and how it will affect our neighborhood. However, I think that it will benefit local businesses and increase appreciation for our neighborhood. Overall, I think it is a good idea.

Traffic congestion is always a concern when you build something new. Our streets are narrow, with parking on both sides. More cars traveling through the neighborhood could cause a lot of congestion. Traffic means parking problems, too. Our neighborhood has very few garages attached to the houses. Most of us depend on finding a space to park on the street. If the new restaurant is built, we'll be competing for those spaces with the restaurant's patrons. Plus, if the restaurant offers valet parking, it'll be even worse. Valet parkers work in teams to grab every possible space available on the street.

I'm also concerned about the type of patrons this new restaurant will bring into our neighborhood. A family restaurant wouldn't be a problem. However, if it's going have a bar and dancing, then there could be problems. The restaurant would stay open later, and people leaving the restaurant might be drunk. Who wouldn't worry about rowdy customers staggering around our neighborhood in the early morning hours, looking for their cars?

I have to admit, though, there are advantages to a new restaurant. Our neighborhood could certainly use the jobs the restaurant would provide. Not only that, the money neighborhood residents would earn there would likely be spent at other neighborhood businesses. This would give a boost to those businesses and make our neighborhood more prosperous.

A new restaurant would also attract a lot of people to our neighborhood. They could see what a nice area this is to live. That might attract new residents to the neighborhood. That would be a good thing, because we've been losing residents to the suburbs the last couple of years.

There are a lot of details to consider, but all in all, I support the idea of this new restaurant in our neighborhood.

▼

| 17 | PR | Some people think that they can learn better by themselves than with a teacher. Others think that it is always better to have a teacher. Which do you prefer? Use specific reasons to develop your essay. |

Most of us can learn how to do something simple on our own with just a set of instructions. However, to learn about something more complex, it's always best to have a teacher.

Teachers bring with them varied and useful backgrounds. They've been trained to teach individuals in different ways depending on their style. For instance, some students learn better by discussing a topic. Others learn more by writing about it. Teachers can help students learn in the way that's best for each student. A textbook or a manual can only give you one way of learning something. Plus they're only as helpful as your ability to understand them. A good teacher can adapt her teaching to your needs.

Teachers help you focus on what you're learning. If you're learning something by yourself, it's easy to become distracted and go on to other activities. Teachers keep your attention on the subject. They also approach a subject logically, taking it one step at a time. On your own, it's tempting to skip parts of the learning process you think you don't need. That can hinder your ability to really understand the subject.

Learning a subject on your own is a very narrow way of learning. You can only use the information you get from the textbook. With a teacher, you get the information in the written materials as well as the teacher's own knowledge of the topic. Teachers can also provide extra materials to broaden the scope of what you're learning.

There's nothing wrong with studying on your own, and a learner can always benefit from some quiet study. For the best possible learning, though, a good teacher is the biggest help you can have.

▼

| 18 | EX | What are some important qualities of a good supervisor (boss)? Use specific details and examples to explain why these qualities are important. |

Even though job situations can be very different, there are several qualities that all good supervisors have in common. A good boss treats all her employees fairly. She doesn't single out one employee for better (or worse) treatment than the others. A poor supervisor has favorites. Sometimes she'll even use her favorites to spy on other employees. She expects them to tell her what the others are saying about her. This can cause a lot of bad feelings among employees.

A good supervisor gives clear and understandable directions. She doesn't constantly change her mind about what she wants employees to do. She also doesn't get angry with an employee who is confused and needs her to explain the directions again or more fully. Delegating authority well is another quality of a good supervisor. She knows how to use the skills of her employees to best advantage. A poor supervisor insists on doing everything herself. She is unwilling to give any authority to others.

A good boss evaluates her employees on a reasonable set of criteria, not on how she feels about them personally. And she lets the employees know what those criteria are, so they have a fair chance of meeting them. She gives both praise and criticism in a straightforward manner. She also offers guidance when needed. A poor supervisor will criticize without giving any suggestions on how to improve.

Most importantly, a good supervisor sets the standards for her employees by her own behavior. She works hard and treats employees like valuable assets to the company. This promotes good morale among her workers, and this is of great benefit to her business.

▼

19	PR	Should governments spend more money on improving roads and highways, or should governments spend more money on improving public transportation (buses, trains, subways)? Why? Use specific reasons and details to develop your essay.

Governments should definitely spend more money on improving all forms of public transportation. These include buses, subways and trains. This is the best way to preserve natural resources and reduce pollution.

As a planet, we're dealing with a finite amount of natural resources. Once they're gone, they can't be replaced. They can't fill our need for oil and gasoline forever. But we seem to forget that and consume them at an incredible rate. In wealthier countries, some families have two or three cars. As soon as teenagers get their driver's licenses, they're given cars so their parents won't have to drive them places.

Public transportation hasn't been sufficiently developed. Because of this, suburban areas surrounding cities have been allowed to sprawl more and more widely. This means that people can't even go to the store without having to hop into the car. Everything is too far away from where they live. If there were better and more frequent public transportation, people would be able to give up their cars for local driving.

As a result of all the cars being driven, we're dealing with terrible pollution problems. In big cities, there are days during the summer when the elderly and people with respiratory problems are advised not to leave the house. Ten years ago this was unheard of! Now it's the norm. Public transportation would cut down considerably on air pollution.

Public transportation also encourages a sense of community. People who travel to work together all the time get to know each other. Cars isolate us from our neighbors. However, people feel they need to drive because they can't depend on public transportation to fit their schedules. If more money were available, buses, subways and trains could run 24 hours a day. Then they would be available all the time to the people who need them.

I always try to take public transportation whenever possible, and I encourage friends and neighbors to try it to. I think we must support public transportation in order to create a better world.

▼

20	AD	It is better for children to grow up in the countryside than in a big city. Do you agree or disagree? Use specific reasons and examples to develop your essay.

There are advantages and disadvantages to a childhood in either the country or a city. It's hard to say which is better. Growing up in the country means a certain amount of isolation. You're in a small town or on a farm and not with a lot of people. Even more important, the people you meet every day tend to be just like you. Most will be the same race as you, have the same background as you, and will have gone to the same schools as you. In the city, the people you meet are all different. There are different races and different cultures. You get a more interesting mix.

City people tend to come from a lot of different places and move around a lot. So, there isn't the sense of community in the city that you have in the country. People in the city can live in the same apartment building for twenty years and never get to know their neighbors. In the country, everybody knows everybody. For a child, this means the country is more secure. A child can get lost or hurt in the city and have no one to turn to. In the country, everyone's a neighbor. People in the country feel connected to each other.

A child growing up in the city has the advantage of a lot of interesting and excit-ing places to visit. He or she can go to the zoo, museums, art galleries and concerts. There are a lot of restaurants with different kinds of food. It's easy to see every new movie that comes out. Children in the country don't have a lot of these activities nearby.

All in all, I think a childhood in the city is better because it prepares you more for what real life is like.

▼

21	EX	In general, people are living longer now. Discuss the causes of this phenomenon. Use specific reasons and details to develop your essay.

Today people are living to be much older than ever before. Some of the main reasons for this are the improved health care and better nutrition available to everyone.

Medical care is more available to people. Although not everyone can get the best health care, everyone can get basic health care and advice. When people are seriously ill, they can go to a public hospital and be taken care of. Years ago, health care wasn't available to everyone. Some people didn't live near a doctor or a hospital, and others couldn't pay for the care they needed. They made do with herbal medicines or folk remedies. Of course, some of these worked, but not for the more serious diseases.

The quality of medical care has improved. That's also a factor in longevity. Doctors know more now about what causes disease and how to cure it. Years ago, doctors only knew about the most basic diseases and cures. Medicine was not very advanced. You could die from something as simple as an infection from a cut. Now we have antibiotics and other medicines to help cure infections.

People are also living longer now because of better nutrition. We're eating better and more healthfully than we used to. That's reduced the number of people with heart disease and cancer. We try to eat low-fat foods and eat more vegetables and fruits, which are now available year-round.

Improved medical care and healthy eating habits has greatly expanded our life spans. What we need to do now is make sure that everyone in the world has these benefits.

▼

22	EX	We all work or will work in our jobs with many different kinds of people. In your opinion, what are some important characteristics of a co-worker (someone you work closely with)? Use reasons and specific examples to explain why these characteristics are important.

We spend more time with our co-workers during a week then we do with our family. Thus, it's important for our co-workers to be people we can get along with. I've worked in a lot of offices, and I've found there are certain characteristics that all good co-workers have in common.

A good co-worker is very cooperative. She does her best to get along with others. She tries to keep her end of things flowing smoothly to help others in the office. She realizes that if one person doesn't get her work done, it can hold up everyone else. She has a positive attitude that creates a pleasant working environment.

A good co-worker is adaptable. She is not stubborn about changes in schedules or routines, and doesn't object to having her job description revised. That can make life miserable for everyone around her. A good co-worker is willing to change her schedule to accommodate another worker's emergency. She has no problem with new procedures and welcomes changes when they come.

A good co-worker is helpful. She pitches in when someone falls behind in his or her work. She's willing to do whatever it takes to get the job done. She doesn't keep track of how often she has to finish another's work or take on extra work. Some co-workers do their own job, period. They have no sense of office community. They only want to do their work, get paid and go home.

A good co-worker is a sympathetic listener, and never uses what she learns against people. She doesn't gossip. A bad co-worker uses negative rumors to take advantage of others.

Being a good co-worker isn't too hard, but some people just can't seem to manage it. Wouldn't it be a wonderful world if everyone could?

▼

23	AD	Do you agree or disagree with the following statement? Sometimes it is better not to tell the truth. Use specific reasons and details to support your answer.

I agree that sometimes it is better not to tell the truth. In some cases the truth is going to hurt someone and no good will be gained by it. If so, then I don't think that person should be told the truth. There are times when a person needs to know the truth in order to make an important decision. There are also times when telling the truth is the only way to help someone who's being self-destructive. However, often telling the truth only benefits the teller, not the person being told.

If someone has said something nasty about a person, those words don't need to be repeated. However, what if a person has told a shameful secret to a friend, and that friend has told the secret to others? Then that person needs to know that she can't trust her friend. Otherwise, she might tell that friend other secrets.

What if someone is doing something self-destructive, like partying all night in college instead of studying? Then he needs to be told that this behavior is upsetting his friends, who are worried about him. However, if he skips class and the teacher asks his friend why he isn't there, it's not necessary for the friend to tell the truth. He doesn't have to lie, but he also doesn't have to give information about his friend's behavior.

Sometimes people need to know the truth before they can make an important decision. Suppose you're selling your house and you know there's water in the basement. Then you should tell the truth about that to anyone interested in buying your house. If you don't, you could be in trouble legally as well as ethically! However, you don't need to tell the truth about the cranky neighbor who lives next door. The neighbor may not be as cranky with someone else as he was with you. Sometimes it's better not to tell.

▼

24	AD	In some countries, teenagers have jobs while they are still students. Do you think this is a good idea? Support your opinion by using specific reasons and details.

I don't think it is a good idea for teenagers to have jobs while they are still students. It can interfere with their studies, it can disrupt their home life, and it takes away part of their childhood that they can never replace.

Education today is very complex and difficult. In order to learn and get good grades, a student must work very hard and concentrate. This means attending classes from early in the morning until late afternoon, then doing research for projects, then going home and doing homework. It's a busy schedule for anyone. For someone trying to hold down a job, it's even harder. Students need all their energy for their studies. If they're working after class at night, they're going to be tired the next day. They won't be able to concentrate. This will have a negative impact on their learning, and eventually on their grades.

Having a job can also disrupt a teenager's home life. Families spend less and less time together. If a teenager has a job to go to after school, he won't be home for dinner. He won't be home after dinner, either, and may not get home until late at night. This means he doesn't have a lot of time to spend with his family. If he doesn't have a car, it can mean changes in his parents' schedules, too. They have to drive him to work and pick him up.

The main drawback of a teenager having a job while he's still a student is that he's missing out on the fun of being young. He has a whole lifetime in which he'll have to earn a living. This is the last free time he'll have. It's the last chance he'll have to hang out with friends and just enjoy himself. Soon enough he'll have to worry about paying the rent and buying food.

Jobs bring money, but money isn't everything. A teenager with a job gives up too much. No one should spend all his time at work, and especially not a teenager.

▼

25	PR	A person you know is planning to move to your town or city. What do you think this person would like and dislike about living in your town or city? Why? Use specific reasons and details to develop your essay.

A friend of mine from college is moving to my city, so I have been thinking about what she would and wouldn't like about it. I'd say the quality of life here, as far as fun and activities are concerned, is very good. The quality of life isn't very good, though, in other important ways.

Living in a large city is exciting, but you pay a price for it. There are lots of interesting things to do, and good restaurants with food from around the world. There are museums, art galleries, and lots of movie theaters. However, the crime rate is high, and people have to be careful about where they go at night. There's a lot of traffic most of the time, and finding a parking space can be a problem. There are also a lot of people living here. Sometimes it feels too crowded.

In a big city like mine, housing is very expensive. It costs a lot even if you're just renting an efficiency apartment. The good side is that there's a lot of choice about where you want to live and how you want to live. You can find apartments of all sizes in different settings. Houses of equal variety are available for sale or rent.

If my friend likes the great outdoors, she might be disappointed. Unfortunately, my city doesn't have a lot of wide open green spaces, and there aren't a lot of trees on the streets. We're not near the ocean, and the mountains are a day's drive from here. Still, we do have some natural areas. For example, we have a beautiful big park. It even has a lake in the middle that's used for ice skating in the winter. There's a different kind of beauty in the city.

Thinking about it, I suppose whether my friend likes my city will depend on whether or not she likes exciting places. I hope she likes a lot of variety as far as housing and activities are concerned. If she does, then this is the place for her.

▼

26	AD	It has recently been announced that a large shopping center may be built in your neighborhood. Do you support or oppose this plan? Why? Use specific reasons and details to support your answer.

There would be both advantages and disadvantages to having a shopping center built in my neighborhood. One advantage would be the convenience. I would like to have all those stores close by. Shopping would be much easier and faster because I wouldn't have to drive great distances to get to the stores.

A shopping center would mean more choices, because there would be more stores selling different products. I might have a movie theater nearby, because so many shopping centers these days include movie theaters in their plans. Most shopping centers also have restaurants and a food court. That means a greater variety of places to eat in our area.

Having a shopping center built in the neighborhood would also mean more jobs for the community. Initially, these jobs would be in the building of the center. Later the jobs would be in the stores, theaters, and food establishments.

Of course, there would be some disadvantages, too. Probably the biggest problem would be traffic. A lot of people would be coming to the shopping center. They'd drive through our neighborhood to get to the center. In addition, if there wasn't enough parking at the center, they might look for parking spaces near our homes.

A shopping center might also invite more crime into our neighborhood. Parking lots after dark are a big temptation to robbers. They know people are there with money to spend. The shopping center might also become a place where unruly teenagers would gather. This could cause trouble. Our town would need a community center for them to go to instead.

On the whole, though, I think my neighborhood should support having a shopping center built here. It would bring more variety to our shopping, give us the opportunity to amuse ourselves at movie theaters and restaurants, and bring more jobs into the area.

▼

| 27 | AD | It has recently been announced that a new movie theater may be built in your neighborhood. Do you support or oppose this plan? Why? Use specific reasons and details to support your answer. |

Some people will say that a new movie theater in our neighborhood would be a bad thing. However, I fully support the plan to build one. I feel that a movie theater would bring more opportunities for recreation, reduce teenage delinquency, and lead to several improvements in the town.

As it stands, there is little to do in my town. There are no parks here, and there is certainly no nightlife. Additionally, the nearest movie theater is more than thirty minutes away. That is inconvenient for everyone here. Many movies end late at night. Who wants a long drive home at 11:30 p.m. or midnight?

Building a new movie theater here will reduce juvenile delinquency. Like everyone else, teens here are bored. They need activities to keep them busy and out of trouble. The jobs that the theatre will provide will help teens, too. We need more businesses that are willing and eager to employ young people.

Overall, the new theater will bring many improvements to the town. For example, it will help other businesses. That is because the movie theater will attract customers from neighboring towns. Those neighbors do not have a reason to come to this town now. However, if they are coming here for a movie, they will be more likely to stay here to shop. If we get more visitors, we'll need better roads. While this may be costly, it will also make travel easier for people living here. We will be able to get around faster. Safety will be improved with the new roads, because they will be in better condition than many that we have now.

I believe that our town needs a new movie theater. Again, I support it fully. I hope that others in our community will join me to convince residents and local government.

▼

| 28 | AD | Do you agree or disagree with the following statement? People should sometimes do things that they do not enjoy doing. Use specific reasons and examples to support your answer. |

I agree that people should sometimes do things that they don't enjoy doing. This is a basic part of being an adult. Plus, some things that aren't "fun" are still good for us in the long run.

Take personal tasks. Who enjoys going to the dentist? Very few people enjoy having their annual check-up with the doctor. Not a lot of people enjoy changing the oil in their car or mowing their lawns. These are all things we do because we have to, not because we want to. We realize that taking care of our physical health is the sensible thing to do. We know that if we don't change the oil in our cars, our cars won't run. We understand that grass grows and if we don't mow it, our lawns will look like tropical forests.

Professional tasks are another part of the same equation. No one likes to be stuck with a boring assignment or to be told we have to work with someone no one else gets along with. Sometimes we have to put up with unfair criticism from a supervisor or resentment from those we supervise. If we're in management, we may have had the unpleasant task of having to fire someone. None of these are fun things. Unfortunately, they're all part of earning a living, something the majority of adults have to do.

On the other hand, sometimes doing something we don't enjoy doing can lead to enjoyment. Simply by trying it again, we may decide we like doing it. For instance, we may have convinced ourselves we hate to dance. We agree to go to a club only to please someone else. Yet, for some reason, this time we enjoy dancing. We've been cheating ourselves of enjoyment without even knowing it. The same can be true of trying new foods or going to a new type of museum.

Doing what we don't enjoy doesn't always have to be a bother, does it? It's just part of life.

▼

| 29 | AD | Do you agree or disagree with the following statement? Television, newspapers, magazines, and other media pay too much attention to the personal lives of famous people such as public figures and celebrities. Use specific reasons and details to explain your opinion. |

I think the media pay too much attention to the private lives of famous people. Television, newspapers, magazines and web sites dig up all kinds of past bad actions. They say that these are true reflections of a person's character. This may be true if they occurred only a few years before, but some of these are things people did as teenagers. People in their forties are expected to explain something they did when they were fifteen. If they killed someone, obviously that's more than a youthful mistake. Usually, though, these incidents involve experiments with drugs or being reckless in a car. They're not something that the public needs to know.

The media love to say that the public has a right to know. That's not true. We don't need to know if a movie star or politician has had an extramarital affair. That is something of concern only to the people involved. We do need to know if someone we're electing to public office has been involved in shady business deals, but we don't need to know if he or she defaulted on a loan twenty years ago.

It seems the media dig up these facts without giving thoughtful consideration to what might happen. It has an effect on the celebrity's family, especially the children. A celebrity's good name and credibility may be ruined before he or she can prove that rumors are false. If a case goes to court, paying a lawyer can use up all their money. Even if it doesn't come to that, they may find their career ruined.

When are we, the public, going to make it clear to the media that we're tired of having to watch this kind of thing on the news? Wouldn't it be better if they would concentrate on more important issues?

▼

30	PR	Some people believe that the Earth is being harmed (damaged) by human activity. Others feel that human activity makes the Earth a better place to live. What is your opinion? Use specific reasons and examples to support your answer.

The quality of human life has improved greatly over the past few centuries, but Earth is being harmed more and more by human activity. As we develop our technology, we demand more from our planet. Eventually, this will harm people as well.

Our planet gives us everything we need, but natural resources are not endless. Strip mining devastates whole regions, leaving bare and useless ground. Deforestation removes old growth trees that can't be replaced. Too much fishing may harm fish populations to the point where they can't recover. We are too careless in taking what we want without giving anything back.

There are more people than ever, living longer than ever. So is it any surprise that many areas suffer from too much development? Anyone living in or near a city has experienced "urban sprawl." There is a new shopping area on every corner and new houses, townhouses and apartments everywhere. Traffic gets worse and worse because planners can't keep up with growth. Keeping up with human demand is hard enough. Environmental concerns come in last.

With growth comes pollution. Companies and communities dump waste into water. Landfills are full of trash. Emissions from factories pollute the air. Barrels of industrial waste and worse, radioactive waste, have no safe place to go. If we're not careful, we can harm our planet beyond repair.

People need to respect the Earth and try to preserve it. If we don't, what kind of future will we have?

▼

31	AD	It has recently been announced that a new high school may be built in your neighborhood. Do you support or oppose this plan? Why? Use specific reasons and details in your answer.

I oppose having a new high school built in my neighborhood. Although I know there's a real need for a new facility, I have to say that I don't want one built so close to me. I think it would cause a lot of problems.

First of all, there are very few teenagers in this neighborhood, or in our suburban subdivision, for that matter. Most of the residents here are either retired or are just starting out with young children. This means that the kids coming to the new high school wouldn't be walking. They would come on buses or would be driving to the school. Either way, this would mean a lot more traffic on our streets.

In addition to the traffic on school days, there also would be traffic whenever there was a sporting event, such as a basketball or football game, or activities at the school. Would there be enough parking in the school lot for everyone attending those events? Probably not. Consequently, those extra cars would end up in our neighborhood.

My neighbors and I would also be upset about the loss of the park, which is the site that's been selected for the high school. Mothers with young children gather there every morning for their kids to play together. People my age like to take a walk after dinner. On weekends, that park is a place for picnics and relaxation. We'd be sorry to lose our neighborhood park.

I also have some concerns about all those young people being in our neighborhood. Would there be problems with drugs or fights? Could the school district guarantee us that security would be a priority? These are concerns that I don't think can be addressed sufficiently for me to support a new high school in my neighborhood.

▼

32	PR	Some people spend their entire lives in one place. Others move a number of times throughout their lives, looking for a better job, house, community, or even climate. Which do you prefer: staying in one place or moving in search of another place? Use reasons and specific examples to support your opinion.

Even though I have lived in the same house, in the same neighborhood, in the same city my entire life, I know I would be happy living in a variety of places. Moving would expose me to new people, new weather, and new housing.

Even if I were to move to another part of my city, I would encounter new people. Each neighborhood has a distinct personality. When I move to that neighborhood, I would meet the shopkeepers and residents that shape that personality. I may even adopt part of their manner as my own so I could be recognized as part of that community.

If I want to encounter different weather patterns, I would have to move beyond my city. Where I live now, it is the same temperature all year. I would like to go to a place where there are four seasons so I can experience really cold temperatures. I would like to walk in the snow and perhaps go skiing. I could learn winter sports if I lived in the north.

Now, of course, I live with my parents in their home. It is a one story house built around a courtyard where our family spends a lot of time. If I were to move, I would like to live in an apartment on a very high floor so I could see all around me. I could also meet my neighbors in the elevator and we could get together for coffee in my apartment.

The more I move the more I would experience change. I would meet new people in every place I lived; I could move to sample countries with four seasons or even a continent like Antarctica which only has two. Wherever I lived, I would experience living in housing particular to that area. I would then be a citizen of the world, wouldn't I? Could you call me a foreigner if I called everyplace my home?

| 33 | PR | Is it better to enjoy your money when you earn it or is it better to save your money for some time in the future? Use specific reasons and examples to support your opinion. |

"Save it for rainy day." That's my motto. When I have a choice between spending my money or putting it in my savings account at the bank, I always put it in the bank. I will have a lot of expenses in the future like my education, travel, and unforeseen emergencies. I need to have money set aside for these expenses.

Education is expensive. I can't depend on my parents to pay all my bills. I have tuition, room and board, books, and incidental expenses to pay for. I'll try to get a scholarship to cover some of these costs, but I know I will be responsible for a lot of the expenses. If I spend my money now, I won't be able to pay for my education. I need to save money for my education.

Travel is also very expensive. I don't mean vacation travel. I mean travel to get to and from school. Transpacific airfare costs a lot even special reduced fares. I first have to get to school and then, of course, I want to return to my family for important festivals and occasions. Going back and forth will be costly, but worth it. I need to save money for these trips.

Emergencies could arrive at any moment. I might have an unexpected illness while I am at school. There might be costs that aren't covered by the school insurance. One of my family members may need help. I will have to send them money. You can't predict emergencies like this, but you can be prepared. I need to save money for these emergencies.

When you are not rich, you cannot spend your money carelessly. You must plan ahead. I know in my life, I will have expenses for my schooling and for travelling to and from my home. I know that I will also have unexpected expenses related to unforseen emergencies. I must be prepared. I need to save money for these events.

| 34 | PR | You have received a gift of money. The money is enough to buy either a piece of jewelry you like or tickets to a concert you want to attend. Which would you buy? Use specific reasons and details to support your answer. |

The choice between spending money on tickets to a concert or spending money on jewelry is an easy one. Given this choice, I would buy jewelry. The reasons are obvious. Jewelry is an investment; it is permanent; and it is fashionable.

Jewelry like a gold bracelet for example is a very good investment. It is important for women (and for men, too) to have gold jewelry. If you have some serious financial problem, you could always sell your jewelry to help you over any rough spots. You could not sell your used concert ticket.

Jewelry, unless you sell it, is permanent. You always have it to wear. Each time you put it on, you will remember the day you bought it. It will give you pleasure for years and years. You could not wear the ticket stub from the concert.

Jewelry is very fashionable. I would feel very smart wearing a beautiful gold bracelet or diamond pin. People would comment and tell me how much they loved my jewelry. They would compliment me on my good taste.

I would feel very rich with my jewelry. I would have a good investment which is permanent and fashionable. Then, when someone invites me to a concert (and pays for my ticket), I will have something beautiful to wear.

▼

35	MA	You must select a person to teach others to do a job. Which one of the following is the most important for you to consider in making your selection? • the person's education • the person's work experience • the quality of the person's previous work Use specific reasons and examples to support your answer.

Training someone to do a job is an important task. It requires a good education, work experience, and skilled job performance. Of these three requirements, I believe it is most important that a potential job trainer be judged on the quality of his or her previous work.

A person may be well educated, but not able to perform a job proficiently. A doctor may know how to treat childhood diseases, but not be able to train medical students to perform surgery. An accountant may be able to balance a company's accounts, but not be able to help the company's executives invest their money.

A person may have a lot of work experience, but not be able to do the job well. Time is not the best measure of quality. A mother may spend 17-years raising her children, but not be able to train young mothers to care for their infants. A typist may have typed ten-years worth of letters, but may not type over 30 words a minute.

A person who does a job well is the one you want to be a trainer. I want to learn to fly a plane from a pilot who has faced a lot of mechanical problems in flight and never had an accident. I want to learn how to make money from a billionaire not from a salaried investment broker.

As in all things, it is quality that we look for, not general knowledge or time spent in an occupation. I want others to learn from the best so they can be the best, too.

▼

36	AD	Business should hire employees for their entire lives. Do you agree or disagree? Use specific reasons and examples to support your answer.

In some business cultures it is the practice to hire workers when they are young and employ them until they retire. In other business cultures companies hire people to do a job and then fire them when they are not needed. To me, the important considerations in today's economy is job performance, speed and change. Loyalty is not a consideration.

Today there is a lot of competition and we need to hire workers who can perform a task well. We need to find skilled workers who can do a job without a lot of training. We need to match the job to the worker, and, if the job changes, we change the worker.

Because of this increased competition, we need to be able to produce our goods or services quickly. We need young people who are willing to put in long hours. We need young people who are aggressive and will push themselves to do their job faster.

In order to compete, we have to be innovative. By changing our workforce frequently, we can bring in new ideas. We must constantly be looking for new ways to do new things. We need fresh workers with fresh points of view.

Although a company's loyalty to a worker and a workers loyalty to a company is a noble idea, it is not practical today. Skilled workers do not want to be tied down to one company; they want the flexibility to improve their opportunities. Change makes the economy powerful.

▼

| 37 | EX | Countries, businesses, and schools are three areas that need good leaders. Choose one of these three areas and describe the most important qualities of a leader in that area. Explain why these qualities are important, using specific examples and details. |

The principal of a school is one of our first encounters with a figure of authority. Consequently, he or she must be a good example of a leader. The principal must be firm, fair, and foresighted which are important qualities of a principal.

When a principal announces a rule, you must understand that he or she means it. If a rule requires all students to be in their seats when the bell rings, the rule must be enforced. If students are out of their seats, they should be punished. If a rule requires that students not wear hats in school, the rule must be enforced. If students wear hats, the hats must be taken away from them. A principal must be firm.

When a principal enforces a rule, you must understand that he or she will treat everyone equally. If I get caught eating at my desk, I must receive the same punishment that my classmate got when she got caught eating at her desk. If a sophomore is late for school, he or she must receive the same punishment that a senior would. A principal must be fair.

When a principal establishes a rule, you must understand that he or she has a good reason for it. If a rule requires that students must participate in extracurricular sports, you should understand that the principal knows that a strong body as well as a strong mind will help us in the future. If a rule requires that students must do two hours of volunteer work in the community each week, you should understand that the principal knows that close involvement in the community builds strong character. A principal must be foresighted.

A principal's job is not as easy one. I only hope that in the future, I can model my own leadership abilities on the ones I observed in school. I hope I can be as firm, fair, and foresighted as my principal.

▼

| 38 | EX | Choose one of the following transportation vehicles and explain why you think it has changed people's lives.
• automobiles
• bicycles
• airplanes
Use specific reasons and examples to support your answer. |

An airplane is a form of transportation that has changed people's lives. Thanks to the plane, our lives are now faster, more exciting, and more convenient that before.

You cannot deny that a plane is fast. For example, the Concorde flies at supersonic speed. A businessman can leave Paris at 11 a.m. in the morning and arrive in New York at 8 a.m. the same morning in time for a day's work. Many business people in Europe will fly to London for a noon meeting and then return home to Rome or Madrid for dinner.

It is always exciting to take a plane trip. When you take a trip by plane, you know that you might cross many time zones, many oceans, and many countries. When you get off the plane, you could be in a place that speaks a different language. A plane is like a magician's trick. You get in a box and you come out somewhere totally different.

Nothing can beat the convenience of a plane. In the old days, it might take you days to do what the plane can do it an hour. Boats, for example, only leave on certain days of the week and take a long time to get to their destination. Planes give you the option to leave several times a day and get you to your destination quickly.

Although other forms of transportation may be more comfortable, none has changed the way we do business and live our lives more than the plane. Thanks to the speed, excitement, and convenience of the planes, our lives are richer.

▼

| 39 | AD | Do you agree or disagree that progress is always good? Use specific reasons and examples to support your answer. |

Who would disagree with the statement "progress is good"? Without progress, there would be no change. Without progress, there would be no change in our economy, our standard of living, or our health.

Progress is required to keep the economy moving forward. New products need to be developed; new services need to be created. Without progress, our economy would stand still. There would be no change. Without progress, there would be no supermarkets with fresh produce brought in from all over the world.

Progress is required to improve our standard of living. Our homes today are more efficient and use less natural resources thanks to improvement in home construction techniques. Our clothes are warmer and safer thanks to developments in textile manufacturing. Our educational system is better thanks to the use of the computers and the Internet.

Progress is required to improve the health of the world population. Without progress, there would be no vaccines against deadly diseases like smallpox. Without progress, there would be increased infant mortality. Thanks to progress, our lives are longer and healthier.

Progress is a natural state. Without it, we would not evolve. Without it, our economy, our standard of living, and our health would deteriorate. Who could deny the necessity of progress?

▼

| 40 | AD | Learning about the past has no value for those of us living in the present. Do you agree or disagree? Use specific reasons and examples to support your answer. |

People often say "Those who don't understand history will repeat the mistakes of the past." I totally disagree. I don't see any evidence that people have made smart decisions based on their knowledge of the past. To me, the present is what is important, not the past. I think that people, the weather, and politics determine what happens, not the past.

People can change. We can't assume that people will continue to hate one another just because they have had hated one another for years. Look at Turkey and Greece. When Turkey had an earthquake, Greece sent aid. When Greece had an earthquake, Turkey sent aid. Now, these two countries are cooperating and looking forward to improved relations. No doubt, if we looked at the past, we would have thought this was a lost cause. But people change.

The weather can change. Farmers think that they can plant certain crops because these crops have always grown well in their fields before. But the weather can change. There can be a long drought. The crops that have always worked well, will die. A drought-resistant crop needs to be tried. If we looked at the past, we would not have changed our crop and we would have lost our farm. Weather changes.

Politics can change. According to my way of thinking, politicians must be responsive to changes in the people. If politicians looked only at the past, they would always say the same thing. People change. On the whole, people today care about human rights. They want all people to have the equal rights. If we looked at the past in the United States, we would see a lot of discrimination against races, women, and sexual orientation. Now, that is changing. Politicians change, too.

As a rule what is important today is to follow the mood of the moment. We can't be locked into the past. It doesn't do us any good to think about the past. People, the weather, and politics can change in any direction. The direction of this change, in my opinion, can not be predicted by studying the past.

▼

| 41 | AD | The expression "Never, never give up" means to keep trying and never stop working for your goals. Do you agree or disagree with this statement? Use specific reasons and examples to support your answer. |

"If at first you don't succeed, try, try again." These are wise words. One should never give up. There is always another opportunity, another goal, or another option.

Once I ran for president of my class. Unfortunately, I lost. I lost because I did not promote myself enough. I looked at my mistakes and decided how to correct them. The following year, I ran for president again. This time I gave speeches, called voters on the phone, and handed out brochures. This time I won. Never give up. There is always another opportunity.

Once I wanted to study medicine. Unfortunately, I didn't like science. I failed all my science courses at school. Then I realized that what I liked about medicine was helping people. I changed my goal from healing people to helping people. Now, I'm studying psychology. There is always another goal.

Once I wanted to talk with my friend. Unfortunately, his computer was down and I couldn't e-mail him. His phone line was busy so I couldn't call him. Mail would take too long so I couldn't write him. Since I realy wanted to talk with him, I got on the bus and went across town to visit him. There is always another option.

If you give up, you might as well die. My advice is to always look for another opportunity, another goal, or another option. There is always something else. Don't give up.

▼

42	AD	Do you agree or disagree with the following statement? With the help of technology, students nowadays can learn more information and learn it more quickly. Use specific reasons and examples to support your answer.

Technology has greatly improved the way we get information. Students can now get more information, get it more quickly, and get it more conveniently.

The Internet and the World Wide Web has opened every major library and database to students around the world. Information comes not only in print form, but also in multimedia. You can get audio and video data. You can get information about events in the past as well as events that unfold as you watch your computer monitor.

Information comes at the speed of the Internet which is to say in nanoseconds. You can type in a few key words in your search engine, and the engine will search the entire WWW to find information on your topic. You don't have to spend hours pouring over card catalogs in the library and looking at the shelves. This research is done for you instantly on the Web.

It is certainly more convenient to sit at home and do research on your computer. Your computer is open 24-hours a day, unlike a library or office which has limited hours and limited resources. You can do research in your pajamas while you eat breakfast. What could be more convenient?

Technology, especially the Internet, has certainly changed the quantity and quality of the information we get. The speed and convenience of a computer helps students learn more, more quickly.

| 43 | AD | Do you agree or disagree with the following statement? Games are as important for adults as they are for children. Use specific reasons and examples to support your answer. |

Everyone likes to play games. Games are important at any age to keep your mind sharp, learn new things, and maintain social skills.

People say you can't teach an old dog new tricks. Modern research has shown that senior citizens can continue to grow brain cells by exercising their mind. Games are a great way to exercise your mind. By concentrating on the tactics of the game, memorizing moves, keeping track of your opponents strategies, you can keep your brain functioning and growing.

Some games can teach you a lot. Games that ask questions, for example, will show you what you don't know. (Name the capital of Albania, for example.) It is always easier to learn something when you realize you don't know it.

When you play a game, you have to be considerate of your opponents. You can observe people's reactions and the way they interact as they play. It is always interesting to watch people. Maintaining personal contacts is important for everyone.

Regardless of your age, playing games can help you keep your mind alert, learn new things, and build friendships.

| 44 | EX | Awards and prizes are given for excellence in various fields. Do these awards and prizes serve a useful purpose? Use specific reasons and examples to support your answer. |

A prize or award, whether it's the Nobel Prize, the Academy Award, or Best Handwriting Prize, is important. Such prizes can have economic, personal, and social effects that enrich the life of the recipient.

Prizes like the Nobel Prize can be a cash award. But even for prizes that don't, like the Academy Award, an actress who wins Best Actress will be offered more roles and a higher pay than actresses who don't win the award. Even for the elementary student who received the school's Best Handwriting award may get a congratulations gift from proud grandparents.

The personal benefits of receiving any award are evident. Any award winner is pleased that he or she has been recognized for his or her work. When people receive the Academy Award, they often cry they are so happy.

Everyone likes to be with a winner. A person who gets a prize often has many new, best friends. A winner's social life is much better than a loser's social life. The winner of the Best Handwriting prize may not be very popular with his or her jealous classmates, however.

Awards serve a very useful purpose in that their economic, personal, and social benefits add to the recognition.

▼

| 45 | AD | Some people think that human needs for farmland, housing, and industry are more important than saving land for endangered animals. Do you agree or disagree with this point of view? Why or why not? Use specific reasons and examples to support your answer. |

In the past, there have been many endangered animals. Now they are extinct. Does it matter? Has our environment been affected by their absence? Has the quality of our own life been changed? The answer to these questions is "Yes."

Yes. It does matter if we destroy an endangered species habitat to develop more farmland, housing or industrial parks. There is a delicate balance of nature. If one small part is removed, it will effect all the other parts. For example, if certain trees are cut down, bats will have no place to roost. If they cannot roost, they cannot breed. If there are no bats, there will be no animal, or bird to eat certain insects that plague our crops.

Yes. Our environment has been affected by the absence of certain animals. Certain flowers are pollinated by butterflies which migrate from Canada to Mexico. Some of the breeding grounds of these butterflies was destroyed. Now these flowers are disappearing from certain areas. We will no longer be able to enjoy their beauty.

Yes. The quality of our life has been changed. America used to be covered with giant trees. Now we have to visit them in one small park. Rain forests around the world are being cut down to make room for humans. We will never be able to see or study this fragile ecosystem.

I would encourage us humans to look for other alternatives for our farmlands, housing, and industries. We have alternatives; the animals do not.

▼

| 46 | MA | What is a very important skill a person should learn in order to be successful in the world today? Choose one skill and use specific reasons and examples to support your choice. |

The one skill I would choose for success is tolerance. I do not define success economically; I define success socially. To succeed in the future, we will need to be tolerant of one another's background, opinions, lifestyle.

The world is becoming increasingly mobile. We no longer are able to live and work only with people who went to the same schools and went to the same parties as we and our parents did. Now, we will work directly with people whose backgrounds are completely different from ours. We must be tolerant of these differences as they must be tolerant of us if we are to live and work together amiably.

We cannot stop speaking to people or start a war just because there is a difference in opinion. We must learn to be tolerant of one another and respect these differences in opinion. We have to find a common ground, an idea we can both agree on. Once we have agreement on one subject, it will be easier to settle differences in other subjects.

Different people have different lifestyles. We must accept these differences even though they may be different than what we are used to. Women can live on their own, hold important jobs, and raise children on their own. Men can stay home and take care of children. Social roles can change and we must be tolerant of these changes.

To succeed socially, you must be adapt to differences. You must be tolerant of all peoples regardless of their background, their opinions, or their lifestyles.

▼

47	MA	Resolving problems between individuals or groups is important. What should be considered or kept in mind in resolving problems between individuals or groups? Use specific reasons and examples to support your answer.

Conflict resolution is very important. The technique is the same whether it's between people, between groups, or between nations. You need to find a common ground; you need to learn what both sides want; and you need to plan steps to resolve the conflict.

Finding a common ground is the first important step in any conflict resolution. For example, if two countries are fighting, a mediator could ask what is the single thing that both countries are concerned about. One answer might be their children's future. Agreeing on the future of their children is an important first step.

The next step would be to try to determine what both sides want for their children. For example, Country X says, "Security from Country Y." Country Y says, "Security from Country X." Obviously, they feel threatened by one another.

The third step is to plan steps to resolve the conflict. A mediator might ask what would make each side more secure: Stronger borders? Increased trade? Smaller military forces? Once the steps are established, the peace process has begun.

I don't mean to imply that this is easy. Resolving long-term disputes is not simple. But the process can be broken down into three steps (common ground, needs, steps to resolution) and then repeated and repeated until there is peace.

▼

48	AD	Do you agree or disagree with the following statement? Self-confidence is the most important factor for success in school or at work. Use specific reasons and examples to support your opinion.

Self-confidence is one very important factor for success, but there are two other equally important factors: knowledge and sensitivity. All three are required for success in any area.

One needs to feel one can accomplish a task. If one thinks he or she is incapable of doing something, he or she will not succeed. For example, if you think you are going to do poorly on an exam, you will probably do poorly. It is important to tell yourself that you can do well. If you have confidence in yourself, you will probably do well.

Even if you have a great deal of self-confidence, you won't be able to do well on the exam without knowledge. You have to understand your subject very well. With knowledge and self-confidence you have a better chance of success.

In areas other than exams, you will need to be sensitive to your surroundings in order to succeed. You will need to know whether to boast about yourself or be modest;

you will need to know whether you should take the lead or let others. This is a difficult skill to learn, but an important one for success.

To be successful in school or work, you need three qualities: self-confidence, knowledge, and sensitivity. Alone, none of these factors will help you succeed. But together, they ensure success.

▼

49	EX	Why do you think some people are attracted to dangerous sports or other dangerous activities? Use specific reasons and examples to support your answer.

Dangerous sports or activities attract a certain type of person. This person is often a risk taker, an optimist, and a fatalist.

People who take risks are found both in dangerous sports and business. But it is a special person who takes a risk with his own life as opposed to his money. My father was a risk taker. He put everything he owned into his business, but he stopped playing risky sports like horseback riding and skiing. Once his business was a success and he no longer had to worry about providing for us, he returned, at the age of 60, to the risky sports that he did as a youth.

Someone who plays a dangerous sports must be an optimist. They cannot imagine that anything will happen to them. They never think about breaking their leg while skiing, falling off a cliff while rock climbing, falling on their head while sky diving. They live for the thrill of the moment without a thought to the many things that could go wrong.

Rock climbers and sports car drivers must be fatalist. They might plan for potential problems, but once they have done everything they can do, the outcome is out of their hands. A motorcyclist who jumps across a narrow canyon will get the fastest, strongest bike available that will carry him or her across the canyon. However, wind conditions or other problems might interfere and the cyclist may fall short of his goal.

Many people have the same traits of course. Many of us are risk takers, optimists, and fatalists. But I think people who play dangerous sports must have these characteristics in abundance.

▼

50	EX	Which is more important for success: the natural ability you are born with or hard work? Explain your opinion, using specific reasons and examples.

Without a doubt, hard work is a much better predictor of success than natural ability. In my experience, I have seen this at work in sports, school, and work.

Many athletes have a natural ability to run the fastest mile or kick the ball the most accurately. Unless they work hard though, they will not be a star. They need to train daily, eat properly, live correctly. It takes hard work to be Number One.

At school, I have seen many very bright students do poorly on exams. They count on their intelligence to get them through. However, unless they do their homework every day, participate in class discussions, and study for exams, they will be at the bottom of the class.

Many salespeople can talk with anyone and convince them to buy something. They have a natural ability to sell. They must however apply some hard work to this skill. They must learn a lot about their customers, about the product they are selling, and about the market. They must put some effort into the paper work that goes along with the sale. If they don't follow through, the sale will not be made.

Whatever the area, whether on the playing field, at school, or on the sales floor, a person must not rely on his natural ability alone if he or she wants to succeed. They must work hard to be a success.

▼

| 51 | AD | Do you agree or disagree with the following statement? Parents or other adult relatives should make important decisions for their older (15 to 18 year-old) teenaged children. Use specific reasons and examples to support your opinion. |

No one knows me as well as my parents. No one wants the best for me like my parents. It is natural that I should allow my parents to make important decisions for me. I think all older teenagers (15 to 18 year-olds) should take their parents advice on decisions that concern their education, their social life, and their future careers.

My parents have always chosen the best schools for me to attend. They have encouraged me to attend special prep classes to make sure that I was well prepared for the exams. They have given me tutors to make sure that I understood my subjects well. When it comes to choosing a college, I will trust my parents to make that decision. They know what they can afford and what will give me a good education.

When I was young, my parents would invite children over to play with me. Over the years, I have become very close to these children. They are like my family. We celebrate holidays and birthdays together. We even go to the mountains together in the summer. My parents do not want me to fall into the wrong crowd. They do not want me to meet and fall in love with someone they do not know. I understand that and I want to make them happy.

My father runs a very successful business and my mother is a well-known politician. They are very well connected and they have many friends who would like me to work for them when I finish school. This is a very good arrangement for me.

If all children follow their parents wishes, they would probably be happier. Parents only want the best for their children.

▼

| 52 | PR | Some people like to travel with a companion. Other people prefer to travel alone. Which do you prefer? Use specific reasons and examples to support your choice. |

Travelling alone is the only way to travel. If you take someone with you, you take your home with you. When you travel alone, you meet new people, have new experiences, and learn more about yourself.

When I travel with a friend, I spend all my time with that friend. We eat together and sightsee together. When I travel alone, I spend my time looking for new friends. It is easy to find other people, either other tourists or locals, to eat with or have a coffee with. When you share meals with strangers, they become friends.

When I travel with a friend, my routine is predictable. We maintain the same schedule that we do at home. When I travel alone, I adopt the rhythm of the place I visit. I might take a nap in the afternoon and eat dinner at 11 pm. I might go to a disco and dance all night.

When I travel with a friend, we know how we will react to things. When I travel alone, each new experience requires a new reaction. If I don't try new things, I won't be able to decide if I like something or not. Shall I ride an ostrich or eat one?

I think it is always important to do things on your own. You can find new friends, collect new memories, and adopt different ways of doing things. Isn't that the point of travel?

▼

53	PR	Some people prefer to get up early in the morning and start the day's work. Others prefer to get up later in the day and work until late at night. Which do you prefer? Use specific reasons and examples to support your choice.

I prefer sleeping late and staying up late at night. This routine fits my body's rhythm, my work schedule, and my social life.

I believe in following my body's natural rhythm. My body tells me to sleep until I am ready to get up and go to bed when I am sleepy. This means I never get up early in the morning. My body tells me it likes me to get 8 to 10 hours of sleep a day.

Sleeping late also fits my work schedule. Actually I don't have that much work to do. I can easily finish my work between lunch and dinner. I think that if one works too much, there is not enough time left to enjoy one's self.

My active social life is another reason I prefer to sleep late. Who gets up early in the morning to have fun? No one. Anything amusing, such as concerts, dances, parties, dinners, all happen at night. If I got up early in the morning, I would be too tired to enjoy myself in the evening.

I will maintain this pattern forever I hope. I think it is always important to listen to your body and if your body tells you to stay in bed, you should listen to it. By listening to your body, you will never let work interfere with your social life.

▼

54	EX	What are the important qualities of a good son or daughter? Have these qualities changed or remained the same over time in your culture? Use specific reasons and examples to support your answer.

The qualities of a good son and daughter—obedience, loyalty, respect—have not changed. Any parent will tell you that, like their ancestors, they expect these qualities from their children. However, they do not always get what they expect from their children.

Parents demand that their sons and daughters, regardless of age, obey them. Even if the children are married and have their own children, they should still do whatever their parents ask of them. At least, that's the way it was. Now, children tend to obey their parents until the children are of college age. Then they feel they are adult enough and can make their own decisions even if these decisions are against the parent's wishes.

Parents also expect loyalty from their children. If there was a dispute in the neighborhood or between families, the parents would expect their children to side with their own family. This quality is probably still very common. Most children today will support their family against others.

Parents, of course, demand respect. As people become more mobile, and children are introduced to non-traditional ways of doing things, this quality may not endure. Parents are sometimes viewed as old-fashioned. Children don't think their parents can appreciate the way life really is. They think their parents are too old to understand. They lose respect for their parents.

Obedience, loyalty, and respect are virtues that are being challenged today. We may not obey our parent, give them the loyalty or respect they wish or deserve, but I hope my children obey me, are loyal to me, and respect me.

▼

| 55 | PR | Some people prefer to work for a large company. Others prefer to work for a small company. Which would you prefer? Use specific reasons and details to support your choice. |

I would prefer to work in a large company rather than a small one. A large company has more to offer in terms of advancement, training, and prestige.

In a large company, I can start at an entry-level position and work myself up to the top. I could start in the mailroom and, once I know the company, can apply for a managerial position. In a small company, there is not as much room to grow.

In a large company, there are a variety of jobs. I could work in sales, in marketing, in distribution, in shipping, or in any department I applied for. I could be trained in a variety of positions and would have valuable experience. In a small company, there would not be the same opportunity.

In a large company, there would be more prestige. I could brag to my friends that I worked for one of the biggest companies in the world. I would always have something to talk about when I met strangers. If I worked for a small company, I would always have to explain what the company did.

Working for a small company would not give me the same opportunities for advancement or on-the-job training as working for a larger company would. Nor would I be as proud to work for a small company—unless the small company was my own.

| 56 | EX | People work because they need money to live. What are some other reasons that people work? Discuss one or more of these reasons. Use specific examples and details to support your answer. |

Although people work to earn money, money is not the main reason people stay in their jobs. They also work because they enjoy working, they receive job satisfaction, and they like the sense of accomplishment.

Most people work for work's sake. They enjoy going to an office, or store, or school each day. They like to interact with other people. They like to help people solve problems, learn something, or get a product. People like to help other people.

A lot of people keep the same job because the job gives them a lot of satisfaction. They genuinely enjoy what they do. This is true for most teachers. A teacher's pay is not very great, but the job satisfaction can be very high. Helping someone learn is one of the greatest things anyone can do.

People enjoy their work because they like the sense of accomplishment. They like to know that they finished a project. People who work in factories take pride in the car they produce or the television they assemble. When they see a car on the street, they can feel a sense of accomplishment. They helped make that car.

Money is nice, but it is not the only reason people get up and go to work each day. I believe that people work because they enjoy the act of working; they find their work personally rewarding; and they like the feeling of a job well done.

| 57 | AD | Do you agree or disagree with the following statement? Face-to-face communication is better than other types of communication, such as letters, e-mail, or telephone calls. Use specific reasons and details to support your answer. |

I would have to agree that face-to-face communication is the best type of communication. Face-to-face communication can eliminate misunderstandings immediately, cement relationships, and encourage continued interaction.

If you are talking to someone directly, you can see right away if they don't under-stand you. A person's body language will tell you they disagree or don't follow your line of thought. You can repeat yourself or paraphrase your argument. If you had sent an e-mail, the person may have misinterpreted what you wanted to say. He or she could be insulted and you would have to waste time explaining yourself in another e-mail.

When you talk face-to-face, you communicate with more than words. You com-municate with your eyes and your hands. You communicate with your whole body. People can sense that you really want to communicate with them. This energy bonds people together. Your relationship with a person can grow much stronger when you communicate in person.

Face-to-face encounters tend to go on longer than other forms of communication. An e-mail lasts a second; a telephone call, a few minutes. However, when you meet face-to-face, you've made an effort to meet with the person, and the person has made an effort to meet with you. You will probably spend longer together talking. The longer you talk, the more you say. The more you say, the stronger your relationship will be.

In summary, if you want to establish a relationship with another human being, the best way is talking face-to-face. When you communicate directly, you can avoid misunderstandings that may occur in writing. You can communicate on levels other than just words and you can spend more time doing it.

▼

58	PR	Some people like to do only what they already do well. Other people prefer to try new things and take risks. Which do you prefer? Use specific reasons and examples to support your choice.

I am not a risk taker. I like to do just those things that I am proficient at. I have learned that it is better to focus my attention, do one thing and do it well, and not try anything new.

When I was younger, I was always experimenting with a lot of different things. First I wanted to be a dress designer so I studied drawing. I couldn't draw so I decided to be a veterinarian, because I liked animals. I didn't like to see sick animals so I decided to be a historian. That suited me perfectly since all I had to do was sit in a library and read. I learned to focus my attention on one subject.

I am a very good reader and history is very interesting to me. I decided not to read any other subject. I only read history books. I even focused my attention on Chinese history. I only read history books on Chinese history. I do one thing and I do it well.

I don't like to try anything new. If I read things in another area, I don't do well. I don't understand American history or English history. The names are confusing and the stories not interesting to me. I don't want to learn about anything else. Chinese history is my subject.

I may seem a bit stubborn, but I have learned what makes me happy. I don't like to take a risk with new things. I like to focus my attention on one subject, do it well, and not try anything new.

▼

59	EX	Some people believe that success in life comes from taking risks or chances. Others believe that success results from careful planning. In your opinion, what does success come from? Use specific reasons and examples to support your answer.

Nothing ventured. Nothing gained. If our great explorers and scientists did not live by this creed, where would we be? I think that we must all take risks in our lives, but these must be calculated risks. Like the great thinkers of our time, we must plan carefully, seize all opportunities, and reevaluate our plans.

There is no such thing as a chance occurrence. Columbus in his search for the Indies drew maps, plotted his route carefully, and set out. Madame Curie worked diligently in her laboratory recording every aspect of her experiments. You need to have a careful plan so you can measure your success.

Even with a careful plan, changes occur. Columbus was looking for the Indies, but ended up in the Caribbean. Lewis and Clark were looking for a river passage west, but discovered much more. You have to be ready to take advantage of new things as they occur.

When things go against plan, you must be ready to change direction. Columbus didn't bring back spices from the East Indies, he brought back gold from the West Indies. It is important to see the positive side of things. Make your mistakes work for you.

You will never succeed in life if you don't take chances. But before you start, you must plan carefully so you are ready to take advantage of every opportunity and turn mistakes to your advantage.

▼

60	MA	What change would make your hometown more appealing to people your age? Use specific reasons and examples to support your opinion.

I think that people my age would like to have a place to go after school. They could go there to socialize, have meetings, and just relax.

In my town, there are a few tea houses, but these are reserved for our fathers and their friends. Teenagers do not go there unless it's to carry messages to their fathers. We need a place where we can meet after school to talk about school and other subjects that interest us.

At our own tea house, we could also have meetings. These would be like club meetings. We could have a debating society, a poetry reading group, or a political club. We could meet after school one night a week and have our meeting.

We need a place where we could just relax away from our family. Our home life is very hectic; there are a lot of younger children making a lot of noise in the evening. We need a quiet place to study, read the paper, or just sit.

If our town had a tea house reserved for teenagers, it would be good for our parents since they would always know where we were. They would know that we were just socializing, or meeting, or just relaxing with our friends.

▼

61	AD	Do you agree or disagree with the following statement? The most important aspect of a job is the money a person earns. Use specific reasons and examples to support your answer.

Yes. Yes. Yes. The most important aspect of a job is the money a person earns. When I get a job, I want to earn a lot of money. If I earn a lot of money, people will know I am successful, smart, and a good candidate for marriage.

Money equals success. If I earn a lot of money, I can wear nice clothes, get a big car, buy my parents a nice apartment, and spend a lot of money on my friends. Everyone will know I am rich and very successful.

Earning a lot of money will show people how smart I am. Everyone knows you can't be stupid and earn a lot of money. Who will trust someone stupid to do a job?

When I earn a lot of money, my mother will be able to find me a good wife. She will be able to tell everyone what an important job I have. It will make it easy for her to find someone for me since all girls want to marry a rich man.

I don't care what kind of work I do as long as I earn a lot of money. That's the most important thing for me. Having a well paying job will show everyone that I am successful, smart, and a good catch!

▼

| 62 | AD | Do you agree or disagree with the following statement? One should never judge a person by external appearances. Use specific reasons and details to support your answer. |

In most cases, one should never judge a person by external appearances. Sometimes when I walk down the street at night, I avoid people who are acting tough and loud, but in general, I prefer to reserve judgement until I get to know someone. Judging someone by external appearance can be deceptive. Judgements based on external appearances prevent you from getting to know a person, reinforce stereotypes, and are superficial and limiting.

In high school I stayed away from students who were called the "bad students" because they dressed a certain way. I wanted nothing to do with them. I later had the chance to meet one of these "bad students" because his mother was a friend of my mother. Since we had to be polite to each other because of our mothers, we started talking and I realized that we had a lot in common. My impression of him was very different once I got to know him.

If you form an opinion of someone based on stereotypes, you risk never getting to know someone who is different. You may be missing out on an opportunity to make a good friend. In addition, you are reinforcing that stereotype by believing it without given the person a chance. If you take the time to get to know the person, you might become friends.

Judging people by external appearance is superficial and often unfair. After all, you don't know what circumstances the person might be facing or who the person really is. Perhaps the person comes from a less fortunate family than you and cannot afford the kind of stylish clothes your friends wear. However, that does not mean the person is less intelligent or interesting than you are.

People should not be naive about new people they meet, but should take time to get to know them. External appearance often does not tell us anything about a person. Judging someone by their appearance is misleading, reinforces stereotypes, and is limiting. Doing so could prevent you from making a true friend.

▼

| 63 | AD | Do you agree or disagree with the following statement? A person should never make an important decision alone. Use specific reasons and examples to support your answer. |

A person should never make an important decision alone. Important decisions should be well thought out. People who know you well, know what is best for you. People close to you can give you good advice, give you a different perspective, or share their own experience.

When I had difficulty deciding which classes to take in college, I talked to my teachers and advisors. They had the knowledge and expertise to help me determine which classes were the best ones to take for my future career. Without their advice, I might have chosen unsuitable courses.

In college, I had convinced myself that I was not good enough to act in the school play. Therefore, I decided not to audition even though drama had always been my passion. The day of the auditions, a friend of mine asked me why I wasn't auditioning. When I told her I didn't feel I was good enough, she was shocked. She was able to provide me with another perspective on myself and my talents. I rethought my decision and tried out . . . and got a lead in the play.

Last year when I was trying to decide whether or not I should study overseas, I talked to my friend. This was the best thing I could have done. This was a big decision for me because I had never been overseas on my own and I wasn't sure I could do it. She had studied overseas the previous year. She told me about the challenges and opportunities I might encounter and helped me make the right decision. I went and it was amazing!

Whenever I am faced with an important decision, I seek advice from others so that I am well-informed and have the benefit of their perspective and experience.

▼

| 64 | MA | A company is going to give some money either to support the arts or to protect the environment. Which do you think the company should choose? Use specific reasons and examples to support your answer. |

Deciding between supporting the arts and protecting the environment is a difficult choice to make, but I think I would choose protecting the environment. Arts help to maintain our culture and serve as a source of entertainment. However, we need a healthy environment in order to survive so we must protect it. We need to protect the environment now to help prevent health problems, to maintain the ecosystem, and to preserve the Earth for our children.

Pollution from factories and cars can cause damage to the environment. Moreover, pollution causes health problems particularly for children and the elderly who have weaker immune systems. We need to ensure that there are controls on the amount of pollution when possible so as to prevent health problems caused by breathing dirty air.

We also need to pay attention to the ecosystem. Trees, plant life, and people all depend on each other. An unhealthy environment can have harmful effects on the ecosystem. For example, if a plant dies because of changes to the environment and that plant is food for a animal, that animal won't have any food. If humans use that animal as a food source, there could be big problems.

If we do not respect our environment now, it will continue to get worse and our children will suffer the consequences. They would not have the same quality of air to breathe or natural beauty to admire. That would be sad.

Without clean air to breathe, a healthy ecosystem, and a future for our children, the human race would not survive. That's why protecting our environment is important. If we have a healthy environment, we have healthy children who will be able to participate and appreciate the arts.

▼

| 65 | PR | Some movies are serious, designed to make the audience think. Other movies are designed primarily to amuse and entertain. Which type of movie do you prefer? Use specific reasons and examples to support your answer. |

Movies have the power to make you laugh, cry, or think about an issue that you might not otherwise think about. Although I sometime watch movies that are serious in nature, I prefer movies that amuse and entertain. When I see an amusing movie it makes me relax, laugh, and keeps me in good spirits.

After a long day at school and work, I need a break and something to take my mind off of the troubles of the day. I can do that with an entertaining movie. When I watch an amusing movie, I don't have to think. I just want to sit back and relax. After a movie, I then feel ready to get back to work on my studies.

Amusing movies make people laugh. Laughing is important for the soul. Laughing not only makes people feel good, but also connects people. When people laugh together, they become friends.

After watching an entertaining movie, which relaxes me and makes me laugh, I feel good. When I feel good I can focus more on other important things like my studies and work. Being in good spirits makes me feel better about myself and gives me a positive outlook on life.

While I can appreciate serious movies that make you think, I prefer to be amused and entertained after a long day of work. Such movies allow me to take a break from the rigors of life by making me laugh and putting me in a good mood.

▼

| 66 | AD | Do you agree or disagree with the following statement? Business should do anything they can to make a profit. Use specific reasons and examples to support your position. |

After I get my degree, I plan to start a business. My goal is to make money, a lot of money. However, I can't forget that there are more important things in life than earning a profit. I must consider the people I work with, the customers I serve, and the community I live in.

My colleagues are a very important part of my business. Without them, I would not have a business. I depend on them to help me carry on the day-to-day operations. I depend on them for their advice on what to sell and how to sell it. I must compensate them for their work. I can't take large profits without sharing with the people who made it responsible.

Similarly, I would not have a business without my customers. I can never forget that they could take their business elsewhere. I must give them good value for their money. I can't overcharge them. I must also remember that money is as important to them as it is to me. I want my customers to trust me and keep coming back.

My employees and I all live in the same community as our customers. We are a part of the social life of our community. We can't ignore it. We must play an active part in it. I feel it is important that some of the profits my business earns from the community be returned to the community. We need to support community programs like summer jobs for high school students, campaigns to clean up the parks, and efforts to make the shopping area more attractive.

A business must make profits, but we all—workers, customers, community—must profit from a successful business.

▼

| 67 | PR | Some people are always in a hurry to go places and get things done. Other people prefer to take their time and live life at a slower pace. Which do you prefer? Use specific reasons and examples to support your answer. |

Life is short. Haste makes waste. What's your hurry? These three sayings character-ize the way I manage my day to day chores. I don't want to rush through things; I prefer to take my time.

Life is short. You never know what may happen tomorrow so it is important to enjoy today. Of course, some people will say that's why it is important to cram a lot into a day. But then, how would you possibly have time to enjoy all of those experiences. By doing a few things slowly and doing them well, you can savor the experience.

Haste makes waste. We are not machines. We can't rush through things mechani-cally. If we do, we might forget something; we might take shortcuts. By taking our time, we can do a chore carefully, completely, and correctly.

What's your hurry? Where's the fire? I don't see any need to rush to the next experience. There's still a lot to see and learn from the chores around you. Taking care of your baby brother for instance can be very rewarding. You could simply keep him near you while you watch TV and write a letter and talk on the phone. Or you could devote your whole attention to him and observe his reactions to his environment. You can observe carefully, if you are trying to do four things at the same time.

To twist a common saying, "Don't just do something, sit there!" Take life easy and savor each minute. Life is shorter than you think.

▼

| 68 | PR | Some people think governments should spend as much money as possible exploring outer space (for example, traveling to the Moon and to other planets). Other people disagree and think governments should spend this money for our basic needs on Earth. Which of these two opinions do you agree with? Use specific reasons and details to support your answer. |

When we see photographs of starving children, it's hard to say that we should spend billions of dollars on space exploration. But that's just what we should do. Children don't need to be starving, but we do need to explore space. Right now, we have enough money to feed every person on Earth. Children are starving because of mismanagement of resources and simple human greed. Those are problems we can solve right here on earth. That shouldn't stop our need to find out what's beyond our own solar system.

We may never make contact with whatever other species there may be out there in space. Even so, there are still two very practical and positive consequences of space exploration. One is a certainty and the other is a possibility. The certainty is medical research. Yes, we can conduct research here on earth. But much of the research done in space, for example, on the effects of gravity on bone marrow, is making a difference in medicine here on Earth. When we do research in space, we also learn more about space exploration. Also, many of the inventions that were developed for space travel have been adapted to good use on Earth.

The possible consequence of space exploration is finding another planet human beings can colonize. Overpopulation is a huge problem on our planet. People are living longer, more healthful lives, and that's a good thing. But it means there are fewer people dying and more people being born. Eventually we'll have less space, fewer resources, and major distribution problems. If we can find another planet to live on, we can relieve the problems of overpopulation on our planet.

It's a tragedy that there are human beings suffering on Earth. However, if we wait until everyone has a perfect life, we will never explore space—and that, too, would be a kind of tragedy.

▼

69	EX	People have different ways of escaping the stress and difficulties of modern life. Some read; some exercise; others work in their gardens. What do you think are the best ways of reducing stress? Use specific details and examples to support your answer.

Stress is one of our biggest enemies. It affects our health, our personality, and our relationships with others. In order to get rid of stress, I first have to identify the cause. I have different antidotes to stress depending on the cause. The most common types of stress I face are with work, with friends, and with myself.

Work-related stress is the easiest to combat. I simply stop working for a while. If I find myself picking up the same piece of paper four times a day and never doing anything with it, I blame stress. If I find myself staring at the computer without finishing a report, I blame stress. The best thing to do is to do something else. Sometimes, I get up from my desk and go down the hall to talk to my colleagues, but I don't talk about work related subjects. Other times, I will take a short walk around the block and get some fresh air. Work-related stress can be cured by getting away from the work.

Stress caused by friends is more difficult to cure. Often the cause is more complicated. My friends could have a personal problem that causes them and me both anxiety. Or my friends could be angry at me or vice versa. Here, the cure for stress is talking about the problem and being with my friends. Unlike work, you can't walk away from your friends.

Stress I cause myself is also not so easy to get rid of. If I feel bothered by an exam or anxious about the future, there is very little for me to do. I just have to tell myself that I can only do my best and leave the rest up to fate.

It is important to try to lead a stress-free life. If you can avoid stress by walking away from it (like at work), talking through it (like with your freinds) or facng it head on (like with yourself), your health, personality and relationships will benefit.

▼

70	AD	Do you agree or disagree with the following statement? Teachers should be paid according to how much their students learn. Give specific reasons and examples to support your opinion.

Some communities have decided to base evaluations of teachers on students' test scores. It's these evaluations that determine how much teachers will be paid. I don't think this is a very good idea for several reasons.

First of all, if teachers' salaries are going to be based on how much students learn, then some teachers will start to teach their students only what they need to get high test scores. This means that students will miss out on a lot of education that can't be measured on a test.

For instance, one of the best methods to help students understand a subject is encouraging them to discuss it. A common practice is to divide the class into groups, have each group discuss the subject, and then have them report back to the whole class. This kind of shared learning can lead to a fuller understanding. It also teaches students how to discuss and debate ideas. However, it doesn't supply facts to show off on a test.

Another problem with basing teachers' salaries on how much their students learn is that teachers may ignore students who have learning difficulties. Some students learn more slowly than others and need more personal attention. If a teacher is worried about tests, he may feel he has to push the majority of the students to cram facts. That effort will take all his time. He won't be able to help the less able students.

It's true there are teachers who "burn out" after many years teaching and just don't care how much their students learn. Basing their salaries on their students' test scores may improve their efforts. However, it's not fair for the majority of teachers. They deserve and need to be judged by other criteria.

▼

71	MA	If you were asked to send one thing representing your country to an international exhibition, what would you choose? Why? Use specific reasons and details to explain your choice.

If I were asked to send one thing representing my country to an international exhibition, I'd send something unexpected: one week's worth of television programming. These programs would best represent my country. They show how the citizens of my country live and what they think and feel.

The dramas on television are very realistic. They show how people in different parts of the country go about their daily lives. They show how they earn their livings, how they deal with crime, and how they interact with each other. The dramas also show how people in various economic groups dress, what kinds of houses they live in, and what kinds of education their children receive.

The comedies indicate what people in my country think is funny. Even though the situations are exaggerated, they reflect how my culture deals with very basic human situations. People everywhere understand falling in love, raising a family, and earning a living.

The documentaries show what issues we're concerned about and how we want to resolve them. Some documentaries tell stories from our history. Others look into the future. They speculate on how we'll function as a country in the new millennium. Still others examine our political system, its failures and its successes.

The sports programs show what we think about winning and losing. They demonstrate how we feel about fairness. Some of the wealthiest people in our country are the athletes we watch playing professional sports. This, also, is a reflection of our values.

Television is a common cultural experience in my country. It reflects my country's unique personality. I think it would be the perfect way to show what my country is like.

▼

| 72 | PR | You have been told that dormitory rooms at your university must be shared by two students. Would you rather have the university assign a student to share a room with you, or would you rather choose your own roommate? Use specific reasons and details to explain your answer. |

I'd rather have the university assign a roommate to share a room with me. As far as I'm concerned, this is part of the university experience. Students should meet new people and be open to new experiences. I like leaving this up to chance.

Actually, even though the university will choose, it's not totally a matter of chance. We all filled out information sheets. The school knows what we're majoring in, what our interests are, and our study habits and our goals. I think they're probably very good at matching roommates using this information. They've had a lot of practice. Besides, if a mistake is made, I can change my room assignment next semester.

If I did want to choose my own roommate, I'd first pick some candidates from the list supplied by the university. Then I'd write to them and they'd write back. Through our letters, we'd find out if we shared common interests, such as sports or movies. More importantly, we'd find out if we liked doing the same things in our free time. Because of my investigation, I'd probably get someone compatible with me. It's a lot of work to go through, though. Besides, the process of finding similar interests isn't all that different from what the university does.

Trying to predict whom I'm going to get along with is not a science. I might choose someone who sounds just like me and still find that the two of us just don't get along as roommates. Besides, I think it would be boring to room with somebody who's just the same as me. I'd rather be with someone who has different interests and likes to do different things. Maybe I'd even get a roommate from another culture. After all, one of the reasons I'm going to the university is to be exposed to a lot of new experiences. So, I'd rather have the university choose my roommate for me.

▼

| 73 | PR | Some people think that governments should spend as much money as possible on developing or buying computer technology. Other people disagree and think that this money should be spent on more basic needs. Which one of these opinions do you agree with? Use specific reasons and details to support your answer. |

I realize that it's important to stay up to date with our technology. So much, like our space and defense programs, depends on it. I've also read that we shouldn't let other governments get ahead of ours in the race for better technology. This could eventually put us at a disadvantage and our whole economy could suffer. Despite all this, I think our government should spend our tax dollars on more basic items before it gets into the business of developing computer technology.

We have so many problems in our society, and it seems every solution needs money. For instance, we talk about getting people off welfare. To do that we need money to give them jobs until they can support themselves. That means support training, day care for their children, and probably a monthly rent subsidy. All of those things can cost hundreds of millions of dollars. However, if we could solve a major problem like that, wouldn't it improve our society even more than new technology?

Another problem is that our transportation system is falling apart. Bridges have cracks in them. Highways buckle. Accidents happen because of these problems. We shouldn't put money into improving a computer chip when we have basic needs like these.

Besides, why should the government be in the business of developing technology? Aren't there several very successful corporations doing just that? Yes, it's probably less expensive in the long run for the government to develop the technology. Nevertheless, in the short run, there are basic needs in our society that aren't being met. I think that's where the money should go.

▼

| 74 | PR | Some people like doing work by hand. Others prefer using machines. Which do you prefer? Use specific reasons and examples to support your answer. |

Here's the problem. I'm sloppy. That's why I like to use machines to do my work rather than do things by hand. Machines can be creative, precise, and efficient.

Most people think that you can only be creative if you do things by hand. However, it takes creativity to set the machine up. Once it's set up, it can repeat the same task over and over and over perfectly. If you want to write ten letters, you can set up your word processor to do it, press a button, and ten letters will be printed. It would take me forever by hand, and I would make a lot of mistakes. By hand, each letter would be different. By machine, each one is perfect.

Machines are very precise. They don't get tired and cut the wrong way. They don't get distracted and drop some mustard on the paper. As I said, I'm sloppy, but I like neatness. That's why I prefer to use machines.

Machines are also more efficient. I'm too tired to pick up the phone and see who is calling me. My answering machine isn't tired. It's always on duty. It doesn't get tired, upset, or moody.

I can depend on my machines, but I can't always depend on my hand to be creative, precise, or efficient.

▼

75	AD	Schools should ask students to evaluate their teachers. Do you agree or disagree? Use specific reasons and examples to support your answer.

I think it's a good idea for schools to ask students to evaluate their teachers. This informs teachers of how students react both to their teaching methods and to them as individuals. Teachers can weigh the criticisms and change what they think needs to be changed. Praise from students is also valuable. It can reinforce teachers' opinions about how they're teaching and give them confidence.

It's also helpful for school administrators to hear what students think about their teachers. It keeps administrators in touch with what's going on in the school. It also gives them some idea of which teachers effectively reach the students. However, good administrators know that student evaluations need to be reviewed with a keen eye for prejudice and adolescent attitudes. After all, an evaluation is a good way for students to get back at teachers who expect more of them than they want to give.

Evaluating teachers is also a good exercise for the students. They have to organize their thoughts about what they think of their teachers. In that way, they pinpoint for themselves what they expect of those teachers. They begin to understand what they value in a teacher and what is phony or useless. Evaluating their teachers is also a way for students to think about how they would evaluate themselves. Are they working as hard as they should in class? Is that why their teachers are sometimes critical of their work? Isn't that what a teacher should do—push us to try harder? Thinking about these things can help students do better in class. At the very least, they will understand better what is expected of them.

Student evaluations of teachers also make students feel as if they have a voice in what happens in their schools. It makes them feel as if they're part of the education process when their opinion is valued by the administration. Finally, it teaches them responsibility.

▼

76	EX	In your opinion, what is the most important characteristic (for example, honesty, intelligence, a sense of humor) that a person can have to be successful in life? Use specific reasons and examples from your experience to explain your answer. When you write your answer, you are not limited to the examples listed in the prompt.

Although honesty, intelligence, and a sense of humor are all worthwhile characteristics, I feel the most important one in life to have is sensitivity. A sensitive person is aware of him/herself and the way their actions affect others. A sensitive person knows the place of honesty, intelligence, and a sense of humor.

Honesty is not always the best policy. There is such a thing as a white lie. You don't want to insult someone by saying that their new dress doesn't fit properly or that you wouldn't live in their new house if they paid you. You must be sensitive to when it is necessary to tell the truth and when it is better to tell a white lie.

Intelligence is a wonderful thing to have, but not all intelligent people use their intelligence sensitively. You don't want to show off and make others feel stupid. You must be sensitive to the reactions of the people around you. It might be appropriate for you to admit that you have the right answer, but in some cases, you might have to say, "I think this is the answer, but we might want to check it." A sensitive person would not make someone else look dumb.

A sense of humor is always valued. Different people, however, laugh at different things. You don't want to make someone feel uncomfortable by laughing at his/her mistakes. A sensitive person would understand whether a person could be teased or whether a person would appreciate a certain joke.

A sensitive person would make everyone feel comfortable. A sensitive person understands that people are different and that the values of honesty, intelligence and humor can be applied differently.

▼

| 77 | PR | It is generally agreed that society benefits from the work of its members. Compare the contributions of artists to society with the contributions of scientists to society. Which type of contribution do you think is valued more by your society? Give specific reasons to support your answer. |

Artists and scientists both make valuable contributions to our society. It may seem sometimes that artists are more valued. That's because those artists who are famous make a lot of money. However, they are relatively few. The fact is that scientists are more valued. They get more respect from society for the work they do.

Artists reflect their times and their culture. A painter or a writer shows us in pictures and words what we're like as a people. They record our culture for future generations. Actors and other performers, like singers and dancers, entertain us. They take our minds off our troubles, and remind us how beautiful and exciting our imaginations can be. Artists also help keep their societies mentally and emotionally healthy. For example, children that participate in the arts, such as painting or music, in school do better in their other studies. Art of all types is necessary to the human spirit.

The contributions scientists make to society are more obvious. They include the cars we drive, the computers we use at home and at work, and the appliances that help us cook our meals and clean our houses. All of these come from the ideas and hard work of scientists. Because of scientific discoveries, we're living longer and more healthful lives. Scientists also contribute to the arts. Movies are the result of science. So are television, radio, and the recording of music on CDs.

Generally, scientists don't make as much money as famous artists like film stars, opera singers or successful painters. However, our society gives them more respect, and they generally make a good living. Scientists are considered to be serious professionals, while artists are sometimes viewed as flaky, irresponsible people. So overall, I'd have to conclude that we value scientists more.

▼

78	PR	Students at universities often have a choice of places to live. They may choose to live in university dormitories, or they may choose to live in apartments in the community. Compare the advantages of living in university housing with the advantages of living in an apartment in the community. Where would you prefer to live? Give reasons for your preference.

I think it's better for college students to live on-campus their first two years, and then move into an apartment off-campus their last two years. Freshmen and sophomores need the stability of campus life, while juniors and seniors need the independence of off-campus life. Students' needs change over four years, so their housing should too.

Living on-campus makes it easier to get oriented to the way things are done. You get the whole university experience. Plus, you interact more with other students. This includes not only your roommates, but everyone in your dormitory. The older students in the dormitory can be a big help for the new students. Keeping up with studies your first year is hard enough. You shouldn't have to worry about finding your way around and figuring out the university bureaucracy.

Living in the dormitory also makes a student feel more a part of the university community. There are more opportunities for becoming involved in university activities and networking with student leaders and university administration.

Living off-campus, however, is a definite advantage for older students. Finding an apartment, dealing with leases and the landlord's regulations, cooking meals, and figuring out budgets are all good practice for life after graduation. This kind of independence helps older students grow into adulthood.

Off-campus housing also gives students a better perspective on what's going on around them. Campuses can be like little worlds of their own. There are few children or older people and everyone is focused on education. Getting to know neighbors who aren't students is good for students coming from different places. It's a chance to find out what other people think and feel.

I think a combination of two years on-campus and two years off-campus is a winning combination for most students.

▼

79	PR	You need to travel from your home to a place 40 miles (64 kilometers) away. Compare the different kinds of transportation you could use. Tell which method of travel you would choose. Give specific reasons for your choice.

Choosing the Best Transportation

There are many different types of transportation which I could use to travel 40 miles from my home. The type of transportation I would choose depends mainly on how fast I need to get there and how much money I have. Some possibilities are walking, horseback riding, driving, or using a taxi, bus, or train.

The most economical choice is walking. It costs nothing, is healthful, but it is time consuming. The average person can walk about 4-5 miles per hour, so this trip would take at least 10 hours to complete. That means I would probably have to spend the night somewhere along the way. If I have to spend money for a hotel, then this choice really isn't free. Plus, I might arrive at the end tired and with sore feet! After walking comes animal transportation. In my area, horses are not common, so it wouldn't be a likely choice. I believe that a 40-mile trip would take 2 or 3 hours on a horse. If I had free access to a horse, the cost would be minimal. Of course, I'd have to know how to ride!

With a car, the travel time is minimal (under one hour), with only the cost of gasoline to consider. However, I don't own a car, and car rentals are expensive. Shared taxis are one form of affordable transportation, with 4 or 5 people sharing the cost of a car trip to a common destination. The only downside is finding people to share the fare with me. Fortunately, I live in an urban area, where there are buses and trains to ride. One of these would be my first choice.

In short, the kind of transportation depends on how fast I need to get to my destination and how much money I have. If I need to get there fast, and money isn't important, I can hire a private taxi. Since I don't own my own car, I don't have that option, and I have never walked 40 miles in one trip. I usually depend on the bus and trains, and would do so in this circumstance. They are cheap, dependable and reliable.

▼

| 80 | PR | Some people believe that a college or university education should be available to all students. Others believe that higher education should be available only to good students. Discuss these views. Which view do you agree with? Explain why. |

Both good and bad students should have the opportunity to attend college. Everyone should have a period to learn about themselves before they begin to work and earn money. An education is an investment in yourself and in your future. Good or bad, a student must decide to invest real money and real time.

Higher education is very expensive. It might seem like a waste of money to send someone to college who might not be able to handle the course work. Still, education is a valuable investment in future career earnings. People with college degrees make more money and have more opportunities later. If people have a desire to improve their lives, do we have the right to say no?

Higher education is also a big investment of time. Some people think a weak student should get a job and earn some money. They think poor students shouldn't waste their time at college. But college is a time to meet different people, separate from your parents, and begin to define yourself as a person. I think that's an experience every student should have.

I think every student should be given a chance to see how far she can go. Students who got poor grades in high school might do very well in a different environment. College may be expensive and take time, but it's an investment in one's self and one's future.

▼

81	PR	Some people believe that the best way of learning about life is by listening to the advice of family and friends. Other people believe that the best way of learning about life is through personal experience. Compare the advantages of these two different ways of learning about life. Which do you think is preferable? Use specific examples to support your preference.

Both learning through personal experience and learning through the advice of others can help you in life. If you don't have a lot of knowledge about something, the advice of people you trust can be very valuable. They can tell you about their own experiences, and about the advantages and disadvantages of a situation. Then you can consider your own wants and needs and decide what you should do. Pretty soon, you'll have more experience of your own.

When you're thinking about what you want to do with your life, friends and relatives are a great resource. They can give you information about things like jobs, school, volunteering, and traveling to other parts of the world. They've done a lot of learning in their lives, and you can use it to decide what you want to do with yours.

In some cases, there's no real substitute for personal experience. For example, I really don't like to make presentations in class. I know I'll make mistakes, even if I'm thoroughly prepared and know all about my topic. Nothing but experience can help me deal with the nervousness I feel. I know that the feedback I get from the teacher and from the other students will help me learn from those mistakes. At least I'm confident that the next class presentation I make will be much better than the last one.

In the end, I think that the best way to learn about life is by experiencing it first-hand. No one else can teach you how to get along with other people, how to realistically judge your own abilities, or how to understand who you are. You can only learn these things by dealing with situations every day. Experience is the best teacher.

▼

82	PR	When people move to another country, some of them decide to follow the customs of the new country. Others prefer to keep their own customs. Compare these two choices. Which one do you prefer? Support your answer with specific details.

Some people adapt quickly to the customs of a new country while others keep their own customs. How do they decide? It's a difficult choice, and the decision is not always conscious. Many practical and social factors influence people.

Very often it depends on age. Older people have spent a lifetime doing things a certain way. Their social customs are part of who they are as people. It's very hard for them to start doing things differently. The younger generation finds it easier to leave behind the culture of their native country and adapt to the customs of their new country. They're not as set in their ways as adults are. Children also feel the pressure to fit in from the other kids in school.

A major part of adapting to the customs of a new country is learning that country's language. Children learn the language in school, and use it all day while going to class and playing with other children. But many times adults coming to a new country don't have time for formal language classes. Their first priority is getting a job. Sometimes they work with people from their own country, and they don't have to use the new language. Or they may find a job that doesn't require much speaking at all. This means even if they're trying to learn the language, they don't have a lot of opportunities to practice it.

Another way of adapting to the customs of a new country has to do with how family members interact. Different countries have different ideas about how family members should relate to each other. Sometimes the adults will oppose changing what was normal in their native country. This can be a difficult adjustment to make, especially if their children are visiting new friends at home and seeing how different things are in the new country.

I believe that people who want to make their home in a new country need to find a balance. They should keep the best of their native culture and adopt the good things they find in their new country.

▼

| 83 | PR | Some people prefer to spend most of their time alone. Others like to be with friends most of the time. Do you prefer to spend your time alone or with friends? Use specific reasons to support your answer. |

If I had to choose between spending time alone or spending time with my friends, I'd rather be alone. I need this time alone to "recharge my batteries," to re-energize my mind and spirit. Being with friends can be fun and can help you get through the rough spots in life, but it's the time alone, I think, that forms you as a person.

When I'm alone, I have time to think about my goals and to develop a strategy to reach them. Of course, I can think about these things when I'm with others, but it's harder to concentrate in a crowd. Being alone gives me the quiet time to really think about my life and what I want to do with it.

Being by myself is also a good way to listen to the silence and relax completely. When I'm alone I can practice meditation and lower my stress level. That's a very good way to sharpen my powers of concentration. Too much time with friends means filling my mind with a lot of chitchat. That's enjoyable for a moment, but can dull my concentration.

Being with other people can also distort my view of things. It's easy sometimes to become too worried about what other people think of me, or what other people have that I don't. When I'm alone I have time to step back. I can see the real value of things, without being influenced by the opinions of my friends.

It's natural to want to be with other people, but I find the time I spend alone is more valuable to me in the long run.

<table>
<tr><td>84</td><td>PR</td><td>Some people prefer to spend time with one or two close friends. Others choose to spend time with a large number of friends. Compare the advantages of each choice. Which of these two ways of spending time do you prefer? Use specific reasons to support your answer.</td></tr>
</table>

We all need to have friends, and I think the more friends we have the better. Friendship helps us learn how to trust others, what to expect from others, and how to profit from experiences. I want to have a lot of friends around me so I can learn more about myself from different people.

I want to have people around me that I trust and that I can depend on. We all need friends, both in times of trouble and in times of happiness. If I only have a few friends, it is possible that they might not be available if I need them. If I have a lot of friends, it is more likely that they will be able to share my troubles or my good fortune.

I want to have people around me that surprise me. If I have just one or two friends, I know what to expect from them. I know how they will react. If I have a lot of friends around me, I will always be surprised. Each will have a different way of reacting to a situation. Observing this reaction and responding to it will teach me how to deal with strangers whom I might meet.

I want to have people around me that can teach me something about life. If I only have a couple of friends, I will know everything about them very quickly. If I have hundreds of friends, think what I will learn. Each day they'll teach me something new and show me a new way of thinking about something.

I have a lot to learn in life, so I want as many people as possible to help me. I want a lot of friends to show me how to have a good time. I'll do the same for them.

<table>
<tr><td>85</td><td>PR</td><td>Some people think that children should begin their formal education at a very early age and should spend most of their time on school studies. Others believe that young children should spend most of their time playing. Compare these two views. Which view do you agree with? Why?</td></tr>
</table>

Should children play more or study more? The question is what will be better for the child. There are benefits to both activities, but the answer depends on the details of the situation.

There are many things that could affect the outcome of the argument. What kind of a school is it? It could be a school where children sit at their desks all day long memorizing dates and facts. Or it could be a school where the teacher helps the children learn what they want to learn. I think the second kind is a lot better for a child than the first kind.

Similarly, what kind of play are we talking about? The child could be alone all day long watching television, which could make him or her bored and lonely. Or the child could be involved in group activities with neighborhood children of the same age, which could help him or her learn how to get along with others.

I think both study and play are valuable, so I would prefer to send my child to a school where there is a combination. I think a variety of activities makes learning easier for anyone at any age.

▼

| 86 | PR | The government has announced that it plans to build a new university. Some people think that your community would be a good place to locate the university. Compare the advantages and disadvantages of establishing a new university in your community. Use specific details in your discussion. |

The first advantage of having a new university built in my community would be the jobs it would bring to the community. Initially, the jobs would be those connected with the actual building of the university structures, such as brick layers and carpenters. Once the buildings were completed, the jobs would be those on the campus itself. Those would include teachers, office workers, custodians, and librarians.

Not all of the people the university hired would already be members of the community, so that would mean a lot of new people coming to town. Of course, a lot of students would come too. Two advantages of new people in town would be more taxpayers and a more diverse population. With more people paying taxes, there would be more money for schools, libraries and other community needs. With a more diverse population, there would be new stores, new restaurants (to serve different tastes) and new cultural influences.

Of course, there would also be disadvantages. More people living in the community could mean more houses being built. There would be more traffic on the streets, with the combination of new residents and students who bring their cars. Plus, more people would mean more public services would be needed. These services could include everything from trash collection to more schools to hold all the children of the new residents. New services might mean local taxes would have to go up, even though there would be more taxpayers.

Another disadvantage is that the personality of our community would change. It would go from being a place where everybody knows everybody else to a place where a lot of people are strangers. It would become a place with a lot of short-term residents, like the university students, who might not care as much about the town.

Communities always change over time, though, and overall I like the atmosphere of a "college town." A new university would bring a lot of challenges, but I think it would be worth it.

▼

| 87 | PR | Some people think that the family is the most important influence on young adults. Other people think that friends are the most important influence on young adults. Which view do you agree with? Use examples to support your position. |

Although friends make an impression on your life, they do not have the same influence that your family has. Nothing is as important to me as my family. From them, I learned everything that is important. I learned about trust, ambition, and love.

Your family is with you forever. They are not going to leave you because they find another daughter they like better. They are not going to leave you because they think you are too much trouble. A family is permanent, while friends come and go.

Your parents are your role models. They will encourage you to do your best, to push yourself, and to improve yourself. Friends want you to stay the same; they don't want you to be different. A family is ambitious for you. Friends are not.

Your family teaches you about love. A family's love is not judgmental. They love you for everything you are. Friends may love you because you have a new car or because you go out with them on Saturdays. A family loves you. Friends only like you.

Without my family, I wouldn't know what to do. I wouldn't feel as secure. I might not have the ambition to go to school. I probably would be afraid to love. My family is my greatest influence.

▼

88	PR	Some people prefer to plan activities for their free time very carefully. Others choose not to make any plans at all for their free time. Compare the benefits of planning free-time activities with the benefits of not making plans. Which do you prefer—planning or not planning for your leisure time? Use specific reasons and examples to explain your choice.

I think that free time is a precious thing for most of us. When we're working hard, it's nice to imagine what we'll do when the weekend comes. We juggle one idea with another, trying to decide what best suits our budget and the amount of time we have. After all, anticipating free time is part of the pleasure.

It's good to plan what we're going to do with our free time. That way we won't waste any of it trying to decide. It's so easy to just sit around and think about this or that activity. Before we know it, half the day is gone. If we decide ahead of time, we can get started in plenty of time, and we can get the most benefit out of the time we have. For instance, if we're going on a picnic, we can get all our supplies ready to go. Or if we're going to a movie, we can find out the time and how long it'll take us to get there. Also, if we plan what we're going to do with our free time, we can invite others to join us. If we wait until the last minute, our friends may have other plans.

On the other hand, it's also fun sometimes to do things without a plan. We can just leave the house and walk around and see what catches our attention. Often, this is how we discover places we never knew existed. We might end up doing something we never thought we'd try. We might just happen to find ourselves outside a new bookstore or a bowling alley and go in on a whim, because we have some free time.

It's nice if we can have the best of both worlds. We can plan our free time activities for one day of the weekend, and let the other day plan itself. This way our free time also gives us the enjoyment of having it both ways.

▼

| 89 | PR | People learn in different ways. Some people learn by doing things; other people learn by reading about things; others learn by listening to people talk about things. Which of these methods of learning is best for you? Use specific examples to support your choice. |

The effectiveness of a learning method varies from person to person and also from activity to activity. Learning by doing, learning by reading, and learning by listening all have the transfer of information as their goal, but the information is transferred in very different ways in each case. Each has its benefits. In my own opinion, learning by doing is the method that works best for me.

Learning by doing works because it gives a learner first-hand experience. Other methods are more passive; you're either listening to a conversation or trying to pay attention to words on a page. However, learning by doing means actually participating in the activity. Can you imagine learning how to play a musical instrument from a book? As the saying goes, practice makes perfect. Frankly, I can't think of a way that better ensures one has truly learned than by seeing and doing.

In contrast, reading makes learning less easy to visualize. Not only that, learning by reading often requires extra research, such as looking up unfamiliar words. Also, you might not be a good reader, or you might be learning in a second language. If so, you might find it hard to concentrate or become frustrated by the slow pace. So while reading is fun and useful for many people, for others it may not be the best way.

Learning by listening can be enjoyable. Lively debate is interesting, and interesting things are usually easier to learn about. Plus, unlike reading, you can ask questions if you don't understand. However, as with reading, it is all too easy to become a passive listener and not truly learn anything. If you get bored, you might even fall asleep while you're listening! When you're actively participating in something, you're more likely to stay alert.

Overall, when it comes to learning, I believe that nothing substitutes for the first-hand experience that physically doing an activity provides.

▼

| 90 | PR | Some people choose friends who are different from themselves. Others choose friends who are similar to themselves. Compare the advantages of having friends who are different from you with the advantages of having friends who are similar to you. Which kind of friend do you prefer for yourself? Why? |

There are a lot of advantages to having friends who are different from you. For one thing, they'll give you a different way of looking at the world. Friends who are different can introduce you to foods, music, politics, and books you've never tried before. If you're a spontaneous kind of person, someone who is more scheduled can help you get better organized. You, on the other hand, can help them loosen up a little bit, and do things more on the spur of the moment.

Someone who is different from you won't have the same reaction to situations. This can be a big help. If you're the kind of person who gets very impatient waiting for your meal in a restaurant, it helps to have someone calm with you. Your friend can help you keep your temper. If you're a little timid about standing up for yourself, a more assertive friend can help you develop a little more self-respect.

However, there can also be advantages to having friends who are similar to you. You usually enjoy doing the same things, so you don't have to argue about what you want to do. Sometimes it's fun experiencing new things. Other times, it's more fun doing what you know you'll enjoy.

All things considered, I think I'd like to have a lot of acquaintances who are different and a few close friends who are similar to me. That seems the best of both worlds.

▼

| 91 | PR | Some people enjoy change, and they look forward to new experiences. Others like their lives to stay the same, and they do not change their usual habits. Compare these two approaches to life. Which approach do you prefer? Explain why. |

There are those who prefer things to stay the same, while there are others who prefer change. My personal preference is to establish a routine and stick to it, though this has not always been true of me.

When I was younger, I wasn't a creature of habit. I enjoyed change. When summers came and I was free from the responsibilities of school, I would travel, take off with friends at a moment's notice, and make decisions from day to day. In this way, I had lots of new experiences, met new and interesting people, and learned a lot about life.

These days, I enjoy sticking to a routine. This is partially due to the fact that I am a mother of two small children. I find that their lives are happier if I don't upset their schedules too much. For example, we give the children a bath every night at 8:00, put them in their pajamas, read them stories and put them to sleep by 9:00. There are times when this is inconvenient, but everyone in the household is happier if we stick to our routine. In addition, our friends know when to find us at home and when we are free. This makes visiting easier.

In conclusion, the type of person I am has changed with the circumstances of my life. The obligations of my family force me to have a routine. When I was young, I enjoyed the suspense and adventure of living a crazy life. Now the stability of a household routine suits me better. I think that while most people need a minimum amount of security, those who depend on you often make a difference in your lifestyle.

▼

| 92 | AD | Do you agree or disagree with the following statement? People behave differently when they wear different clothes. Do you agree that different clothes influence the way people behave? Use specific examples to support your answer. |

People do behave differently depending on what they are wearing. The reason is not because they have changed, but because people's reactions to them has changed.

Certain clothes are appropriate for certain situations. A man can wear a suit to work and a woman can wear something professional looking like a skirt and jacket.

When everyone dresses the same, there is no problem. It is like a uniform. Imagine going to a law office to hire a lawyer. One of the lawyers is wearing a suit; the other is wearing jeans. Which lawyer do you want to hire? Similarly, a mechanic works on cars all day and wears clothes that can get dirty. It would be strange to find a mechanic wearing a coat and tie to repair an engine.

People will treat you differently depending on what you are wearing. It will depend on how well they know you and where you are. If your clothes are unusual for the situation, they may treat you with disrespect. I remember once I had an old army coat. I wore it into a fancy candy shop to buy some chocolates. The woman was very suspicious and a little afraid. I couldn't understand her reaction since it was still me underneath my big, old ugly green coat. I was dressed like a bum and this caused the salesperson to react negatively to me. Consequently, I was even more polite than usual.

This experience shows me that sometimes I do behave differently because of what I'm wearing. In this case, I had to balance my appearance. Still, that doesn't mean that I'm rude if I dress up.

▼

| 93 | AD | Decisions can be made quickly, or they can be made after careful thought. Do you agree or disagree with the following statement? The decisions that people make quickly are always wrong. Use reasons and specific examples to support your opinion. |

I disagree with the statement that the decisions people make quickly are always wrong. However, I think those decisions probably turn out to be wrong more often than carefully made decisions do. Usually, fast decisions are based on what we call our "gut reactions," or feelings we have about a situation. Sometimes these gut reactions are based on good sense backed by experience, but sometimes they're based on nonsense or poor reasoning.

Let's say you're at work and the boss calls you to his office and tells you there's a big project that needs to be done. He thinks you're the best person for the job, but he needs an answer from you on the spot. He hasn't told you what the project is, but you make the quick decision to accept. This is the right quick decision, because you're basing it on a lot of factors that will occur to you later. One is that it wouldn't make sense for the boss to ask you to do something he didn't think you could handle. That would only hurt his business. Plus, doing a good job on this project might help your career. You realize it's good to reach higher, if you want to get ahead.

But let's say you're on a deserted highway late at night and your car breaks down. Along comes a car driven by someone who doesn't seem quite right to you. He offers you a ride to the nearest gas station. You make the quick decision to accept the ride because it's late, you're cold and tired and you don't want to sit there waiting for the highway patrol to arrive. This is a case where a quick decision is a wrong decision. You shouldn't trade your personal safety for physical comfort, and if you thought about it, you wouldn't.

How do you know when it's okay to make a quick decision? You have to be able to guess at the possible benefits versus the possible dangers. If it's a small decision like where to go to lunch, who cares? However, if my whole future were at stake, I'd want as much time as I could get to think about it.

▼

| 94 | PR | Some people trust their first impressions about a person's character because they believe these judgments are generally correct. Other people do not judge a person's character quickly because they believe first impressions are often wrong. Compare these two attitudes. Which attitude do you agree with? Support your choice with specific examples. |

Any opinion is, in fact, a judgment. I feel that as Americans we would do well to judge others less often. Still, we must be able to decide whom to spend our time with and whom we'd rather forget. In my opinion, this type of judgment is best after we get to know other people. First impressions are not always accurate impressions.

Judging a person based on a first impression does save time. There are more people than anyone could possibly get to know in one lifetime. It is frustrating to waste time getting to know someone, only to find out that your first impression was correct and that you really don't like him or her. So is it a waste of time getting to know people you probably won't like? That seems to be a valid point of view, but I believe that it is not the best attitude to take.

It's more humane to spend time getting to know people before judging them. I know that I don't always make a good first impression, even when I truly like the person with whom I am interacting. We all have bad days. I wouldn't want to lose a job or a potential friendship simply because I picked out the wrong clothing or said something wrong. I think everyone deserves the chance to make a second impression.

If we all based our final opinion of others on first impressions, it would be hard to get to know anyone. There is always more to people than meets the eye. If we don't give someone a chance, we may be missing out on meeting a life-long friend. That would truly be a shame.

▼

| 95 | AD | Do you agree or disagree with the following statement? People are never satisfied with what they have; they always want something more or something different. Use specific reasons to support your answer. |

I think it's probably true that people are never satisfied with what they have. They always want something more or something different from what is theirs. This just seems to be part of our human nature. Look at a toddler. Give her a toy to play with and she's happy—until she sees something else. Then she wants that other toy to play with. If she and her brother are each given a cookie, she'll look to see whose cookie is bigger. She'll protest loudly if she thinks her brother is getting more.

"The grass is always greener" is an old expression, but it's a good expression of how many of us feel. We're always striving for a better job, a nicer place to live, a fancier car, or more expensive clothes. Part of this reaching for more and better is because we care about what other people think and want to impress them. Part of it is trying to make ourselves feel successful. But there's also something in our nature that tells us we can do better and reach higher.

This isn't always a negative quality. There's another saying: "A man's reach should exceed his grasp, or what's a heaven for?" It's a good thing to be constantly pushing ourselves and looking for something different. If we don't try for more and different things, we begin to stagnate, like a pool that doesn't get any fresh water.

The problem comes when we won't let ourselves be satisfied with anything we have. If we have a comfortable life and still feel as if something's missing, then we need to look inward. The something that's missing may be in our spirit.

▼

96	AD	Do you agree or disagree with the following statement? People should read only those books that are about real events, real people, and established facts. Use specific reasons and details to support your opinion.

The Importance of Fiction

How could anyone suggest that people should only read about real events, real people, and established facts? For one thing, that means people wouldn't be reading half of all the great books that have ever been written, not to mention the plays, short stories and poetry. For another, it would mean that people's imaginations would not develop as children and would remain dulled throughout their lives.

Reading stories as a child helps develop our creativity by teaching us a lot about how to use words to create mental images. It opens our world up, exposing us to other times and different ways of living. Reading histories of those times would serve kind of the same purpose, but it probably wouldn't stick in our minds as sharply. Reading an essay about poverty in Victorian England is not the same thing as reading Charles Dicken's Oliver Twist. The images of a small boy being sold are more horrifying than simply reading the statement, "Children were sold into labor" because a novel makes that small boy seem real to us. Reading fiction makes a more lasting impression on our minds and emotions.

Besides, storytelling is an emotional need for human beings. From earliest times, humans have taught their children about life, not by telling them facts and figures, but by telling them stories. Some of these stories show what people are like (human nature), and help us experience a wide range of feelings. Some make us think about how we should act. Telling a child that it's wrong to lie will make little impression, but telling him the story of a little boy whose nose grows longer every time he tells a lie will make a big impression.

Fiction is too important to our culture, our minds, and our emotions. How could we ever give it up?

▼

97	AD	Do you agree or disagree with the following statement? It is more important for students to study history and literature than it is for them to study science and mathematics. Use specific reasons and examples to support your opinion.

I think it's more important for students to study history and literature. These subjects help us understand the human race and feed our spirits and our imaginations. That's more important than understanding how to split the atom or do algebra.

People talk about a crisis of spirit in our country. They mean we've forgotten how to believe in and understand our own better natures. I think part of this is because we've become too excited about facts and not enough about things we can't see and measure. Reading books from our own culture helps us understand our roots. Reading books from other cultures helps us understand the way other people think and react to situations. It also teaches us that we're not so very different from others, and that leads to better relations between cultures.

Reading literature also feeds our spirits. Even when the material we're reading is about terrible sadness and hardship, it still brings us in touch with our inner selves. It makes us think about issues other than the new car we want to drive or how much money we're making.

Studying history gives us more information than just who died when or who won which war. It tells us about how human beings have related to each other at different periods in our development. It gives us the big picture. So often, when international crises occur, we only see the problem of the moment. We have no idea how something that happened twenty years ago was the beginning of this current problem. Without that information, we can have only a shallow understanding of what's going on in the world.

Both history and literature are necessary subjects for students to prepare for more than just careers. These subjects prepare students for the way they want to live their lives.

▼

98	AD	Do you agree or disagree with the following statement? All students should be required to study art and music in secondary school. Use specific reasons to support your answer.

I agree that all students should be required to study art and music in high school. I've read that young children who study art and music in grade school do better in their other studies. That argument aside, we should study art and music for its sake alone. We should study art and music to learn more about ourselves, our culture, and our world.

Both art and music feed students' imaginations and help them express themselves. There's a reason our ancestors in caves drew on the walls and made music with drums. Wanting to express ourselves is natural. It gives us an avenue for our emotions and fears. It may not always be music other people want to hear or art others will appreciate, but the activity itself is enjoyable. It shouldn't matter if the end result isn't perfect. In the process, we learn what we like and dislike.

Studying art and music means more than drawing or playing an instrument. Students usually go to art galleries and concerts, too. By studying the pictures on the museums' walls or by reading the program notes at a recital, students will learn what society has decided is worthy of praise. They learn what is important in their own culture.

Students may also learn about other cultures by looking at art and listening to music from other countries. When they do that, they'll see similarities and differences with their own. They'll learn about what is important in other societies. Students will also learn how the art and music of other cultures affect our own.

By studying art and music in high school, students begin to understand themselves as well as their own culture and other cultures. What could have more value than that?

▼

| 99 | AD | Do you agree or disagree with the following statement? There is nothing that young people can teach older people. Use specific reasons and examples to support your position. |

Many of us believe that young people have nothing valuable to teach older people. However, that is not always the case. Young people can teach older people about technology, youth culture, and youth-related social issues.

Young people are usually better at using new forms of technology than older people. Children these days become familiar with computers at an early age. Older people can learn to use computers from young people. This is true of other technology too. For example, I taught my grandparents how to use a video cassette recorder when I was thirteen years old. They didn't know what it could do until I showed them. Now they use it regularly.

Older people are usually not familiar with youth culture, and younger people can help here too. This is important because it can help older people live a more enjoyable life. For example, popular music is generally youth-oriented, and older people don't always listen to it. However, when young people teach them about it, they may come to enjoy it. My grandmother, for example, never listened to popular music before I introduced her to it. Now she and I listen and dance all the time. I plan to teach her about another piece of youth culture—rollerblading—very soon!

Of course, there are more serious issues about which younger people can teach older people. As with computers, today's children have grown up knowing about AIDS and school violence. That is not true for older generations. Here, again, children can teach older people about things that are important to everyone.

I know there are people who would say "you can't teach an old dog new tricks." However, it's plain to me that the young have plenty to teach the old if they take the time to try. When they do, I think both gain a new appreciation for each other.

▼

| 100 | AD | Do you agree or disagree with the following statement? Reading fiction (such as novels and short stories) is more enjoyable than watching movies. Use specific reasons and examples to explain your position. |

Reading fiction, such as novels and short stories, is more enjoyable than watching a movie. Of course, the images in a movie are much more vivid, because you're seeing them on a large screen in a dark room. The images you "see" in a novel are only as strong as your own imagination. But the more you read, the stronger your imagination becomes. Reading exercises your imaginative powers. Watching a movie dulls them. Imagination, like a muscle, needs to be used. Otherwise it can disappear.

When you read, you're an active participant in your own enjoyment. That's one reason reading develops the imagination. You're reading the words on the page and translating them into images in your mind. When you're watching a movie, you're a passive viewer. The movie is giving you everything. Nothing comes from you except your reaction to what you're seeing, and even that can be given you by the movie. Some movie plots are so simple, you can predict what's going to happen before it does.

Reading fiction also develops your storytelling skills. The more reading you do, the better you become at creating plots and characters. The plots and characters in movies are often very simple, because the emphasis is on action rather than on language or character development.

Still, going to the movies is a great community experience. Sitting in a large theater with a lot of other people is fun. You experience the same reactions to what you're seeing together. Reading is a one-person experience. It's a chance to go into an imaginary world by yourself. Both experiences can be fun and rewarding, but I think reading fiction is more enjoyable.

▼

| 101 | PR | Some people say that physical exercise should be a required part of every school day. Other people believe that students should spend the whole school day on academic studies. Which opinion do you agree with? Give specific reasons and details to support your answer. |

While physical exercise is important, I do not believe that it is the school's responsibility to provide physical training for its students. That is something that everyone can take care of on his or her own.

Many students get plenty of physical exercise as part of their daily life or recreation. A student who bicycles ten miles to and from school does not need more exercise. A good physical education program must take a student's outside activity into consideration. Otherwise, some students will spend valuable class hours repeating physical exercise.

If a school offers such activities, it also suggests that students will be graded on them. The range of possible physical activities is great: football, swimming, weight lifting, ballet, ballroom dance, yoga, skiing, horseback riding, and golf are just a few. However, the number that a school could offer is small. Some students could get bad grades in physical education simply because the school could not provide an activity they enjoy or do well. This seems unfair. Research suggests that participation, not excellence, in these activities determines the physical benefits the body will get.

Another issue is economic. Many schools do not have the money to provide gym facilities, playing fields, and athletic equipment for their students. Other schools are located in cities where that kind of space just isn't available. A few schools would rather keep money for academic purposes.

Schools can certainly encourage physical activity. They can provide space for notices about activities, events, and classes for physical activities. They can encourage students to plan time away from academic studies to get some exercise. However, I think that providing exercise should not be the school's responsibility.

▼

| 102 | PR | A university plans to develop a new research center in your country. Some people want a center for business research. Other people want a center for research in agriculture (farming). Which of these two kinds of research centers do you recommend for your country? Use specific reasons in your recommendation. |

The importance of agricultural and business research centers cannot be underestimated. Success in farming and success in business each can improve a country's standing. I think that agricultural research tends to improve the quality of individual citizens' lives, whereas successful business practices improve a country's economy in relation to other nations. Choosing between an agricultural and a business research center is a difficult decision. However, I believe that the agricultural research center would be most beneficial because its benefits are more widespread.

Business practices in the United States already serve as a model for many other countries. While we certainly have much to learn, the U.S. already has a fairly solid economic basis. Further, businesses are already well-connected internationally. They have the advantage of the Internet and other means of electronic information transmission. I think that a business research center would really only help a few directly. Businessmen would get richer. For the rest of the country's people, there might be little obvious benefit.

On the other hand, an agricultural research center would help all people. No country can survive without adequate means of food production. While the U.S. is able to produce or import enough food now, that may not remain the case if current trends continue. Natural resources are eroding, and more and more American farms are closing. Farmers need to build stronger networks across the country and internationally, much as businessmen already have done. Ultimately, better systems for farming will help all people. For example, food prices can be reduced as farmers discover more effective means of food production.

Morally, I believe that it is best to do what will benefit the most people. I believe that the university's decision to build an agricultural research center could do just that.

▼

| 103 | PR | Some young children spend a great amount of their time practicing sports. Discuss the advantages and disadvantages of this. Use specific reasons and examples to support your answer. |

Most kids love to play sports. It's important to them, but for the majority, it's just one type of activity out of many that they do. For a small number of kids, though, a sport becomes their whole life. They spend almost all their time and energy practicing. This has both advantages and disadvantages.

Sports are good for young children in many ways. Kids who enjoy sports are likely to have better health. They develop good habits of daily exercise that will keep them healthy as adults, too. Today, many children and adults are overweight, but those who love sports stay in shape. Plus, by developing their physical abilities, they will learn how to work hard towards a goal. Their achievements in sports will make them feel good about themselves. They'll also make friends and learn teamwork. Sports, whether a little or a lot, can have positive effects.

We admire the talent and dedication of young athletes, but we also wonder if they're losing something. Their focus is very narrow. If they devote most of their time to sports, are they neglecting schoolwork? What about other interests? Children should try out many different activities. In addition, many young athletes are pressured by parents or coaches to succeed. Kids whose drive comes from inside usually do okay, but others can be unhappy and have health and emotional problems. So sports, like anything else in excess, can have negative effects too.

When I was young, I liked books and hated sports. I saw other people who loved sports and hated school. Now that I'm older, I've found a better balance. People have to figure out what's right for them. Is there such a thing as too much sports? There is no right answer, because there is no "right amount." Everyone is different.

▼

| 104 | AD | Do you agree or disagree with the following statement? Only people who earn a lot of money are successful. Use specific reasons and examples to support your answer. |

Many people believe that a large income equals success. I believe, however, that success is more than how much money you make. Some of those measures of success include fame, respect, and knowledge.

Most people assume that famous people are rich people, but that isn't always true. For example, some day I would like to be a famous researcher. Few scientists are rich by today's standards. Still, I will feel myself to be successful if I am well-known. Additionally, there are many famous humanitarians who are not rich. Mother Theresa was one. Certainly, no one would say she was not successful.

I also believe that being respected by coworkers indicates success. Without that respect, money means little. For example, I once did some work for a top attorney in a law firm. He made a very good salary, but he wasn't a nice man. No one ever did work for him willingly. He ordered everyone around, and we didn't respect him. In contrast, however, I had a wonderful band director in high school. He had to take extra jobs just to make enough money to support his family. However, his students had great respect for him and always listened to what he said. As a result, we were a very good band. In my opinion, my band director was more successful than the attorney was.

Finally, I think one of the most important indicators of success is knowledge. Wealthy people don't know all the answers. For example, in the movie Good Will Hunting, *the only person who could solve some complex problems was the janitor. He knew a lot, and decided what he wanted to do with that knowledge rather than just think about money. In my opinion, he was extremely successful.*

When we think of history, there are few people that we remember simply because they were rich. Overall, we remember people who did something with their lives—they were influential in politics, or contributed to science or art or religion. If history is the ultimate judge of success, then money surely isn't everything.

▼

| 105 | MA | If you could invent something new, what product would you develop? Use specific details to explain why this invention is needed. |

If I could invent something new, I'd invent a device or pill that could put people to sleep immediately and would have no side effects. The proper amount of sleep is important for our concentration, mental health, and physical health.

Getting enough sleep is a vital human need. For one thing, without sleep our concentration is strongly affected. We're easily distracted, we can't remember things, and we don't notice what's happening around us. For example, a lot of car accidents are caused by tired drivers. When we get enough sleep, our powers of concentration are sharper. We're more focused on what we're doing. We perform better.

Mental health is also affected by lack of sleep. It's easy to tell if people don't get enough sleep. They're on edge, cranky, and out of sorts. They lose their tempers easily and over-react to situations. In fact, experiments have shown that lack of sleep over a long period of time can cause a complete mental breakdown. When we get our proper rest, we're more alert and responsive. Our outlook is positive, and we're much easier to get along with.

Our physical health shows the strain of sleeplessness, too. We have less energy, and everything seems like a major effort. Over a long period of time, we become slow and unresponsive. The wear and tear on the body from lack of sleep can be a very serious health problem. Every doctor will tell you that getting enough sleep is a basic factor in maintaining good health.

Wouldn't it be great to go to bed every night knowing you'd have no problem getting to sleep, no matter what's going on in your life? Getting enough sleep is always going to be an important part of how you respond to your situation. I think this device would be very helpful to all of us.

▼

| 106 | AD | Do you agree or disagree with the following statement? A person's childhood years (the time from birth to twelve years of age) are the most important years of a person's life. Use specific reasons and examples to support your answer. |

I agree that a person's childhood years, from birth until twelve years of age, are the most important. All the information I've read about that time of life states that these are the years that form us. These years determine what kind of a person the child will become. During these years we learn about relationships, begin our formal education, and develop our moral sense of right and wrong.

The early years are the time when we learn about relationships. First we learn about our parents and siblings, then about rest of the world. We learn how to respond to others based the treatment we're given. If we're loved, then we know how to love others. If we're treated harshly, we may grow up to treat others harshly. We also form our ideas about our own self-worth from the way others treat us during these years. They can convince us we're worthless, or they can teach us we deserve love and respect.

These are the years when we begin our formal education. We acquire the basic skills—reading, writing, working with numbers—that we'll use throughout our lives. We need a good foundation in these subjects. Otherwise, anything we try to do later will be undermined by our lack of skills. Perhaps the most important thing we can learn during these years is how to analyze information and use it. These are skills that will always be useful.

Most important, from my point of view, these are the years when we develop our moral sense of what's right and wrong. Others teach us about good and bad, but later in our early years we begin to decide for ourselves. It's also during this time that we begin to develop the self-discipline to live according to our morals.

I believe a person grows and changes for the better throughout the many stages of life. However, the foundation is laid in those first few years of life.

▼

| 107 | AD | Do you agree or disagree with the following statement? Children should be required to help with household tasks as soon as they are able to do so. Use specific reasons and examples to support your answer. |

In the past in America, children were valuable workers. For example, they helped on the farm or in the family business in order to bring in money. Just a couple of generations later, attitudes have changed. Now children are hardly expected to work at all. Modern children often don't even do household chores. This is sad, because I think that they are missing something if they don't help out at home. Sharing in household tasks benefits children of all ages.

First of all, household tasks build skills. Very young children learn motor skills and classification skills when they pick up their toys and put them away. Talking about how to do things helps them learn to analyze situations. Older children learn skills they'll need as an adult. Cleaning and cooking may seem dull, but knowing how to do them well makes life a lot easier. How many young adults leave for college unable to do their own laundry or cook anything besides a frozen microwave dinner? It's amazingly common.

When everyone in a family helps out, the family is happier. Nowadays it's common for both parents to work. When they come home, they have more work to do. Life is stressful and there's no time for fun. By sharing household tasks, everyone gains. Children can help their parents with simple tasks such as picking up their own rooms, putting away their own laundry, starting dinner occasionally, or taking care of younger siblings. Then the family can relax together, and parents won't feel like servants to their "couch potato" offspring.

The most important thing children learn from helping with household tasks is responsibility. Handling everyday tasks teaches organization and time management skills. Children learn that chores have to be completed before they can play, or before they get their allowances. Children who understand that effort pays off will be more successful later in life.

Kids should not work all the time. A happy life needs balance. But if they can successfully handle tasks at home, they will handle life better too. They will know the satisfaction of doing a good job, be involved in family life, and become more confident and responsible adults.

▼

| 108 | PR | Some high schools require all students to wear school uniforms. Other high schools permit students to decide what to wear to school. Which of these two school policies do you think is better? Use specific reasons and examples to support your opinion. |

Many high schools, both public and private, require students to wear uniforms. I think that such a policy is an excellent idea because uniforms can make things more equal for all students.

First, uniforms make students equal on an economic level. With uniforms, students from poor families dress the same as students from rich families. This can prevent envy and jealousy about stylish clothes. It can also encourage students to form friendships based on personality, not clothes.

Second, uniforms can reduce unequal treatment by teachers. Research suggests that teachers often have higher expectations for more attractive students, which include those students with nicer clothes. This special attention can include providing more challenges and opportunities for these students. Uniforms help teachers make judgements based on ability, not appearance.

Finally, uniforms encourage the individual students of a school to feel like part of a bigger group. Their feelings of being together, working together and having something in common are all helped by uniforms.

It is my opinion that all schools should have a policy requiring uniforms. Uniforms give every student an equal chance.

▼

| 109 | AD | Do you agree or disagree with the following statement? Playing a game is fun only when you win. Use specific reasons and examples to support your answer. |

I agree with the old saying, "It's not whether you win or lose, it's how you play the game." I don't need to win. I have fun playing all games because it gives me time to be with friends, learn new things, and work as a team.

Tennis is one game that I enjoy. It's a great opportunity to socialize. Of course, you can't carry on a conversation while you're playing, but my tennis partner and I talk a lot before the game. Since we have to reserve a court, we have to talk to one another to find a convenient time to meet. Then we have to make sure that the court is available at that time. This often takes many phone calls and, of course, we talk about many other things during the same conversation. Once we get to the court, we often have to wait. That gives us another opportunity to chat. After the game, we usually go out for a soda or a meal and talk some more. We don't even talk about how well or how poorly we played. Tennis is just an excuse for us to get together.

The board game Scrabble, on the other hand, is a real skill builder. It's a challenge to form words from the letters in front of you and on the board. I always learn a new word from my opponent, although sometimes I'm suspicious whether the word really exists. Often we don't even keep score. We just do it because it's fun and we learn new English words.

Soccer is the most competitive sport I'm involved in. I do my best, but it doesn't matter to me if my team loses. I enjoy just being with my friends and travelling to different schools in different cities to play. I learn a lot about teamwork when we practice. Our coach tells us the most important thing is to play well as a team. It seems she just wants us to have fun and not worry about winning.

All in all, I just enjoy having a good time. Presumably that's our purpose in life. Isn't that better than worrying about who wins and who loses all the time?

▼

110	AD	Do you agree or disagree with the following statement? High schools should allow students to study the courses that students want to study. Use specific reasons and examples to support your opinion.

I think high school students should be allowed to choose some of the subjects they study. However, the basic subjects, like mathematics, literature, and science, should be mandatory for all students.

When I was in high school, we were allowed to choose three electives each semester. Electives were subjects that weren't part of the basic curriculum. They included things like music, journalism, art, and various kinds of team sports. Choosing some of these subjects to study gave me a chance to experiment. I was able to get a head start on what I was going to study in college.

However, college preparation shouldn't be the main factor. I think all students should be allowed to take a certain number of courses just because they're interested in them. For many students, high school is the last chance to learn about things they're interested in. Maybe once they have a job there won't be time for studying.

Of course, it's also important that students study certain basic subjects. If I'd had a choice, I know I wouldn't have studied mathematics or science. I wasn't very interested in them. However, once I was in class, I found myself getting interested. I wouldn't have known this if I'd been given the choice, because I would have chosen not to take the courses.

High school students aren't always the best judges of what they'll find useful in the years ahead. They need the guidance of experts in the field of education. However, they also need some freedom to follow their curiosity and individual interests. They should be given the freedom to choose some courses, while being required to take others.

▼

111	AD	Do you agree or disagree with the following statement? It is better to be a member of a group than to be the leader of a group. Use specific reasons and examples to support your answer.

According to my opinion, it's always better to be a leader than a follower. True leaders show initiative. They take action and they assume responsibility. A leader makes a decision. Some followers may approve of the decision; others may complain about it. However, these followers all chose to follow, not to lead. They chose not to make a decision. That's how I'm different. I'm not a follower. I want to make the decisions.

Good leaders will not react to events, but will anticipate them. A leader will start a plan of action and then will persuade others to follow. For example, a class president at a local college may feel that the relationship between the community and the campus is not a good one. The citizens may feel that the college kids make too much noise on the street, litter public areas, and shop in other communities. A good class president will recognize that the community and the campus depend on one another. The president will ask the student body to keep noise down, help clean up the neighborhoods, and work with businesses to attract students. A good leader takes the initiative.

Good leaders must be action-oriented. Having taken the initiative, they must see the job through. They have to take charge and lead the followers. They have to motivate and encourage the followers. The followers (in this example, the student body) must understand why good relations with the community are necessary. The followers must be persuaded to do something about it.

Good leaders must be ready to accept responsibility. They accept responsibility for their actions as well as those of the followers. In the end, any credit will be shared with the group; any blame will be the leader's fault. The leader who fails is always alone.

I enjoy taking the initiative, determining the direction, and being responsible for my actions. I don't want to suffer through other people's stupid decisions. If there are going to be stupid ways to do something, let them be mine. Wouldn't you agree?

▼

112	**EX**	What do you consider to be the most important room in a house? Why is this room more important to you than any other room? Use specific reasons and examples to support your opinion.

The kitchen is my favorite room in a house, because it is where families gather. To me, that is the most important thing. So many of the memories people have of growing up revolve around the kitchen. My childhood memories concern the kitchens in my grandparents' homes.

My mother's family lived in a row house in the city. The rooms were all small, and that included the kitchen. In the summertime, when we'd visit, the back door of the house would be left open. People would be sitting on the back porch and in the kitchen, talking and laughing, while my grandmother made dinner. There was no air-conditioning, but I don't ever remember feeling too hot. There was always a breeze coming through, along with the sounds of traffic and kids playing ball in the street.

My father's family lived on a farm in the country, and their house had a huge kitchen with windows on three sides. It seems like the windows were always open and the curtains blowing with the breeze. The main door to the house was almost never used. Everyone came in through the kitchen, and sat at the big table in the middle of the room. When dinner was being prepared, all the women would bustle around, while the men sat at the table talking about farm prices. Sometimes my grandmother wouldn't even sit down during dinner, but would be refilling bowls of food and people's glasses. From outside, we could hear the cows in the field near the house.

These two kitchens are the background for some of my happiest memories. From the beginning of time, human beings have gathered together near the fire where the food was being prepared. I hope that never changes.

▼

| 113 | MA | If you could make one important change in a school that you attended, what change would you make? Use reasons and specific examples to support your answer. |

Most of the schools that I attended had excellent programs and instructors. Unfortunately, at one school this was not the case. The foreign language program there needed both better planning and better instructors. If I could, I would make changes in three major areas.

The first step would be to offer third and fourth year language classes. This particular school had no language programs above the second year level. Students who started language classes in the first year ran out of classes to take by the time they were halfway through the school. This was frustrating for those of us who loved learning languages. It also had bad effects when we tried to resume language studies in college after a two-year break.

Next, the foreign language program should be staffed with well-trained instructors. The current teachers in the program don't speak the languages well enough. In our classes teachers frequently made errors which the students repeated. If the teachers were well-trained, they would be good models for the students.

Finally, the materials in the language courses should be updated. They need to use modern technology. Even though the school has a computer laboratory, our language class never used it. We were limited to using the assigned textbook. If software was available, the students could search the Internet for current, real-life materials, such as newspapers from other countries.

Understanding people from other countries depends on being able to communicate with them. Poor language instruction makes this impossible. Improving the foreign language program would really make a difference to the students of the school.

▼

| 114 | MA | A gift (such as a camera, a soccer ball, or an animal) can contribute to a child's development. What gift would you give to help a child develop? Why? Use reasons and specific examples to support your choice. |

When I was about 10 years old, my older sister gave me a present. It was my first real grown-up bicycle: a three-speed, yellow and black, shiny and new. I still remember how excited I was. That bicycle was very important to me over the next few years. If I wanted to give a gift that would contribute to a child's development, I would choose a bicycle.

Bikes are great exercise. They encourage outdoor play. Television and video games, which are the most popular children's activities nowadays, involve mostly sitting and staring. Riding a bike makes exercise fun.

Bikes are convenient transportation, too. Without a bike you have to depend on an adult to drive you almost everywhere. With a bike you can go farther. You can ride to your friends' houses. If your school is close enough, you can take yourself to school. You have control over where you go, and you're not always waiting or begging for a ride. Now you can say "Can I go...?" instead of "Please take me!"

To me as a child, a bicycle meant independence. Not only could I go farther, but no one was watching where I went. The road went past the park, the pond, the woods, the 7-11 store, and more. I saw the network of little neighborhood roads from a different viewpoint. Everything was much more interesting up close than it was through a car window. I could stop anywhere and look at whatever I wanted. Everything was my choice. Bike riding was active, not passive.

My bicycle gave me fun exercise, easy transportation, and freedom. For all these reasons, I think that a bicycle is a special present for a child.

▼

115	PR	Some people believe that students should be given one long vacation each year. Others believe that students should have several short vacations throughout the year. Which viewpoint do you agree with? Use specific reasons and examples to support your choice.

I like the idea of students having several short vacations throughout the year. I'm a working parent with two school-age children. Every summer I have to come up with a plan for keeping my children safe and entertained for three months, while my husband and I are at work. Summer camps are expensive, and finding the one your children will enjoy can be a challenge. Getting rid of that one long vacation would make life a lot easier.

Having several shorter vacations would also make it easier to schedule vacations. My husband and I both work in small offices with other working parents. All of us need vacation time during the same three months. This is hard on our businesses and our careers.

We also find that wherever we go in the summer, it's crowded. It would be nice to go places throughout the year and find smaller crowds. I'm sure the attractions themselves would like that better, too. It would be better for the economy to spread things out, too.

I think my children would be more focused on their studies if their vacation time was divided up throughout the year. The final month of the school year, they're just not paying attention. They've been in school for nine long months and they don't have a lot of energy. Plus, they're anticipating vacation time. If vacations were throughout the year, they would concentrate better on studies.

Of course, many older school buildings aren't air-conditioned, because usually people aren't there during the hottest months. That might be a problem. I think, though, that new air-conditioning would be worth the cost. During the last few weeks of summer, my children are bored with their long vacation. I doubt that would happen if there were several vacations throughout the year.

| 116 | PR | Would you prefer to live in a traditional house or in a modern apartment building? Use specific reasons and details to support your choice. |

I know there are advantages to living in a modern apartment, but I'd prefer to live in a traditional house. My main reason is that I love traditional design. It's graceful and warm and inviting. I think modern design is very empty and sterile and not very inviting. So, because of the way it looks, I'd choose a traditional house.

I recognize the fact that a modern apartment is going to be in much better shape. Being new probably means all the plumbing works, the roof isn't going to leak, the windows are properly sealed, and the kitchen appliances are in working order. A traditional house can't guarantee any of that. In fact, it's likely that things will break down or need replacement, simply because of age.

Still, if the appliances are old, so is the wood, and that's a big advantage as far as I'm concerned. Very few new buildings have the kind of beautiful woods that were used years ago. It's something that can't be copied.

Space is always important to me, too. I need a lot of room for my home office, my clothes, and to display all the knickknacks I've picked up in my travels. I also like to have interesting space. I don't want all the rooms and windows the same size or a boxy design. A modern apartment usually comes in one size and shape. A traditional house is going to have a variety of spaces where I can put a little table or a window seat. And it will have lots of room, from basement to attic. These are all good reasons for me to prefer living in a traditional house.

Some people love modern design, but it's not for me. The space and beauty of a traditional home are more important to me than having everything new and perfect.

| 117 | PR | Some people say that advertising encourages us to buy things that we really do not need. Others say that advertisements tell us about new products that may improve our lives. Which viewpoint do you agree with? Use specific reasons and examples to support your answer. |

The whole point of advertising is to encourage us to buy things we don't need. Advertisers are in the business of making money for themselves and their clients. If they manage to sell us something that's good for us too, that's fine. But their primary goal is profit.

It begins when we're children. Saturday morning children's television is full of commercials. Over and over again, children see images of toys and games. They see other children who are having the time of their lives. They watch these children and get the message that if they want to have that much fun, they need to buy those things. Thus, at a very early age, we're introduced to two ideas: that we want to be like everyone else, and we want to have what everyone else has.

This continues throughout our lives. We spend a lot of our money trying to keep up with our neighbors. We buy the latest model cars, have all the latest gadgets in our homes, and live a lifestyle beyond our budgets. Advertising encourages us to define ourselves by what we own rather than by who we are. It encourages a competition of false values and shallow measurements of what matters in our lives.

Advertising can be damaging. However, it is also one of the ways in which our economy keeps growing. People need to buy products in order for other people to have jobs manufacturing, transporting and selling those products. Advertising also keeps us informed about new products that may actually help us in some way. For these reasons, you could say advertising is a necessary evil.

▼

| 118 | PR | Some people prefer to spend their free time outdoors. Other people prefer to spend their leisure time indoors. Would you prefer to be outside or would you prefer to be inside for your leisure activities? Use specific reasons and examples to support your choice. |

Enjoying Time with Mother Nature

If I had to choose where to spend my leisure time, I'd rather spend it outdoors. I spend all my working hours inside at a desk. When I have some free time, I want to completely change my environment. Getting outdoors gives me a new perspective and helps clear my mind.

Being outdoors gives me the opportunity to try new things, see new sights, and meet new people. Staying indoors means reading a book or watching television. Sometimes it involves visiting with friends. Those are all relatively inactive. Being outdoors means a chance to stretch my mental and physical muscles. I can go hiking in an area I've never been before. I can go swimming or rafting on the river. I can go on a nature walk with a ranger and learn about flowers and trees. I can visit all the outdoor monuments in my city that I've never seen before. In each case, I'm doing something that helps me relax while also enjoying the excitement of something new.

Of course, weather is a factor. I have a hard time functioning in extremely hot or cold weather and like to stay indoors when it's below freezing or the heat is scorching. At times like that, it's fun to sit inside with a good book or a good friend looking out at the weather and enjoying the comforts of home. But if the weather cooperates, it's fun to read that book outside on a park bench or go swimming with that friend.

Enjoying leisure time outdoors can also mean making new friends. Getting outside my own environment gives me the opportunity to meet new people. All in all, leisure time is better when it's spent with Mother Nature rather than a television set.

▼

| 119 | MA | Your school has received a gift of money. What do you think is the best way for your school to spend this money? Use specific reasons and details to support your choice. |

A gift of money is generous and welcomed at our school. There are many things that my school could use. To decide, one must consider the amount of the gift and understand that it is a one-time thing. Keeping this in mind, I think that my school could most benefit from new classroom fixtures.

If you looked at our school, you would agree that nearly all of the classrooms could use new desks, chairs, chalkboards, bookshelves and cabinets. Our school is old and the people who live here aren't very wealthy. New equipment would provide students with the tools that they need to learn. It is hard to write papers if there aren't enough desks and chairs. It is hard to learn when the blackboards are so old that they can't be erased properly. It is also difficult to organize school supplies without proper bookshelves and cabinets.

Another plus that new equipment would provide is that it would make the school more attractive to the community. It is hard for a community to be proud of a school that is falling apart. If the community felt that our school was important, perhaps others would give more money in the future. That would allow us to further improve our school. In addition, maybe community members would feel encouraged to come and help out in the school. That would make it even better.

Students would be happier with new equipment. It would make them want to come to school and learn. There would be fewer dropouts. By continuing in their education, these students will be able to better contribute to our community in the future—perhaps even becoming future schoolteachers.

While there are many things that can be purchased with a gift of money at our school, I believe that new equipment is the best choice. New equipment would improve the learning environment, the community's attitude, and the students' feelings about their school.

▼

120	AD	Do you agree or disagree with the following statement? Playing games teaches us about life. Use specific reasons and examples to support your answer.

Almost everyone, from little children to adults, loves games. The types of games may change and get more complex as we grow up, but our enjoyment never changes. Playing games is both fun and useful, because games teach us the skills we need in life.

First of all, playing games teaches us that everything we do causes something else to happen. If we hit a ball, it will land somewhere or someone will try to catch it. If we make certain combinations with cards, we'll earn points. So when we play a game, we learn there is always a cause/effect relationship. We learn to pay attention to what's happening around us and see how people react to what we do.

Playing games also teaches us how to deal with other people. We learn about teamwork, if the game has teams. We learn how to assign tasks according to each person's skills. We learn how to get people to do what we want, and we learn that sometimes we have to do what other people want.

Game playing teaches us how to follow rules to achieve something. In a game, the rules have been worked out in advance and make the game go more smoothly. We find out that if we want to reach a goal, we need to know the rules. We learn how to go step by step towards a desired end. We also learn how to make adjustments when things change. We learn how to devise a plan for reaching our goal. We learn strategy.

Most people understand that "all work and no play" is bad for you. Learning all these things would be much slower if we didn't play games. Life would be much duller, too.

| 121 | MA | Imagine that you have received some land to use as you wish. How would you use this land? Use specific details to explain your answer. |

Land is a valuable resource, and it is important to use it effectively. I think it would be most effective to create something that all people can enjoy. I therefore propose to use the land to build a campground. At the present time, there is little low-cost recreation in the area where I live. Building a campground would change that. Ultimately a campground would make a more enjoyable environment for everyone.

Local entertainment is simply too expensive. A nice evening out can cost as much as one hundred dollars. Even movies and other less expensive types of entertainment are no longer cheap. Further, there are no real recreational facilities nearby. There are no parks within 30 miles. There are very few basketball courts, and most of those are in poor condition.

Building a campground could change all that. Staying overnight at a campground is very inexpensive. It can cost as little as thirty dollars. Further, there would be a sports area and picnic tables for use by campers and also those who do not wish to stay overnight. A campground would provide a lot of activities for very little money. That would definitely improve this area.

The result of building a campground will be that many more people will be able to afford an enjoyable evening out. A campground also promotes healthy living. People can get out and breathe fresh air. They can walk and hike and play basketball or other sports. That is certainly better than spending an evening sitting down, eating buttery popcorn in a movie theatre.

A campground will make the area beautiful as well as functional. We have many wonderful natural resources, but we need to cultivate them. In addition to all the other good things it can bring, building a campground will help us do just that.

| 122 | EX | What is the most important animal in your country? Why is the animal important? Use reasons and specific details to explain your answer. |

In the United States there are many important animals. They help us in a wide range of ways from food production to scientific research. An animal that is not only helpful to us but close to us emotionally is the dog. That is why I feel that dogs are the most important animal in my country.

Dogs provide a very important chance to learn or maintain social skills. Children who have dogs learn responsibility while caring for them. Dogs also help older people. The elderly often feel lonely as they get older and have fewer living friends and relatives. They are able to maintain a positive outlook and to feel needed because they are caring for a dog that needs them.

In addition to social benefits, dogs also provide some very important assistance. Seeing-eye dogs help the blind live fulfilling, fully mobile lives. Dogs that act as shepherds on small farms are also very helpful. Lost animals mean lost money for farmers, and that can mean going out of business. Police dogs help find illegal drugs, catch criminals, and protect their handlers. Dogs' intelligence and desire to please people made them ideal for all kinds of work.

Finally, dogs can save lives. Dogs have been known to find lost children. In extremely cold conditions, they have provided them with life-saving warmth. Dogs have alerted people to fires and other dangers. And we cannot forget guard dogs, which save many owners' lives and property each year by scaring off potential burglars.

Again, there are many useful animals in the United States. In terms of the numerous ways in which they can be helpful, however, I believe the dog is the most significant.

▼

123	EX	Many parts of the world are losing important natural resources, such as forests, animals, or clean water. Choose one resource that is disappearing and explain why it needs to be saved. Use specific reasons and examples to support your opinion.

Preserve Our Planet's Trees

Many natural resources are disappearing or being wasted on our planet every day. One of the most important resources we are abusing is our trees. Each year, hundreds of thousands of acres of trees disappear in countries all around the world. In some countries, these trees are used for fuel. In other countries, trees are destroyed to build housing developments and shopping centers. Saving trees has become a major cultural and economic issue in many areas of the world.

Trees are essential to our survival. They are a major part of the process of photosynthesis. Photosynthesis is the process in which green plants use carbon dioxide to produce oxygen, and oxygen is something all of us need. The fewer trees there are, the more this affects our ability to breathe.

Trees are also important in the development of many medicines. The mainstream medical establishment did not recognize this for many years. However, those who use natural medicines have always known how important trees are. Now scientists are agreeing with them. Many drugs come from the leaves of certain trees, along with other herbs and plants.

In rural areas, farmers have always known how important trees are to soil conservation. This is why you'll usually see trees lining a field. Tree roots help keep the soil in place, and are also a factor in water distribution deep beneath the ground.

Finally, we should save trees from disappearing because they provide so much pleasure. "I think that I shall never see a poem as lovely as a tree," wrote a poet. That is the truth. A tall, stately tree is beautiful to look at, and pleasing to the soul. It is also a great place to find shade on a hot summer's day. For practical and emotional reasons, we need to preserve our planet's trees.

▼

124	AD	Do you agree or disagree with the following statement? A zoo has no useful purpose. Use specific reasons and examples to explain your answer.

Zoos are often controversial because many people believe they are unnecessary or even harmful. If properly managed, I feel that zoos have a lot of value. In fact, I believe zoos are useful in two main ways: educating the general public and advancing scientific research.

Zoos can be wonderfully educational places. They provide a safe, controlled environment to learn about a specific species. Children can feel safe exploring the world of the chimpanzee there, and adults can learn about and see types of birds they've never seen before. Unlike in the wild, there's no worry of being physically harmed by an animal.

Zoos are also important for the research opportunities they provide. Research is safer and easier to conduct than in the wild. Scientists can feel secure in the confined area of the zoo. For example, while conducting a medical experiment in an open field, scientists have to worry about both the animal they are working with, and also other animals nearby. In zoos, however, they need only worry about the research subject.

In the wilderness, animals are also much harder to track and monitor. Zoos make research less time-consuming and expensive. Long term follow-ups are easier too, since even with monitors, wild animals often are killed or disappear. In zoos, researchers can observe an animal's entire life span.

Overall, I feel that properly managed zoos provide excellent opportunities for education and research, and are therefore very useful.

▼

125	AD	In some countries people are no longer allowed to smoke in many public places and office buildings. Do you think this is a good rule or a bad rule? Use specific reasons and details to support your position.

Not allowing smoking in public places and office buildings is a very good rule. I believe this for several reasons. Not only will banning smoking improve people's health, it will also increase worker productivity and reduce conflicts.

We all know smoking is not healthy. Unfortunately, when smokers are able to smoke in public buildings, they can make other people sick. They may work with people who are allergic to smoking, for example. In that case, the non-smokers have no choice unless they want to quit their jobs. They can only get sicker, which is unfair. Of course, banning smoking in public buildings and offices will please non-smokers. It will also improve the smokers' health. They will have fewer opportunities to smoke, so they will smoke fewer cigarettes.

Banning smoking in office buildings can also increase worker productivity. Smokers won't interrupt their work all the time to smoke. There will also be fewer worker absences. When smokers cut down the number of cigarettes, they will get fewer smoking-related illnesses.

Finally, it is a good idea to ban smoking in public places and office buildings because a ban can reduce conflicts. Non-smokers tend to get annoyed and jealous because smokers have an excuse to take frequent breaks. The most significant conflict, however, is over whether smokers have a right to smoke in public. As we have already seen, non-smokers feel they are not always given a choice. If smoking in public is allowed, they will be forced to breathe harmful air. This may violate their rights, and nonsmokers are angry with smokers because of it.

It seems clear that banning smoking in public places and office buildings is a good idea. It will reduce conflict and increase productivity. It will also benefit the health of smokers and nonsmokers alike. I believe that just about anything that improves our health is a good idea!

▼

| 126 | EX | Plants can provide food, shelter, clothing, or medicine. What is one kind of plant that is important to you or the people in your country? Use specific reasons and details to support your choice. |

The coconut tree is a very important plant in my country. Coconut tree plantations are important sources of revenue, food and shelter.

Our country earns a lot of money from the export of coconut tree products like copra, coconuts, coconut oil, and coconut milk. This has been the main source of our foreign exchange for over a century. In fact, many of the coconut plantations were planted by various colonial powers and now, since independence, are run by our own citizens.

We not only export the food products of the coconut tree, we eat them ourselves too. The coco is the basis of much of our national cuisine. We are famous for our curries made rich by coconut mlk. We also use the oil to fry our foods as well as to add shine to our skin and hair.

The fronds of the coconut tree are also used to cover the walls and roofs of temporary shelters. The breezes pass through the fronds and cool the interior, but the heavy rains, which fall daily, do not enter.

The coconut tree is a very versatile and useful plant. It is a tree that has served our country well.

▼

| 127 | AD | You have the opportunity to visit a foreign country for two weeks. Which country would you like to visit? Use specific reasons and details to explain your choice. |

If I could visit any foreign country, I'd like to visit Ireland. The scenery there is so beautiful. Ireland has a lot of rain and that makes everything very green and lush. It hasn't become a completely industrialized country yet, so there are still areas where the countryside is unspoiled by pollution. Often, you can drive for miles without seeing another car or coming to a big city. I'd like to take my set of paints and several canvases and try to capture some of the scenes there. It seems every way you turn, you're looking at beautiful scenery. The area near the ocean is especially dramatic, with giant dark cliffs rising out of the water.

I also think I'd enjoy the slower pace of Ireland. It's so different from the busy pace of my country. Of course, Ireland's big cities are just as hectic as any big city anywhere. But many of the Irish live in smaller towns or on farms in rural areas. Visiting these places is very restful. People don't feel the need to stick to a schedule. Things get done, but in a much more relaxed fashion. In my country, there's the feeling that you're always late for something. In Ireland, it feels like you're never late because no one stays on schedule.

Most of all, it would be interesting for me to meet the cousins in my mother's family. They live in Donegal. I could see the house where my grandmother grew up and where my cousins still live. This house is connected to a lighthouse. Visiting there would give me a clearer idea of what my grandmother's childhood was like.

Ireland would be a refreshing break from the life I lead in my own country. I wish I could go there.

▼

128	PR	In the future, students may have the choice of studying at home by using technology such as computers or television or of studying at traditional schools. Which would you prefer? Use reasons and specific details to explain your choice.

If I had a choice between studying at home using computers and television or studying in a traditional school setting, I'd choose the traditional setting. Maybe it's just what I'm used to, but I don't think that technology can replace teachers and classrooms.

After all, technology can fail. Computers go down and computer programs crash. Televisions break, and the electricity can suddenly go off. In those situations, who's going to teach me? If I'm at school, and the television or the computers stop functioning, there's a teacher to step in and change the lesson plan. Teachers can draw on their teaching experience and be creative. Computers and televisions can't.

I'd also miss the chance to interact with other students if I weren't going to school. I think learning to play and work with other people is one of the most important lessons we learn in school. It prepares us for life, and for working with other people. Being with other people also helps us discover who we are.

Another concern I have about studying at home is getting distracted. It's strange, but I think being home alone is more distracting than being at school with a lot of people. At school, we're all focused on the same subjects. At home, it would be so easy to turn off the computer or the television and go do something else. I might tell myself that it's okay to play a computer game now and make up the study hours later. Chances are, I'd never make up the study hours.

I'm all in favor of using technology in the classroom. I think computers and television are great ways for students to have access to a lot of information. I just don't think they should be the only tools I have as a student. I also need teachers and other students to help me get a complete education.

▼

| 129 | AD | When famous people such as actors, athletes, and rock stars give their opinions, many people listen. Do you think we should pay attention to these opinions? Use specific reasons and examples to support your answer. |

Everyone is entitled to have an opinion. When it comes to opinions, though, there's a difference between the majority of people and celebrities like actors, athletes and rocks stars. If you're an average person, only your family and friends care about your opinion. If your famous, the whole world listens, or so it seems sometimes. Is this the way it should be? I don't think so.

We shouldn't pay attention to famous people's opinions just because of who they are. Being a famous basketball player doesn't make someone an expert on environmental issues. However, that basketball player has a better opportunity to be heard than most people do. If that player feels very strongly about an issue, he can use his fame to draw attention to it and get other people involved. Often, people with causes that aren't well-known ask celebrities to get involved. That way they can draw attention and needed dollars to that issue.

People who are rich put their money behind a cause. In the same way, famous people are using their most valuable asset. In their case, it's not money. It's their name recognition. Should people pay attention to what they think just because of who they are? I don't think so. I also don't think we should discount what they think just because of who they are. They have a right to their opinion. If their name draws people to that cause, all the better for the cause.

I think too often we categorize people and try to keep them in their place. Celebrities have brains and should be allowed to use them. When they're advocating a cause, their opinion should be just one of many factors we use to evaluate that cause.

▼

| 130 | EX | The twentieth century saw great change. In your opinion, what is one change that should be remembered about the twentieth century? Use specific reasons and details to explain your choice. |

There have been many changes, both technological and cultural, in the twentieth century. I believe that one stands out above the rest: advances in medical science. The changes in medical science go together with the changes in technological and cultural areas. One can move ahead only with the help of the others. We can see the results of medical advances in three areas: development of vaccines and antibiotics, expanded access to health care, and improved surgical techniques.

When medical researchers learned how to prevent disease and stop it from spreading, the quality of life for many people around the world improved. Today smallpox is a forgotten disease and vaccinations are no longer required. Polio is under control and the vaccine is widely available. The development of penicillin has helped many people recover from serious illnesses.

Although health care is not universal even in developed countries, it is much better than it used to be. Local clinics, visiting nurses, and specialty hospitals have all improved the health care for our communities.

If you should be unfortunate and require surgery, you are still lucky to have the surgery today rather than even ten years ago. Now with microscopic and laser surgery, operations are more efficient. You spend less time in the hospital and you recover faster.

I can't think of any other change that has affected the lives of so many people. Our health is important to all of us. We all are thankful for advances in the area of medical science.

▼

| 131 | PR | When people need to complain about a product or poor service, some prefer to complain in writing and others prefer to complain in person. Which way do you prefer? Use specific reasons and examples to support your answer. |

When I want to make a complaint about a defective product or poor service, I would rather make my complaint in writing. Writing a complaint allows me to organize my points of argument in a logical manner. If I'm really unhappy with the way I'm being treated, I want to present my reasons clearly. I don't want there to be any confusion about why I'm complaining. I like to list my complaints and then list supporting examples. That's the best way of making sure everyone is clear about what I'm saying.

Putting my complaint in writing also ensures it won't seem too emotional. If you feel that you've been treated badly or taken advantage of, it's easy to lash out. Losing your temper, though, is a sure way to lose your argument. Yelling is very satisfying at the moment, but it only makes the person you're yelling at mad at you. It doesn't get them to agree with you or to offer help.

There's also the issue of the person you're dealing with. If you complain in person, you have to talk to whomever is there. Chances are that he or she isn't the person responsible for the defective product or the poor service. Often the people who take complaints are not the people in charge, unless you're dealing with a very small business. Yelling at them isn't fair, and doesn't do anything to get a refund or satisfaction for you. You need to reach the person in charge. The best way to do that is in writing.

Writing about your complaint and sending the letter registered mail also gives you written proof. It's clear that you tried to settle the matter in a reasonable manner within a certain time period. This way, if you need to take further action, you have physical evidence of your actions.

Writing a complaint has the advantages of organization, effectiveness, and fairness. That's why I prefer to write rather than personally present my complaints.

▼

| 132 | EX | People remember special gifts or presents that they have received. Why? Use specific reasons and examples to support your answer. |

I think we remember special gifts we've received because these gifts often are part of a special memory for us. It may be a memory of someone special we've cared deeply about. He or she may no longer be alive. Or it may be a memory of a special event in our lives. It may even be a memory of the person we once were at some particular moment in our lives.

Gifts from other people can make us feel joy every time we look at them. A gift from our parents, or our husband or wife makes us feel loved each time we see or use it. If we have children, the first gift our child made for us in kindergarten is cherished long after the child has grown up. A family heirloom given to us by a grandparent makes us feel connected to our past. A gift from a good friend is a reminder of all the good times we've shared. A memento from a respected colleague is a reminder of a job we worked on successfully together.

Gifts may also pinpoint special events in our lives. Gifts given to us as part of our religious heritage, such as First Communion or Chanukkah gifts, remind us of those celebrations. The same is true for gifts given for birthdays and graduations, and for the anniversaries of special days in our lives, like our wedding day.

Gifts can also be a symbol of the person we were at a particular point in our lives. A gift received in childhood may remind us of a passionate hobby that's now boxed in the attic. A gift received when we left a job may bring to mind the first career we had, now that we're on our third or fourth.

The gifts that are important to us are the ones that remind us of family, friends, and happy times. They're a way of surrounding ourselves with our past.

▼

| 133 | AD | Some famous athletes and entertainers earn millions of dollars every year. Do you think these people deserve such high salaries? Use specific reasons and examples to support your opinion. |

Some athletes and entertainers earn millions of dollars annually. In contrast, an elementary school teacher, on average, probably makes less than $35,000 a year. I think the fact that this difference is commonplace is a sign of our society's misplaced values. It shows that we put more importance on entertaining our children than on educating them. It seems that the careers that are the least valued in our society often are those that are the most important.

Why is this so? The market determines who gets paid what. Teachers are paid by tax dollars. Sports teams make hundreds of millions of dollars every year. These teams earn fabulous profits from radio and television rights, as well as everything sold at the concessions stands. The same is true of movies. They are produced by studios that make huge profits annually. These enterprises can afford to pay their entertainers and sports figures huge salaries, because those athletes and film stars draw people to the entertainment.

Why are we willing to pay so much to see a ball game or a movie, but not for a good teacher? Maybe it's because we want distraction; we want to be entertained. Maybe it's because we think of education as a right, while entertainment seems like a luxury. We expect to pay for our luxuries.

It's not that I begrudge the players and entertainers their huge salaries. Most of them have very short careers. Athletes may be too old in their early 30s. Many of them gamble early in their lives on making it big in the sports or entertainment world, and deny themselves a good education. They have little chance of a stable career, so they *need to earn enough money to support them for a long time. On the other hand, most of us aren't going to earn $10 million in a lifetime of work. So it's hard to sympathize with people who do.*

We have to ask ourselves: who really gives the most value to society?

▼

134	EX	Is the ability to read and write more important today than in the past? Why or why not? Use specific reasons and examples to support your answer.

Today more than at any time in the history of the world it is important to be able to read and write. This change has been brought about by the Internet which we use to communicate with one another, to get our news, and to sell our products.

Millions of people communicate today through e-mail using the Internet. In the past people would have face-to-face meetings or call one another on the phone; today they use e-mail and chat rooms. It is obviously necessary to be able to read and write in order to participate in this technological revolution.

Today, one can subscribe to news and information services on the Net. When you turn on your computer in the morning, you are given the headlines, financial news, sports scores, or social events that you requested. The news is tailored to your specifications. In the not distant past, most people got their news from television or radio—as many still do. Yet, getting your news from the Internet is more efficient since the news is tailored to your specific interests.

E-commerce also demands that people be able to write and read. Of course, the people who design the retail web sites, must be able to express themselves clearly in writing. The potential customers must be able to read the product descriptions. In the past, people would go into stores (as many still do) and point to objects that they would like to buy. This physical approach to shopping does not require any special language skills.

The Internet will force us all to be literate not only in reading and writing, but also with computers. Today, we must be skilled readers and writers to be successful in the high tech world.

▼

135	EX	People do many different things to stay healthy. What do you do for good health? Use specific reasons and examples to support your answer.

Our health is the only thing we really have in the world. You can take away our money, our house, or our clothes and we can survive. Take away our health and we will die. That is why I eat healthfully, exercise regularly, and keep up my social life.

Eating healthfully is important to maintain one's health. I try to avoid foods high in fat like french fries or cookies. I also try to limit the amount of animal protein I consume. I never eat more than a few ounces of fish or chicken a day and I rarely eat meat. I eat a lot of vegetables and fresh fruit which are full of fiber and vitamins. It is important to know how to cook these foods so the nutrients are not lost in the cooking process.

Your muscles must continue to be strong to support your body as it grows older. Exercise helps the bones build density and helps you maintain your posture. A regular exercise program of cardiovascular training and weight training is an important part of keeping you healthy.

Friends are an important part of one's health. Studies have shown that people with a wide range of social contacts get fewer colds and have fewer complaints than those who don't. Laughing is also an important part of health. I like to laugh with my friends and I always feel better when I am with them than when I am alone.

By eating properly and exercising regularly, I can keep my body at an appropriate weight and can maintain my health. By spending time with my friends, I can keep my mind as well as my body happy. It's all a part of my recipe for healthful living.

▼

| 136 | EX | You have decided to give several hours of your time each month to improve the community where you live. What is one thing you will do to improve your community? Why? Use specific reasons and details to explain your choice. |

Volunteering a few hours each week to some communty activity is an important way of investing in the future of our society. I chose to spend my time working with elementary school children helping them to learn to read. Developing good reading skills will help these students keep up with their classmates, open new worlds to them, and help them succeed in life.

Students who are not good readers cannot keep up with their studies. They will not understand the lessons; they will come to school unprepared; they will not be able to perform. By learning to read, students will be on equal footing with their classmates. They will be active participants in class.

Books on different lifestyles, occupations, cultures, or governments will open new doors to students. Students who can't read will only know what they see around them. Students who can read will be able to travel to new worlds and experience new ideas without ever leaving their classrooms.

Today, a person who can't read is severely handicapped. A non-reader will have to work at the most menial jobs. Readers, especially good readers, have the whole universe open to them. They will have the possibility to learn any job that interests them.

By volunteering to help an elementary school child learn to read, I am helping him or her not only today, but for the rest of his or her life. I am helping them keep pace wth their peers and explore the world and themselves through books.

▼

| 137 | MA | Your school has enough money to purchase either computers for students or books for the library. Which should your school choose to buy—computers or books? Use specific reasons and examples to support your recommendation. |

Our school has been given a grant to make necessary improvements to its facilities. We can spend it on new books for the library or on more computers. Our school already has books in its library and it already has computers. Since we have more books than computers, I think that new computers will benefit the students more.

Computers can access up-to-date information on the Internet. Right now, the reference books in our library are very outdated. Our encyclopedia set is eight years old. But if every student had access to a computer, we all could have the latest facts and figures on everything.

Unfortunately, giving every student a computer means we need a lot of computers. Right now, the ratio of computers to students is one to twelve. This means students only get to work on the computers three or four times a week. But if every student had a computer, we could use it whenever we wanted.

"Information on demand" should be our slogan. Students today need lots of information right away. Life goes by too quickly to wait. It takes forever to identify a book that you think might have the information you need. Then you have to go to the library and look for the book. Usually it's not even there.

With a computer, information searches are instantaneous. If we all had computers, we could access more information and access it faster by computer. We could have all the information we needed for our schoolwork. We could all improve our grades. For these reasons, I feel that purchasing more computers will benefit us more than buying more books.

▼

| 138 | MA | Many students choose to attend schools or universities outside their home countries. Why do some students study abroad? Use specific reasons and details to explain your answer. |

Although students can get a good education in most subjects at their home universities, it is important to study abroad for some or part of one's college education. Study abroad can give a student competency in a new language, familiarity with a different culture, and a chance to grow in different ways.

One cannot deny that it is important to be bilingual or even multilingual in today's fast-paced world. We have a global economy and communication by Internet and satellite TV means we must be familiar with other languages in order to keep up with new developments.

Knowing another culture is also important today. Respect for other peoples and their traditions will foster cooperation and peace. We should all do our part to make sure the world is safe for our children. It will only be safe if we understand and respect other people and their culture.

When we are out of our environment, we feel more free to experiment with different ways of doing things. We are all individuals and we need time to be on our own, away from our comfortable nests. We may try different things and reject them. We might also adopt them. People can change and it is easier to change when you are away from your family surroundings.

Study abroad can be enriching. Not only can we learn a new language, understand more about a different culture, but we can learn more about ourselves too. At the same time, of course, we are getting an education in the formal sense.

▼

139	EX	People listen to music for different reasons and at different times. Why is music important to many people? Use specific reasons and examples to support your choice.

Music seems to be a natural need for people. I've read that from ancient times human beings have produced sounds from "instruments" like rocks or skins stretched over a wooden frame. Music is something most people want and need. I think it's important because it can be a major part of both community and individual experience.

Music is a way of sharing a common bond or feeling. When we're children, we learn very simple songs called nursery rhymes. These songs help make us part of our culture by telling us what's acceptable and what's not. We play and sing music in our religious ceremonies because it enhances the worship experience. We play music when we're going to war or celebrating the fact that we've won a war.

We have national anthems to share our love and pride for our particular country. We have music we play for our school, and music we play for our athletic team. In fact, music has become a big part of athletic games. We use it to taunt the other team as well as celebrate when points are scored for our team.

Music is also a major part of individual experiences. When we fall in love, music is usually a part of that experience. People talk about having "our song." That means the song that was playing when they met or a song they both liked when they fell in love. When we get married, we play music before and after and sometimes during the ceremony. It expresses how we feel. We play music to calm our nerves or to stimulate ourselves to get on with a task. We also play music for the simple enjoyment of listening to the sounds.

Music is special to us because it expresses our connection with our culture, and because it enhances our individual experiences. Nothing else seems to capture our feelings quite so well.

▼

140	EX	Groups or organizations are an important part of some people's lives. Why are groups or organizations important to people? Use specific reasons and examples to explain your answer.

Groups or organizations are an important part of our life because we are social people. We like to get together with people whose attitudes and beliefs are like ours. The most important groups for us are our families, our religious organizations, and our political organizations.

Our families are obviously our most important group. You will never find the physical and emotional support from any other group that you will find in your family. Your family is part of you; you are tied to them by blood. They will always be there for you.

Similarly, our religious organizations can provide comfort for us in times of stress. When we are with people who have the same beliefs, we feel better. Our beliefs are based on tradition. These beliefs have been tested over time. These beliefs tell us how to respond and how to act.

Our political organizations change as we change. Some years we may feel conservative; other years we may feel more liberal. Whatever our political philosophy, we can find a political organization that matches our thinking at the moment. These political organizations help us be a part of the larger community.

Whether the group is tightly knit like a family, spiritual like religion, or secular like politics, they all serve a function in our life. They all help us feel as if we belong.

▼

| 141 | MA | Imagine that you are preparing for a trip. You plan to be away from your home for a year. In addition to clothing and personal care items, you can take one additional thing. What would you take and why? Use specific reasons and details to support your choice. |

If I were to leave my home for a year, there is one thing I definitely would take with me: my cell phone. With my cell phone, I could call my friends or family if I ever was lonely, needed advice, or just wanted to talk.

If I were away from home for a year, I would be very lonely, especially in the beginning before I made friends. If I could call my mother and father, I would hear their familiar voices and I would not feel so lonely. Hearing my friends' voices would also help me overcome my sadness.

I've never been on my own so there are many things I am not familiar with. I've never opened a bank account, got a driver's license, or made my own food. If I had to cook chicken or something, I could call up my mother and she could tell me how to make dinner.

Sometimes, I may just want to talk in my own language. With my cell phone, I could call my friends and tell them about my new life. This would make them jealous of me. I would call them a lot so they could hear all the wonderful things I am doing.

For me a cell phone is a necessity. I would need it anytime I was lonely, anytime I needed to do something I didn't know how to do, and anytime I just wanted to talk. Of course, the phone bill will be sent to my parents.

▼

| 142 | MA | When students move to a new school, they sometimes face problems. How can schools help these students with their problems? Use specific reasons and examples to explain your answer. |

Students moving into a new community and attending a new school can face a lot of problems. Their biggest worry is usually fitting in. The school counselor, the school's administration and the students' teachers can all help the students come through this experience successfully. They can engage other students to become involved with the new students, too.

New students in a school need to feel like part of the school community as quickly as possible. A school administrator should begin by giving students a complete orientation to their new school. They should take them on a tour of the school and show them the classrooms, gym, computer lab, band room, and cafeteria. They should tell them about the history of the school, its academic achievements, and its athletic and debating teams. The administrator can talk to the students about what's expected of them in the classroom and what rules the school has.

The school counselor should talk to the students about what they're most interested in studying. If these are older students, the counselor can ask them about career interests. If these are younger students, the counselor can ask them about their favorite subjects at their old school. The counselor can tell the students about all the extracurricular activities there are at the school. For example, the school might offer things like sports, art, music, and working on a school newspaper.

The teachers have the most important job when it comes to new students. It's up to them to help the students meet other students in class. They can also help them learn how classes are conducted in their new school. They can encourage other students to make friends with new people and help them learn the system. Since they're with the students the most, they can keep an eye on them and make sure they're adapting well.

Both the adults and the other students need to help new students feel a part of their new school. It's not easy, but it pays off with happier, more successful students in the end.

▼

143 | AD | It is sometimes said that borrowing money from a friend can harm or damage the friendship. Do you agree? Why or why not? Use reasons and specific examples to explain your answer.

I don't think it's a very good idea to borrow money from a friend. It can cause resentment and awkwardness in the relationship. How do you approach your friend without making him feel he has to do this for you? It's unlikely he'll feel as if he can turn you down. Can he turn you down without insulting you? Probably not.

How do you know whether your friend can afford to lend you the money? He may be embarrassed to admit he's a little short of funds himself. Or he might not want to disappoint you. So he lends you the money and then he needs money, too.

There's also the question of when you'll pay back the loan. It's awkward for your friend to ask for a deadline for repayment. Besides, if you're short of funds, you may not be able to predict when you'll pay him back. What about interest on the loan? If it's a small amount of money, this doesn't matter. However, if large funds are involved, and you won't be paying it back for a while, should you offer to pay interest? Should your friend ask you to pay interest? All these issues can result in hurt feelings and can harm the friendship.

It's possible, of course, that if you borrow money from a friend and pay it back in a timely fashion, this will create a special bond between the two of you. You'll know that you can count on your friend when you need help. He'll know you're trustworthy.

However, more often than not, money issues between friends are an embarrassment. If you need money, it's better to go to a bank for a loan.

▼

| 144 | EX | Every generation of people is different in important ways. How is your generation different from your parents' generation? Use specific reasons and examples to explain your answer. |

The principal differences between my generation and my parents' generation are in how they relate to others. My generation is more tolerant of other people's choices, less concerned about what others think, and more self-centered.

My parents' generation has stricter standards about what kinds of behavior are acceptable. They sometimes have a hard time accepting the fact that other people may have different ideas about what's right and what's wrong. My generation thinks people should have a lot of choices. For example, they choose whom they want to live with, whether or not to have children, whether or not to practice a particular religion, and what to do for a living.

My parents' generation is much more concerned about what other people think of them. Many grew up in tightly knit communities where people knew each other's families. Fitting in meant that you had to act a certain way. Many of my generation grew up in loosely knit communities, where we only knew about our closest neighbors. We didn't care what the rest of the community thought of us. Also, we were a very rebellious generation and often did things just to shock people.

Wherever we grew up, most of my generation didn't have to worry about having enough to eat or a roof over our heads. My parents' generation did. They grew up during the Great Depression, when many people were poor. For this reason, my parents didn't have time to analyze their feelings or think about their inner selves. They were too busy trying to get by. Children of my generation were well taken care of by their parents. Because of that, we had time to think about ourselves and our place in the universe. As adults, many of us have continued to be self-absorbed. We join health clubs to be perfect in body and go into therapy to be perfect in mind.

When I think about our actions, it seems that my parents' generation is more "outer" directed and my generation is more "inner directed."

▼

| 145 | PR | Some students like classes where teachers lecture (do all of the talking) in class. Other students prefer classes where the students do some of the talking. Which type of class do you prefer? Give specific reasons and details to support your choice. |

In my country, the lecture system is the most common system. It is the one I prefer for three reasons: I am used to the lecture system; it is an efficient system; I am too shy to talk in class.

All my life, I have listened to teachers. They come into the room, open their books, and start to lecture. We students sit quietly at our desks and take notes. We never ask questions because we don't want to seem stupid. At the end of the course, we are given a test. If we can repeat on the test what the teacher said in class, we will get a good grade.

The lecture system is an efficient one. The teacher is the one who knows the subject, not the students. It is a waste of time listening to a student's ideas. What good will that do me? Time is short. I want the teacher to give me as much information as he or she can during the class period.

Even if we could talk in class, I would never open my mouth. I am much too shy. I would be afraid the other students would laugh at me and make fun of my ideas. I prefer to listen to the teacher and memorize the teacher's ideas.

I hope I can always study in a school where they use the lecture system. I think it is better to continue with what one is used to. I also think that there is a lot of information that I must learn in the most efficient manner possible. I wouldn't want to interrupt a teacher with my foolish questions.

▼

| 146 | MA | Holidays honor people or events. If you could create a new holiday, what person or event would it honor and how would you want people to celebrate it? Use specific reasons and details to support your answer. |

October 24 is Union Nations Day. The day is noted in the calendars, but not observed as a holiday around the world. I want the entire world to celebrate the birth of the United Nations because of its attempts to promote peace, education, and health around the world.

Peace is the most important thing that we can have today. The sooner that we can stop war the sooner we can all have better lives. There are countries around the world that have been at war for generations. In some of these countries, UN Peacekeepers have temporarily stopped the violence so people can go about their lives. If this peace could be made lasting, the lives of these citizens would be much richer.

The UN actively works to promote education. Universal literacy is one of its important goals. Every child in the world deserves to know how to read and write. The UN is also involved in job training for adults. The age of information technology demands new job skills. The UN works with continuing education programs around the world so workers are not left out of the job market.

The UN has played an instrumental role in the eradication of smallpox. Polio vaccines and AIDS-awareness programs have also helped reduce the incidence of these diseases. There is a lot to be done in these areas.

Much of the work of the UN is unknown and underappreciated. If we want to live in a peaceful world, where every child can attend school and where every citizen has access to health care, we need to support the work of the UN. We need to recognize its importance and celebrate its birthday.

▼

147	PR	A friend of yours has received some money and plans to use all of it either
		• to go on a vacation • to buy a car.
		Your friend has asked you for advice. Compare your friend's two choices and explain which one you think your friend should choose. Use specific reasons and details to support your choice.

Trying to decide how to use your money is always tough. Should you use your money to buy a car or go on a vacation? Both afford lasting pleasure, but of a very different kind. From a vacation you get the pleasure of doing wonderful things and of totally relaxing and enjoying yourself. The memories you bring home with you can give you that same pleasure again every time you think of them.

A car also gives you pleasure, every time you drive it. There's the pleasure of not having to depend on public transportation. You can go places off the beaten track, where public transportation doesn't go. There is also the pleasure of being independent. You are able to go anywhere your car can take you, without depending on others.

A vacation gives you the opportunity to learn new things and meet new and interesting people. However, it's only for a short period of time. A car gives you the same opportunities on a smaller level, but on a more regular basis. With a car, you can go someplace new every weekend. You can also join a car pool. That way you can share travel expenses with the new people you meet.

Some people might say that spending your money on a vacation instead of on a car is being impractical. But nothing is as satisfying as a really good vacation. It's mentally and physically healthy. It gives you a chance to get away from all that is familiar to you and see the world from a new perspective. It lets you do nothing but play, the way you did when you were a child. Being able to play, even for a short period of time, is absolutely necessary for everyone's mental health. I would choose the vacation, because we all deserve to indulge ourselves sometimes.

▼

148	EX	The 21st century has begun. What changes do you think the new century will bring? Use examples and details in your answer.

Now that we are in a new millennium, we can assume there will be changes in the world. I predict that the changes will be in the areas of information dissemination, global alliances, and family structure.

In the past decades, the computer was responsible for changing the way information was organized. Now, the computer plus the Internet is changing the way information is spread. Information will now be universally available to anyone with a computer. You will not have to go to libraries to do research; you will not have to travel to visit scholars; you will not have to go to a bookstore to buy a book. You can do all of this from your home on the computer.

In the past decades, the nations of the world aligned themselves with the United States, the former Soviet Union, or with one another in a loose alliance. In the future, these alliances will be more fluid. Some countries will align politically with one country, but economically with another. Some countries will share technology and other information, but will not trade together. Some countries, which have long been enemies, will align militarily for regional security.

The family structure will not be based on a mother/father/child pattern. Single parent families will be more common and often the child will not be a biological child of the single parent, but will be adopted. Other family structures like domestic partnerships will become more accepted.

Whatever the changes may be, whether in the way we receive information, the way nations align with one another, or the way family units are defined, you can be sure that there will be more change. Change is a constant.

▼

149	EX	What are some of the qualities of a good parent? Use specific details and examples to explain your answer.

I am fortunate to have good parents so it is easy for me to identitfy the qualities that make them good. These qualities are unconditional love, trust, and respect for me and my brothers and sisters.

All mothers and fathers love their children. They nurture them and keep them from harm. But not all love is unconditional. Some parents would not love their children if they married someone of a different religion or from a different ethnic group. Some parents would not love their children if they were of a different sexual orientation. My parents would. My parents would love us regardless of whom we married or whom we chose to love.

Part of unconditional love is trust. My parents trust us to do what is right. They know we would never do anything to hurt them or to disgrace them. They trust us so we trust them. We are confident that they would never do anything to hurt us.

Because our parents love us, they also respect us. They treat us as individuals. They accept our differences. They do not expect us to be like them. They want us to be our own persons. They want us to make our own way in the world, not follow in their footsteps.

Without their love, I would not be as confident as I am. Without their trust, I would not be free to do what I want. Without their respect, I would not feel comfortable being on my own. All children should have such wonderful parents.

▼

150	EX	Movies are popular all over the world. Explain why movies are so popular. Use reasons and specific examples to support your answer.

Movies are popular because people are great watchers. They like to watch other peoples' lives. They like to live vicariously. By going to movies, we can escape our own lives, share other emotions, and imagine ourselves as someone else.

Many of our lives are not as adventurous or glamorous as the lives in movies. We do not battle evil all day long and then go back to our luxurious penthouse apartment. We just go to school, do our homework, eat, talk to our friends, and sleep. We need a little excitement in our lives and we find excitement at the movies.

Humans are very emotional people. We all like to cry and laugh. Fortunately, there is not much to cry about in my life so I like to go to sad movies where my heart strings can be tugged. I also like to go to comedies so I can laugh. I tend to cry and laugh more in a dark movie theater than I do in broad daylight.

Now I am a student, but I know someday I will be a scientist or a politician or a famous model. When I go to the movies, I can see my role models. I see how they act, what they wear, how they talk. I can prepare myself for the day when I will be like them.

Even though my life is quiet, I can go to the movies and watch someone else's life. I can share their emotions and their everyday life. I wonder if they would like to share mine.

▼

151	**PR**	In your country, is there more need for land to be left in its natural condition or is there more need for land to be developed for housing and industry? Use specific reasons and examples to support your answer.

Even though our population is increasing and land is needed for housing and development, I would hope that our country could save the land in its natural state for future generations to enjoy. This land would be good for promoting tourism, for preserving the environment, and for remembering our history.

Although tourism has many negative side effects, it is an industry that can create enormous revenues. Tourists of course need something to see. They would not come to our country to see rows of apartment buildings or new industrial parks. What is interesting for tourists is the pristine countryside that our country is known for.

Preserving the land as it is, would be good for the environment. More factories and other industries would further pollute our rivers and air. We need trees and wide open spaces to make us feel like humans, not machines.

Untouched land reminds us of our history. When we walk through the countryside, we can imagine our ancestors on the same path. If we cover the earth with asphalt and concrete, we will loose touch with our past. We will forget our roots.

Preserving the land is good not only for the economy and the environment, it is good for us as citizens of our soil. We must preserve what little we have left. Can we afford not to?

▼

152	**AD**	Many people have a close relationship with their pets. These people treat their birds, cats, or other animals as members of their family. In your opinion, are such relationships good? Why or why not? Use specific reasons and examples to support your answer.

I think being very close to a pet can be both a positive and a negative thing. Health professionals have concluded that having a pet is very healthy for everyone. People who have heart disease or similar health problems are often urged to get a pet because it can lower your blood pressure. However, some people get anxious about their pets. If you always worry about the pet getting lost or not getting the right food to eat, then that isn't healthy for you.

Many pets are very loving and it's easy to love them back. Some people, though, go overboard. They treat their pets like one of the family. Sometimes they even set a place for them at the table or give them their own rooms in the house. They treat them as if they were children. Some pets are, in fact, substitutes for children. People need to keep their perspective about their pets. Dressing a pet up in clothes like a child is not emotionally healthy. Pets are animals and get confused if you expect them to act like human beings.

There are now stores devoted entirely to pets. They sell pet food, pet toys, pet clothes, pet homes. Pets should be given appropriate food, and they should have a few toys, since they need some enjoyment just like humans do. However, some pet owners spend hundreds of dollars on supplies for their pets. There are children in the world who don't have clothes or food or toys. It would be better to give some of that money to charity.

Feeling close to your pet can be very satisfying and healthy, as long as you don't overdo it.

▼

153	EX	Films can tell us a lot about the country where they were made. What have you learned about a country from watching its movies? Use specific examples and details to support your response.

Do you ever watch movies from other countries? Whenever I do, I think about how similar people really are all around the world. Even though the cultures and languages in those movies are different from mine, people all around the world are alike in their goals and emotions.

One time, I saw a movie made in China that showed parents helping their children with their homework. My parents helped me the same way. Another time I saw a movie from Argentina. It showed school children playing hide and seek, which is a game I used to play with my friends during recess. Seeing these films demonstrated to me that education is a common goal in every country. Parents want their children to learn so their lives will improve. It also showed me that children in schools everywhere want to play with their friends. Sometimes the games are similar to ours and sometimes they're different. Still, they all have the common purpose of fun and learning to work together.

Earning a living is another common goal. I've often seen that in movies about other countries. In some countries, people choose their careers from what they like and are good at. In other countries, careers are chosen for them, following the traditions of their families. But in every country it seems that people care a great deal about earning a living, and working hard is respected.

Showing people having fun together is always an important part of any movie, no matter what country it comes from. People everywhere want to be entertained, and want to spend time with their families and friends. Different cultures sometimes enjoy different activities, but all cultures enjoy some form of sports, music and dancing.

The movies I've seen make it clear to me that no matter the cultural differences between countries, people everywhere have the same basic needs and goals.

▼

| 154 | PR | Some students prefer to study alone. Others prefer to study with a group of students. Which do you prefer? Use specific reasons and examples to support your answer. |

Study habits are a very individual thing. Some people like to study alone, while others like to study with a group. Personally, I would rather study alone, but I can see advantages to both ways.

It can be very helpful to study with other students. For one thing, you can exchange information about the topic. Not everyone is going to hear everything the teacher says in class. Comparing notes is a good way to be sure you get what you missed. You can also discuss various aspects of the topic. Other students can bring a different perspective to the discussion. They can point out things you may not have thought of, and help you make your arguments clearer.

Studying with other students can also help keep you focused on studying. If you're in a study group, you have to be at a particular place to study at a particular time. This is good discipline. The group reviews all the material available and then begins studying. There's not a lot of wasted time, if things work the way they should.

Of course, it doesn't help if you're in a study group that doesn't take studying seriously. Then you'd be much better off studying by yourself. If you're trying to study with friends and all they want to do is talk about other things, you'd get more done going somewhere to study by yourself. Being with people who don't want to study can mean you'll be constantly distracted. There'll be a lot of interruptions, and you won't gain much hearing their points of view on a study subject.

Finally, whether you study alone or in a group depends a lot on your own study habits and on your personality. If you need absolute quiet to study, then you're better off alone. If you're a very social person, then you're better off studying alone, too; you'll be too tempted to socialize instead of studying. This is the reason I prefer studying alone. When I'm with other people, I want to play. I don't want to work.

▼

| 155 | MA | You have enough money to purchase either a house or a business. Which would you choose to buy? Give specific reasons to explain your choice. |

If I had enough money to buy either a house or a business, I'd buy a house. A business may succeed or fail. It's also possible I might change my mind about what I wanted to do in business. However, a home is a lifetime gift to myself.

Right now I'm in a small apartment, with barely enough room for everything. All my furniture and the things I've accumulated since I left college barely fit. I have almost no closet space left. This means my clothes are always wrinkled because they're crushed together. I don't have any place to put my cleaning supplies, nor room for more than one set of sheets and towels. A new house would mean a lot more room for all these things.

I love having plants around. It's very healthy for the air inside and it's cheerful to have living things growing in a room. Right now I have plants sitting on tables. This is the best I can do in an apartment. I'd like to have a garden instead. That way I could grow a lot of different kinds of plants and flowers, and I could have a vegetable garden in the summer.

Besides having a garden, I'd like to have a backyard with lots of trees and a small fountain in the corner. I love watching birds and listening to them sing. On the windowsill of my apartment, I put out bird seed every morning. In the hot weather, I put out a shallow tin plate with water in it for the birds. The trees and the fountain in my backyard would give me pleasure, but they'd really be for the birds. The trees would give them a place to nest, and the fountain would be a source of fresh water when it's hot.

Can you picture my dream house? A business would only give me money. A house would give me someplace special to be myself.

ANSWER KEY

CHAPTER 2
PLANNING THE ESSAY

Practice 1
1. B
2. A
3. A
4. B
5. B
6. B
7. A
8. A
9. A
10. A

Practice 2
1. B and C
2. A
3. B and C
4. A and C
5. B

Practice 3
5.1 weeds
5.2 tables
5.3 safe

Practice 4
5.1 travel
5.2 have lots of new experiences
5.3 read stories
5.4 stability of household routine

Practice 5
5.1 price
5.2 type
5.3 convenience
5.4 interesting mix of people
5.5 complex

Practice 6
5.1 to prepare for a career
5.2 meet new people
5.3 of world

Practice 7
5.1 waste of money
5.2 time
5.3 investment in future career earnings

Practice 8
5.1 Scrabble
5.2 talk before the game
5.3 teamwork
5.4 learn new words from opponents

CHAPTER 3
WRITING THE ESSAY

Practice 1
1.1. Playing games also teaches us how to deal with other people.
1.2. We learn about teamwork, if the game involves being on a team.
1.3. We learn how to divide and assign tasks according to each person's skills.
1.4. We learn how to get people to do what we want, and
1.5. we learn that sometimes we have to do what other people want.
2.1. Cooking takes a lot of time.
2.2. Shopping for the food takes time.
2.3. Cleaning and chopping the food takes time.
2.4. Cleaning up the kitchen after the food is cooked takes time.
3.1. Watching movies and television can give us a broader window on the world.
3.2. For example, seeing movies can expose us to people of different races and cultures that we don't see often.
3.3. We can then overcome some prejudices more easily.
3.4. Recently there have been more handicapped people in films, and this also helps prevent prejudice.
4.1. Our planet gives us everything we need, but natural resources are not endless.
4.2. Strip mining devastates whole regions, leaving bare and useless ground.
4.3. Deforestation removes old growth trees that can't be replaced.
4.4. Too much fishing may harm fish populations to the point where they can't recover.
5.1. The most important lessons can't be taught; they have to be experienced.
5.2. No one can teach us how to get along with others or how to have self-respect.
5.3. As we pass from childhood into adolescence, no one can teach us the judgement we need to decide on how to deal with peer pressure.
5.4. As we leave adolescence behind and enter adult life, no one can teach us how to fall in love and get married or how to raise our children.

Practice 2
1. In my opinion, people's lives are (or are not) easier today.
2. It seems to me that most people prefer (or do not prefer) to spend their leisure time outdoors.
3. To my mind, an apartment building is (or is not) better than a house.
4. From my point of view it is (or is not) good that English is becoming the world language.

Practice 3
1. I believe that high schools should (or should not) allow

students to study what they want.

2. I guess that it is better to be a leader (or member) of a group.

3. I agree that people should (or should not) do things they do not enjoy doing.

4. I suppose that I would rather have the university assign (or not assign) me a room-mate.

Practice 4

1. I am sure that children should (or should not) spend a great amount of time practicing sports.

2. I am positive that a shopping center in my neighborhood will (or will not) be a benefit to our community.

Practice 5

1. No doubt a zoo has (or does not have) a useful purpose.

2. Perhaps growing up in the country-side is (or is not) better than grow-ing up in the city.

3. Certainly, our gen-eration is (or is not) different from that of our parents.

4. Conceivably, a sense of humor can sometimes be helpful (or detri-mental) in a diffi-cult situation.

Practice 6

1. All things consid-ered, the family is (or is not) the most important influ-ence on young adults.

2. In general, parents are (or are not) the best teachers.

3. By and large, peo-ple are never (or are sometimes) too old to attend col-lege.

Practice 7

1. In a way, it is better to make a wrong decision that to make no decision.

   or

   In a way, it is better to make no deci-sion than to make a wrong decision.

2. To some extent, watching movies is (or is not) more enjoyable than reading.

3. More or less, you can/ (or cannot) learn as much by losing as winning.

Practice 8

1. **Opinion:** I think the more friends we have the better.

   Paragraph focus: learn how to trust others

   Paragraph focus: learn what to expect from others

   Paragraph focus: helps us profit from experiences

2. **Opinion:** I believe that playing games is both fun and useful.

   Paragraph focus: teaches cause-effect relationship

   Paragraph focus: teaches us about teamwork

   Paragraph focus: teaches us to follow rules

3. **Opinion:** Nothing is as important to me as my family.

Paragraph focus: learned about trust

Paragraph focus: learned about ambition

Paragraph focus: learned about love

4. **Opinion:** I'd rather be alone.

Paragraph focus: need time to recharge batteries

Paragraph focus: need time to re-energize mind and spirit

Paragraph focus: need time to form as a person

5. **Opinion:** Traveling alone is the only way to travel.

Paragraph focus: meet new people

Paragraph focus: have new experiences

Paragraph focus: learn more about yourself

Practice 9

1.1 big portions

1.2 control ingredients

1.3 control size

2.1 print

2.2 audio

2.3 past

3.1 present opposite views

3.2 give additional information

3.3 show documentary films

Practice 10

1. traveled

2. options

3. going on foot

4. typical

5. require

6. insignificant

7. transit

8. passengers

9. take you where you want to go

10. form

11. quickly

12. turn to

Practice 11

1. a number of

2. benefits

3. introduced to

4. is apt

5. impulsive

6. relax

7. response

8. becomes

9. restless

10. shy

11. confident

12. trade off

Practice 12

1.1 first

1.2 Next

1.3 we

1.4 such as

1.5 Most importantly

1.6 As a result of

2.1 In addition to

2.2 before

2.3 immediately

2.4 whenever

2.5 such as

2.6 Consequently

2.7 our

3.1 A major part

3.2 while

3.2 But

3.4 first priority

3.5 Usually

3.6 If

4.1 In addition

4.2 For example

4.3 her

4.4 merely

4.5 during

4.6 As a result

5.1 On the contrary

5.2 Even though

5.3 Current

5.4 as well as
5.5 if
5.6 much as

Practice 13

1. maintain
2. think
3. advancing
4. in
5. improves
6. interesting
7. You
8. engineers
9. where my cousins still live
10. to

Practice 14

1.1 A
1.2 C
2.1 C
2.2 A
3.1 B
3.2 A

Practice 15

1.1 B
1.2 A and B
2.1 C
3.1 A and B

Practice 16

Paragraph 1
1. Cx
2. S
3. S
4. S
5. Cx

Paragraph 2
6. Cx
7. Cx
8. S
9. S
10. Cx
11. Cx
12. Cx

Paragraph 3
13. S
14. Cx
15. Cx

16. Cx
17. Cx

Paragraph 4
18. S
19. S
20. C
21. C-Cx

Paragraph 5
22. Cx
23. S
24. C-Cx

Practice 17

1.1 A
1.2 C
2.1 C
2.2 A
3.1 A
3.2 C

Practice 18

Paragraph 1
1. bring **active**
2. are outweighed **passive**
3.1 is **active**
3.2 oppose **active**

Paragraph 2
4.1 believe **active**
4.2 would be harmed **passive**
5. would destroy **active**
6. bring **active**
7.1 will be hurt **passive**
7.2 will be affected **passive**
8. is **active**

Paragraph 3
9.1 will say **active**
9.2 will be created **passive**
10. will grow **active**
11. will be needed **passive**
12.1 want **active**
13.1 is going **active**
13.2 would prefer **passive**
14. want **active**

15. must be considered **passive**

Paragraph 4
16.1 believe **active**
16.2 will change **active**
17.1 love **active**
17.2 is **active**
18 is **active**
19.1 must expand **active**
19.2 will be gone **active**
20. would miss **active**

Paragraph 5
21. would be **active**
22.1 feel **active**
22.2 outweigh **active**
23.1 cannot support **active**
23.2 hope **active**
23.3 feel **active**

Practice 19

1. A
2. C
3. A
4. B
5. C

Practice 20

1. B
2. E
3. E
4. B
5. D

Practice 21

Topic Sentences

Introduction I think that people, weather, and politics determine what happens, not the past.

Paragraph 2 People can change.

Paragraph 3 The weather can change.

Paragraph 4 Politics can change.

Conclusion The direction of this change, in my opinion, cannot be predicted by studying the past.

Introduction focus: people, weather, politics

Opinion words
1. I totally disagree
2. To me
3. I think that
4. I don't believe
5. No doubt
6. According to my way of thinking,
7. On the whole
8. As a rule
9. in my opinion

Practice 22

Topic Sentences

Introduction I think I'd have to agree that a person's childhood years, the time from birth until twelve years of age, are the most important.

Paragraph 2 No doubt, the early years are the time when we learn about relationships.

Paragraph 3 These are the years when we begin our formal education.

Paragraph 4 These are the years when we develop our moral sense of what's right and wrong.

Conclusion The foundation is laid, by and large, in those first few years of life.

Introduction focus: begin our formal education, and develop our moral sense of right and wrong

Opinion words
1. I think
2. to agree
3. No doubt
4. Seemingly
5. Perhaps
6. Presumably
7. from my point of view

8. I believe

9. by and large

Practice 23

Topic Sentences

Introduction I believe that success is more than how much money you make.

Paragraph 2 Most people assume that famous people are rich people, but that isn't always true.

Paragraph 3 I also believe that being respected by coworkers indicates success.

Paragraph 4 I think that one of the most important indicators of success is knowledge.

Conclusion If history is the judge of success, than money surely isn't everything.

Introduction focus: fame, respect, knowledge

Opinion words

1. people believe

2. I believe

3. definitely

4. certainly

5. I believe

6. In my opinion

7. I think

8. In my opinion

9. overall

CHAPTER 4
REVISING THE ESSAY

Practice 1

1. I agree that all students should study art and music in high school.

2. Complete sentence

3. I am assuming this would be true of teenagers.

4. All high school students must take

physical education because it is good for their physical health.

5. Complete Sentence

6. Both art and music feed students' imaginations and help them express themselves.

7. Students who've never drawn a sketch will be surprised once they start to draw.

8. Trying something new is always satisfying, even if you find you don't like it.

9. Complete sentence

10. Complete sentence

11. It gives us an avenue for our emotions and fears.

12. It may not always be music other people want to hear or art others will appreciate, but it's the doing that's enjoyable.

13. Complete sentence

Practice 2

1. Sentence OK.

2. This enabled me to get in on the ground floor of computer technology this ensured that I would have a successful and rewarding career.

3. I was in college, computer science was relatively new.

4. Sentence OK.

5. They were learning how to be teachers, journalists, and economists I was learning how to

write computer programs.

6. I graduated I had eight very good job offers.

7. My choice of college major gave me a lucrative career it helped in my married life.

8. I married a Naval officer through the years we've moved six times.

9. Sentence OK.

10. Sentence OK.

Practice 3

1. Students wonder why teachers are critical.

2. A birdbath is a source of water for birds when the weather is hot.

3. I'd like to have a garden where I could grow vegetables.

4. We have all we need, even though we want more.

5. As our population ages, we will need more services for the elderly.

Practice 4

1. There would be more money for schools, libraries, and other community needs.

2. Once the buildings were completed, the jobs would be those on the campus itself and would include teachers, office workers, custodians, and librarians.

3. Our community is a place where everyone knows everyone else.

4. Although playing sports is a wonder-

ful way to learn discipline, it should not be the focus of a university education.

5. Emigrant children learn their new language while playing with other children and while going to school.

Practice 5

1. A child growing up has exciting places to visit in the city.

2. Children who study art do better in all subjects.

3. Reading such as novels and short stories fiction is more enjoyable than watching a movie.

4. English, which is very idiomatic, is the language of diplomacy.

5. Computer science attracts many young people looking for a rewarding career.

Practice 6

Check Essay Model 21 for the correct punctuation.

Practice 7

Note: The asterisked corrections are examples. There are other possible correct revisions.

1. B

2. C

3. C

4. C*, There are many ways to make a difference in a community.

5. C, I believe that the activity learning to read brings hope to the future.

6. C, It teaches them that there are

[other] ways to view situations.

7. C, Reading feeds a child's creativity.

8. C, and other cultures.

9. A

10. A

11. B

12. B, Will the child be strictly logical or will he be a dreamer?

13. C

14. B, . . . what happens to them is their own fault.

15. B, It teaches them that there are other ways to view situations.

Practice 8

1. A
2. A
3. B
4. C*, The entrance to our community is poorly defined.
5. C, A landscaper could plant trees suitable to the area and take care of them.
6. B, beautiful
7. C, more attractive
8. A
9. A
10. B
11. C
12. A, Right now, we don't really have a community recreation area, but we have empty land that is barely used.
13. B and C
14. C, for
15. B, a lot

Practice 9

1. D
2. C
3. C

4. A*, Our school already has books in its library, and it already has computers.
5. B, Right now, the reference books in our library are very outdated.
6. A*, Students today need whatever they want, whenever they want it.
7. B*, If we all had computers, we could [watch] our grades go up.
8. C
9. A
10. A
11. C
12. A
13. C
14. B. too
15. B, watch

Practice 10

Content

1. Thesis statement*; Paragraph 1, sentence 3+; Parents can be very important teachers in our lives; however, they are not always the best teachers.

Grammar

2. Sentence fragment; Paragraph 2, sentence 3; For example, they may limit a child's freedom in the name of safety.
3. Sentence fragment; Paragraph 3, sentence 1; Another problem is that parents may expect their children's interest to be similar to their own.
4. Misplaced modifier; Paragraph 4, sentence 6;

Sometimes parents, especially older ones, can't keep up with rapid social or technological changes.

5. Parallel structure; Paragraph 5, sentence 2; Our parents teach us, our teachers teach us, and our peers teach us.

Punctuation

6. Question mark; Paragraph 4, sentence 2; But should children always believe what their parents do?
7. Period; Paragraph 5, sentence 4; All of them are valuable.
8. Capital letter; Paragraph 3, sentence 3; If they love science…

Spelling

9. Spelling; Paragraph 4, sentence 1; … on their values…

Practice 11

Content

1. Thesis statement*; Paragraph 1, sentence 3; Overall, I believe that team sports have more to offer in this area.
2. Supporting details*; Paragraph 4, sentence 2-4: A child who doesn't give his best to a game will soon hear about it from teammates. He will also be disappointed when his fellow players don't try hard. For example, if one person doesn't show up for practice, everyone suffers.

Grammar

3. Run-on; Paragraph 3, sentence 2 + 3; Players must learn to communicate with other players to succeed. That is not true for individual sports…
4. Misplaced modifier; Paragraph 5, sentence 1; All sports teach important traits.
5. Parallel structure; Paragraph 2, sentence 5; For example, timing is important when throwing and catching are involved.

Punctuation

6. Indent; Paragraph 1, sentence 1.
7. Indent; Paragraph 1, sentence 2.
8. Indent; Paragraph 1, sentence 3.
9. Indent; Paragraph 1, sentence 4.
10. Indent; Paragraph 1, sentence 5.
11. Period; Paragraph 2, sentence 2; Team sports have an added benefit, however.
12. Capital letter; Paragraph 3, sentence 6; That seems to be the opposite…

Spelling

13. Spelling; Paragraph 4, sentence 1; Finally, team sports help…

Practice 12

Content

1. Conclusion*; Paragraph 5, sentences 1-2; By studying art and music in high

school, students begin to understand themselves as well as their own culture and other cultures. What could have more value than that?

Grammar

2. Fragment*; Paragraph 2, sentence 7; In the

process, we learn what we ourselves like and dislike.

3. Misplaced modifiers; Paragraph 2, sentence 2; There's a reason our ancestors in caves drew on the walls and made music with drums.

4. Parallel structure: Paragraph 3, sen-

tence 1; Studying art and music means more than drawing or playing an instrument.

5. Parallel structure: Paragraph 3, sentence 3; By studying the pictures on the museums' walls or by reading the program notes at a recital, …

6. Cohesion: Paragraph 3, sentence 3; They learn what is important in their own culture.

Punctuation

7. Indent; Paragraph 4

8. Capital; Paragraph 4, sentence 2; When they study the art …